HAYEK AND AFTER

This book offers a distinctive treatment of Hayek's ideas as a 'research programme'. It presents a detailed account of aspects of Hayek's intellectual development and problems that arise within his work, and offers some broad suggestions of ways in which the programme initiated in his work might be developed further.

The book opens with an overview, and then discusses how Popper and Lakatos's ideas about research programmes might be applied within political theory. There then follows a distinctive presentation of Hayek's intellectual development up to *The Road to Serfdom*, together with critical engagement with his later ideas. The discussion draws on a full range of his writings, makes use of some neglected earlier work on social theory and law, and also draws on archival material. The book also makes some unusual comparisons, including discussions of Gaventa and of E. P. Thompson, and presents controversial suggestions on how a 'Hayekian' approach should be further developed.

The book will appeal to anyone with an interest in Hayek's work and to those concerned with twentieth century intellectual history. It offers a distinctive interpretation of his views and a particularly wide-ranging survey of what in the author's view now needs to be done in the pursuit of a Hayekian approach to classical liberalism.

Jeremy Shearmur was educated at the London School of Economics, where he also worked as Assistant to Professor Sir Karl Popper. He has taught at the universities of Edinburgh and Manchester, at George Mason University and is a former Director of Studies at the Centre for Policy Studies in London. He is currently a Senior Lecturer at the Department of Political Science at the Australian National University.

ROUTLEDGE STUDIES IN SOCIAL AND POLITICAL THOUGHT

HAYEK AND AFTER

Hayekian liberalism as a
research programme

Jeremy Shearmur

London and New York

First published 1996
by Routledge
11 New Fetter Lane, London EC4P 4EE

Simultaneously published in the USA and Canada
by Routledge
29 West 35th Street, New York, NY 10001

Typeset in Garamond by Routledge
Printed and bound in Great Britain by
Mackays of Chatham PLC, Chatham, Kent

British Library Cataloguing in Publication Data
A catalogue record for this book is available from the British Library

Library of Congress Cataloguing in Publication Data
Shearmur, Jeremy, 1948–
Hayek and after: Hayekian liberalism as a research programme /
Jeremy Shearmur.
(Routledge studies in social and political thought)
Includes bibliographical data and index.
1. Hayek, Friedrich A. von (Friedrich August). 1899–
– Contributions in political science.
2. Liberalism.
3. Free enterprise.
4. Socialism
I. Title.
II. Series
JC273.H382S54
1996
330'.092 – dc20
96–5067
CIP

ISBN 0–415–14058–7

To Pam

CONTENTS

ACKNOWLEDGEMENTS

I have been at work, in various ways, upon this project for so long that proper acknowledgements would amount to an exercise in intellectual autobiography. All that I can sensibly say here, is that I would like to thank again all those whom I thanked in the acknowledgements to my University of London Ph.D. dissertation, 'The Political Thought of F. A. von Hayek', especially Kenneth Minogue, and in addition Norman Barry and John Gray, with whose important work on Hayek I have been engaged over such a period that it is difficult to identify specific influences upon what I have written here. In addition, I would like to thank, in relation to the present volume, Tyler Cowen, David Schmidtz and Leif Wenar for their extensive comments on an earlier version, and also anonymous academic referees for their reactions to successive versions of the manuscript. I would also like to thank Knud Haakonssen and Chandran Kukathas for useful conversations; Bruce Caldwell for his particularly useful comments on a very late version of the manuscript; everyone at the Institute for Humane Studies, George Mason University, for their assistance and encouragement, and finally my wife, for her forbearance in not reminding me too often that the book was not yet finished.

I would also like to thank the Earhart Foundation for their support of research in the Popper Archives at the Hoover Institution.

The ideas set out in this volume build on, and extend, the argument of my 1987 Ph.D. dissertation. In addition, chapters five and six draw on material previously published in, respectively, 'From Hayek to Menger: Biology, Subjectivism and Welfare', in B. Caldwell (1990) (ed.), *Carl Menger and his Legacy in Economics*, *History of Political Economy*, Annual Supplement to vol. 22, Durham, NC and London: Duke University Press; and 'From Dialogue Rights to Property Rights', *Critical Review*, 4(1 and 2), winter–spring, 1990, pp. 106–32.

The argument developed in this volume at several points complements that of my (1996) *The Political Thought of Karl Popper*, London and New York: Routledge.

The reader may wonder why, given the time at which the book is written,

ACKNOWLEDGEMENTS

my examples refer to 'he' rather than to 'she', or some random mix. My reason is not that I think that issues raised by feminists are to be disregarded, but, rather, that I agree with Susan Moller Okin in her *Justice, Gender and the Family* (New York: Basic Books, 1989) that simply swapping 'she' for 'he' is a matter of *false* gender neutrality. It also leaves the reader wondering: was there any special reason why this example used one rather than the other? In my view, the problem of whether the argument advanced here is compatible with feminist concerns is a topic that needs to be taken very seriously. But this would call for several substantive papers, or another book, rather than just playing about with the words used in examples.

Jeremy Shearmur, Bungendore NSW

1

INTRODUCTION

OVERVIEW

I will start by explaining the overall argument that is offered in this book and also the contribution that is made to it by each chapter.

Hayek is well known for having argued for the desirability of a market-based social order, both in broadly consequentialist terms and because of its relation to a particular conception of human freedom. He further argued that if we wish to live in societies in which our economic activities are coordinated with those of numerous other people with whom we cannot have face-to-face relations, we have no option but to make use of market mechanisms. These allow for the transmission of information in ways that cannot be simulated by central planning. In chapter two, I introduce these ideas in the course of a fairly detailed account of some aspects of Hayek's intellectual development. The reason for proceeding in this way, I will explain shortly. First, I will sketch what they look like, in more general terms.

On Hayek's account, a desirable social order turns out to be a complex whole which contains as intrinsic and ineliminable parts things which, in themselves, are not desirable. This idea is of interest not only in itself, but also because it turns out that, on his account, such a social order must be sustained on the basis of behaviour that in key respects is what I will call disaggregated. Hayek, like Hume and Smith before him, stressed the way in which actions in a society of any complexity are not – and can hardly be – taken with the intention of bringing about large-scale social consequences which we find desirable. Instead, they are taken on a basis that is intelligible to us in the concrete situations in which we act; situations in which our knowledge is inevitably very limited.

These ideas are of the greatest importance for social theory. Hayek's writings about the problems of economic calculation under socialism discuss the way in which, under certain conditions, we may be able to sustain some desirable social outcomes on the basis of such actions. But as Hayek himself suggested in what he wrote about social justice, we may not be able to realize other attractive social ideals at the same time. More generally, some features of life in large-scale

1

societies of the kind within which most of us live, and to which Hayek has drawn attention, impose important constraints over what we can aspire to, by way of the realization of normative ideals. It is these ideas about the constraints upon the realization of normative ideals which seem to me of real significance for social theory. It is one thing to decide that it would be desirable if the society in which we live possessed certain characteristics. But it may be quite another thing for it to be possible for such effects to be brought about, as consequences of the actions of citizens within it. Not only may our adoption of any one way of solving certain problems preclude our also being able to solve others, but, as Hayek's work suggests, if individuals have freedom as to the actions that they will perform in the specific situations in which they find themselves, and they are, for the most part, not in a position to know what the relationship will be between their particular actions and the more systematic consequences of those actions, it may not be possible even to bring about consequences the realization of which they would consider desirable, and which they would like to realize if they could do so.[1]

In my view, such ideas pose some interesting challenges to the way in which many issues in normative political theory are customarily considered. At the same time, they also lead to some important problems for *Hayek's* own normative views; not least concerning how a social order of the kind that Hayek favours could be maintained in existence, when it has features which will strike the individual within it as unfair or unjust. If Hayek is right in his broader views, God might well be able to appreciate that all is for the best in the kind of society that Hayek favours. But it is not clear that ordinary citizens within such societies will do so, too.

The ideas to which I have referred may remind the reader of some themes from the work of public choice theorists. There is, there, the same concern with disaggregation.[2] But public choice theory is different in its approach to what one finds in Hayek; not least, because of his concern with individuals who are ignorant and who are influenced in their conduct by specific customs and habits. Later in this book, I argue that these Hayekian themes may usefully be extended beyond the economic style of argument which lies behind much of Hayek's own writing. For example, I suggest in chapter four that fruitful links may be made between these ideas of Hayek's, and ideas about 'street-level bureaucracy', and about the habits and rules of thumb that such bureaucrats follow in the pursuit of their tasks in various specific institutional settings.

The ideas to which I have referred above are introduced in chapter two. Their ramifications are pursued right through this work. But there is also another distinctive theme to chapter two. For I am also concerned there with the *development* of Hayek's views. In chapter two – and also in parts of chapter three – I argue that there are some significant differences between his views at different points in time. In consequence, I think that there is something wrong with those approaches to Hayek which have treated his work as if it were a jigsaw, with the task of the writer on Hayek being to show how all the bits fit together. Where there are differences, I do not think that his later ideas are, simply, improvements upon his earlier views. At the same time, I do not wish to argue that we can just return to his earlier ideas. Rather, we need to follow his development, see how his views change over time, and to look at the implications of some of these changes; implications which, in some cases, Hayek himself did not fully appreciate. Only when this has been done are we in a position to consider how we should, ourselves, proceed.

Three major problems are highlighted by such an approach to Hayek's work. The first relates to his ideas about economic calculation under socialism. Hayek had been impressed by Mises' critique of socialism. In the course of responding to some of Mises' critics, Hayek was led to some interesting ideas about the way in which prices affect the coordination of economic activity. He came to view markets as processes through which coordination takes place between the disaggregated activities of individuals whose knowledge is both limited and fallible. However, once Hayek comes to place emphasis upon such ideas it becomes difficult to see exactly what he can claim about the welfare characteristics of a society in which markets – so described – play a major role. Yet at the same time, Hayek is advancing, in his political writings, a broadly consequentialist argument for classical liberalism. Hayek thus arrives in the strange situation of being a consequentialist who thinks that we cannot say much about consequences; a view which is reinforced by some of his writings about the methodology of the social sciences.[3]

Second, in some of his earlier writings Hayek argues for the need for the reform of social institutions so that they will better play a functional role within a market-based economy. Yet some of his later work would seem to question the possibility of such rationally directed reform – reform which his own views none the less seem to require. There is, in fact, more to this issue than might meet the eye, because of its relation to an oddity about Hayek's political development. It is well known that, as a young man, Hayek was attracted to socialism and that under the impact of Mises' work on economic calculation and Hayek's own further developments of this line of argument, his views shifted in the direction of classical liberalism. There would seem to be two stages to this process: initially, his political sentiments remain much as they were before, but he advocates an approach to policy issues which looks more conservative because he becomes convinced of the indispensability of markets. Later – it seems to me not easy to tell quite when – Hayek's substantive views become more clearly classical liberal in their character. These moves I document in chapter two. What is strange, however, is that Hayek offers an account of the rationale for his shift from socialism which does not seem adequate to explain why he should have made the final move.

What I mean by this is as follows. Hayek, when he was a socialist (of sorts), was attracted to a mild form of Fabianism. He was also familiar with, and seems to have had some initial sympathy for, what one might call the market-wise interventionism of his teacher, Ludwig von Wieser; views which Wieser set out in a book, the proofs of the English translation of which he thanks Hayek for reading. Hayek, after the impact of Mises, depicts the key political choice as being between the use of markets, and central planning. However, there is an ambiguity about where he stands. For he has either become a classical liberal – but without having an argument against a view like that of Wieser, the very kind of view with which, earlier, he was in sympathy; or his repudiation of socialism must be understood to relate *only* to the advocacy of central planning and to certain ideas about the simulation of markets within a socialized economy. If this were the case – and there is some evidence compatible with such a view, at least up to the period of *The Road to Serfdom*[4] – it would give his ideas an ideological thrust rather different from that which they have been understood to have. For this latter interpretation would make his ideas much more compatible with *some* forms of socialism than many have supposed – and from how he usually presented them, himself.

I need, at once, to clarify this point. For there are two ways in which one might understand 'socialism'. The first of these centres – understandably enough – on the idea of the social as opposed to the individual or corporate ownership of the means of production. Hayek has, I believe, telling arguments against socialism in this sense. There is, however, a second way in which one might understand 'socialism'. This centres upon values rather than ownership. It is concerned with such things as material equality; with placing limitations upon the power that individuals or corporations are seen as being able to exercise as a consequence of the private ownership of the means of production; and with a concern, variously, that good administration, altruism or radical democracy should replace the chaos, domination and self-seeking that, in the view of socialists, characterizes 'capitalist' societies. This second conception of socialism – in various different variants – serves to explain socialists' concern with the first kind of socialism. For the social ownership of the means of production is seen as necessary to realize socialist ideals – socialism in my second sense.

My point, for which I will subsequently offer detailed argument, is that Wieser was offering arguments about how certain (mildly) socialist ideals in the second sense, might be realized within an economy that was not socialist in the first sense. Hayek was familiar with these ideas of Wieser's, and he exhibits some sympathy for some such socialist ideals, even in material written after his *Road to Serfdom*.

The problem which concerns me is that while Hayek has some strong arguments against socialism, these are against socialism in my first sense, and also against certain particular forms of economic intervention within a market-based economy. What is not clear is whether he has arguments against the kind of view that one finds in Wieser – what one might call a market-wise interventionism – or against the socialist values that might inspire it. In fact, Hayek's argument largely seems to be of a technical rather than a value-based character. But, as I have indicated, his technical arguments do not seem to hit a

Wieser-style approach; something with which, in the light of his own personal background, one might have expected Hayek to have been personally sympathetic. Indeed, one *might* read some of his writings – including aspects of his Inaugural Address at the LSE, and of *The Road to Serfdom* – as simply suggesting that any values (socialist included) should be pursued by means of markets, rather than central planning.

Hayek clearly did, in the end, come to favour classical liberalism. But we can ask what arguments he has for the change in his views. Hayek's values do seem to change over time, but not in a way that it is easy to pin-point; and, as I have indicated, the thrust of his argument is technical, rather than value-based. Yet, as I have suggested, this argument seems to me telling only against socialism in my first sense, and against certain forms of inept interventionism, rather than against a market-wise interventionism in pursuit of socialist values. Hayek does *later* advance an argument which would be telling against a Wieser-style interventionism. The problem is that it is an argument closely akin to those which have been offered by some public choice theorists. It calls into question any casual assumption that government can be relied upon to perform the kinds of intervention that would be required by a market-wise socialist. But, by the same token, it would seem to me also fatal to Hayek's own interventionism: to the idea – which, for example, one finds in his *Road to Serfdom* – that government can similarly be relied upon to perform various actions, including the reform of the legal system, which will make for the smooth running of a market-based social order. There are some indications that Hayek comes to appreciate this point himself, at least on specific issues; for example, as indicated by the fact that, in his later writings, he prefers a policy for the denationalization of money to one in which government is relied upon to run things in the public interest. But a key problem would seem to me to be that, as he argued in his earlier writings, received social institutions stand in need of reform if they are to play the kind of role that Hayek's overall views require of them. If one accepts Hayek's later argument against intervention, it is not clear how such reform is to be accomplished.

One might, I suppose, try to interpret Hayek's rejection of socialist values as based in argument about values themselves, rather than about economic, social and political organization. But this, it seems to me, is not how Hayek presents his argument himself. And if one did try to interpret his work in this way, one would, in my view, find what he had to say suggestive but almost painfully thin. In my view – for which I will argue later in the volume – a Hayekian case for classical liberalism stands in need of argument of both kinds, and thus for more, and better, argument about ideals than Hayek himself furnished.

From what I have said so far, it will have been clear that in the approach that I take to Hayek's work, a historically based form of appraisal plays a key role. This approach is somewhat unusual within political philosophy, although those who have an interest in the philosophy of science may recognize it as related to Popper and Lakatos's non-foundationalist approach to epistemology.

What Popper and Lakatos offered – though it is seldom understood as such – is a way in which we may combine the rational appraisal of claims to knowledge with a repudiation of the idea that knowledge has reliable foundations. At its simplest, their argument is that we can appraise some new theory on the basis of whether or not it is an improvement upon what we had before. But to appraise theories in this way requires that we trace their development over time. At any point, we must ask: what are the problems towards which a theory is directed, and how successful is it in solving them? And if the theory is then modified, or if additions are made to it, we must ask: what implications has this for its ability still to address the problems to which it was initially addressed? In some cases, we may be happy to let a problem drop: we might, say, come to the conclusion that some problem that we have been attempting to solve rested upon mistaken assumptions, or upon an over-restrictive view of the options that were open to us. But in other cases it may be vital that we do not let a problem drop; indeed, our view may be telling to others only because of its ability to resolve some particular problem.

These ideas may seem uncontroversial. But they are, in my experience, not widely used in normative political theory. Indeed, in this context the historical approach to appraisal, to which they lead, may seem slightly strange. For this reason I set out the rationale for adopting them, in a more systematic manner, in the second and third parts of this introduction.

The approach that I am taking leads me to a distinctive perspective on Hayek's work. For it prompts me to follow his 'progress' carefully, and to ask: is each move that he makes one which, in fact, leads us to an improvement upon the position that he held earlier? As I have indicated, once one looks at Hayek's work in such a light, many things become problematic which have not seemed so to other commentators. A critic of my work has suggested that I am unwilling simply to accept that Hayek has changed his mind. This would be a reasonable enough point, if my concern were just with Hayek. But the title of this volume is *Hayek and After: Hayekian Liberalism as a Research Programme*. The 'after', here, does not refer to writers subsequent to Hayek. Rather, it refers to what would have to be done in order for a 'Hayekian' approach to be successful. And success would here involve these ideas being found telling by, say, the younger, socialist-inclined Hayek.

In my view, Hayek offered a distinctive way of interpreting classical liberalism. He suggested that we should place considerations of political economy and of political and social theory at the centre of the stage when we consider issues in normative political theory. Hayek's approach contrasts significantly with the rights-based approach to classical liberalism which may be found in such writers as Nozick. But it also differs from the kind of economic argument for classical liberalism that may be drawn from the Chicago School, or the proponents of law and economics. Rather, it represents something akin to the sceptical approach of David Hume and of Adam Smith. Hayek's ideas are not only distinctive, but represent an interesting programmatic approach to classical liberalism; one which is well worth further exploration. My concern, in the rest of the volume, is with how such a programme is best pursued.

In part, my concern is with the identification of the problems that those attracted to a Hayekian approach must address. Some of these, which emerge out of my discussion of Hayek's development in chapter two, I have already described. In chapter three, I raise some further problems by way of a discussion of his ideas about freedom, political economy and law. The rest of the book is concerned with discussing how these problems might best be addressed in a manner that would represent progress over Hayek's own views.

That I take this approach relates to a further feature of Popper's philosophy of science, of which I am making use in this volume: his ideas about 'metaphysical research programmes'. It is well known that Popper, when discussing the character of scientific theories, stressed the importance of falsifiability. But, in addition, he drew attention to the role placed in the development of science by programmatic ideas which are not themselves in general falsifiable. Such ideas may play a key role in suggesting how we should understand our subject-matter, and the kinds of explanations for which we may usefully seek.

There are, obviously, connections between these ideas (which were subsequently developed by Lakatos) and Kuhn's ideas about 'paradigms'. However, there are also significant differences between them, some of which are important for our present purposes. In particular, as against Kuhn, Popper stressed that at any one time there typically would – and should – be several research programmes in contention with one another. Further, critical discussion between the proponents of a research programme, and also with the proponents of other programmes, both about the theoretical ideas involved in the programme itself, and the methodological ideas associated with it, can, and should, be undertaken.[5] (An example, outside of the field with which we are concerned here, would be the argument between Gerry Cohen and Jon Elster about the relation between Marxism and functionalist explanation.)[6]

All this is of importance for the approach that I take in this volume, because my concern, here, is with Hayek's approach to liberalism *as a research programme*. Accordingly, my focus is not just upon how Hayek's views changed over time, and thus with the current problem-situation facing those attracted to his work, but also on what approaches might usefully be taken by those who wish to develop this programme in the future.

I would not expect that those whose interest is largely in Hayek will relish my theoretical discussion of these issues in the last two parts of this introduction, and they may well choose to skip over it. But that this discussion is there has important consequences for what follows. For, in chapter three, I discuss critically some aspects of Hayek's later work. My discussion there includes a consideration of his ideas about why individual freedom is important (on which topic he offers more than just a consequentialist argument; but one which seems to me defective); of his ideas on law; and of some of his arguments in political economy. In each of these cases, my discussion reveals problems that, I think, need to be addressed if one is going to develop Hayek's programmatic approach to classical liberalism. In this chapter, I raise a bevy of problems; indeed, more than I am able to respond to in this volume, and I should also warn the reader that, in consequence, this chapter has a less systematic character than the other parts of the book.

The issue of how to take a Hayekian approach further then becomes the theme of the rest of the volume. In this connection, I discuss several issues. My discussion is largely of a programmatic character, just because perhaps the most important question facing those interested in Hayek's approach is: what *kind* of argument is now needed? In this connection, I first discuss Hayek's criticism of the idea of social justice, and Raymond Plant's response to it. I suggest that Hayek's argument may usefully be reinterpreted in terms of one aspect of the transition from a 'moral economy' to a 'great society': the commodification of grain. My argument is that certain economic changes have significant consequences for how we should understand our moral responsibilities towards others. My discussion is couched in terms of a specific historical example. But it is significant in that it marks the opening of an argument about the moral consequences of the development of an international market economy.[7] The relationship between my discussion here and current arguments about 'globalization' and its consequences is, I believe, too obvious to labour. In my view, it is the argument outlined here that also serves to explain why the ideals of even a market-oriented social democracy cannot be seen as morally compelling, and which, thus, offers the response to Wieser which was not, I believe, provided by Hayek himself.

The next issue that I discuss, in chapter five, relates to what would need to be shown in respect of the welfare characteristics of market-based economies of the kind that Hayek favours, for Hayek's appeal to them to be able to play the role that is needed in his political argument. My argument, here, should prove highly controversial among those who have been influenced by Hayek's work. For I suggest that his subjectivism in value theory – while in part correct – is in part badly mistaken. For if his economic arguments are to be able to play their proper role in his political argument, he also stands in need of an *objective* welfare theory; one which relates the likely outcomes of market processes to human well-being in a sense that goes beyond simply the satisfaction of individuals' preferences, and instead pertains to issues the moral importance of which can be recognized, intersubjectively.

I will leave the details of this argument to the chapter, but will here make two points. The first is that I am *not* arguing against the importance of subjective individual choice; indeed, in my view it is of the greatest importance for human well-being and flourishing. My argument, rather, is that this connection has to be *argued* for, in order for an appeal to the satisfaction of preferences to be able to play its proper role in Hayek's political argument. Yet it is from just this task that Hayek himself retreated if one compares his ideas with the (admittedly crude) views of Carl Menger, and from which some of those influenced by Hayek seem to have retreated further still.

The second point is that there is an ambiguity about the way in which these issues have been discussed, introduced by the fact that some of those who address them do so from a rights-based approach. Now if one has strong, prior arguments that individuals have a right to make subjective choices in certain areas, this in itself furnishes an argument as to why others should have to respect those choices, regardless of what their content is. But Hayek, and many other economists, wish subjective choice to stand as morally significant on its own. My argument, here, is that it cannot do this, and that it only becomes something that others have to respect if one can show its connection to other things that more obviously have moral clout, such as considerations of human well-being.

Should my argument here hold water, it is possible that some who are attracted to Hayek's subjectivism may react by saying: we do not wish to try to advance claims about the connections between preferences and well-being of the kind for which you ask. Rather, we will take the other option and pursue, instead, considerations of rights. This leads us to chapter six. I there discuss an issue which, I believe, is pressing, but which few liberals see as problematic: *why* we should treat *each* individual as something like an end in him or her self. I suggest that, historically, this idea had a theological basis, and that contemporary liberals face a problem of how to make such a view plausible in secular terms. In chapter three, I consider what seem to me some of the problems about Hayek's own ideas on this topic. But I also suggest, there, that there are important parallels between Hayek's ideas and those of Karl Popper (and that, where there is a clash, there are arguments for preferring Popper's). The *point* of this argument is brought out by my discussion in chapter six, in which I make use of Popper's ideas to try to extract as much as I think can be done from one of Hayek's ideas about why other people's freedom should matter to us. I believe that, by such means, I am able to improve upon Hayek's own argument, and in a manner which spells out some of Popper's own ideas, and also has some parallels with the later work of Habermas.[8] But at the same time, I think that what I am able to achieve is of somewhat limited value. At best, we can take this line of argument as one which, if added to other arguments as to why each individual matters, may go some way towards making plausible the liberal's view of these issues. But I am conscious of the fact that, even if my argument should work, the case still looks rather less than compelling. All this, in my view, serves to emphasize just how problematic the universalism of the liberal tradition is.

It could perhaps be argued that this is a purely theoretical problem, rather than a practical one, for there seems to be widespread agreement to proceed as if such ideas were unproblematic. Thus, the importance of treating each individual as something like an end in him or her self is one of the few areas in which there is no real conflict between classical and 'modern' liberals. It is also a topic on which many postmodernists seem implicitly also to be in agreement, though why they should be is itself a puzzle. At the same time, given that we are also facing a revival of forms of nationalism which are not morally universalistic in their character, it is important to admit the weakness of liberalism here. The argumentative vindication, rather than the presupposition, of liberal universalism is of pressing importance, and a task to which those who find liberalism attractive need to address themselves.

The final chapter explores a further issue to which Hayek's work gives rise, and which is particularly challenging. As I have already mentioned in this introduction, in the exploration of Hayek's ideas in chapter two I discuss the way in which his work highlights two distinctive problems. His writings on markets bring out the way in which the liberal 'great society' that he favours rests upon actions which may be morally unlovely. It also involves the operation of rules which may generate consequences which are morally problematic. Hayek is not arguing that, in the phrase from *Wall Street*, 'greed is good'. Rather, he is arguing, with Mandeville, that greed *can* have good consequences – which is a rather different matter. Similarly, Hayek argues, with Hume, that the system of justice upon which a 'great society' rests may also generate specific legal decisions which may look grim, from a moral point of view. The problem here, in short, is that Hayek is arguing that we should appreciate that a desirable social order may have, as *ineliminable* parts, mechanisms which are morally unlovely, or rules which generate morally unlovely conclusions.

Why this matters is brought out by the other theme in Hayek's work with which we will again here be concerned: the way in which the kind of society that he favours – and which he argues is the best that we can attain – is maintained by the actions of individuals who are, for the most part, blind to the systematic consequences of their actions. By this, I do not just mean that Hayek's vision of a good society is one in which an important role is played by 'invisible hand' mechanisms. Rather, the problem is that the overall character of the society, and what the relation is between particular individuals' actions, their following of particular rules, and the society's overall character, is not one that is, in general, transparent to them. Indeed, it is only the social theorist who will see what is involved, and even he or she will be able to understand these things only in general terms.

These two ideas, together, generate an interesting problem; namely, that if Hayek is right, there is a problem of moral legitimacy haunting the 'great society'. For if people start to look critically at the institutions within which they are living, they will see much wrong with them: that they are living in forms of social order that may seem morally unjust. If Hayek is right – and if the arguments that I offer in this volume are along the right lines – they would be wrong in making this judgement, if making it is taken to involve the idea that the fundamental organization of society should be changed, such that these problems will not arise. Rather, if Hayek is right, the best that can be done is to palliate these problems, in so far as this can be done without disrupting the large-scale mechanisms which underpin the social order of a liberal society.[9]

However, and here is the rub, the problem is that this judgement – if it is correct – is one that will be appreciated only by the social theorist. It seems unrealistic to believe that such ideas can be made part of popular day-to-day knowledge, and thus of the basis on which we act as we go about our ordinary affairs. (Or, more to the point, it is not clear how ordinary citizens in Hayek's favoured society will possess the resources to enable them to resist the arguments of those who suggest that change is needed; especially when such ideas are developed in the setting of consciousness-raising groups, or other forms of contemporary activism, which remove those involved from the pressures towards conformity that are part and parcel of everyday life.) This presents the liberal political theorist with a difficult problem. It is akin to that which faced Plato's guardians, and there is a danger that it may lead them to think of solutions in terms of a regime which, from the perspective of ordinary citizens, is as repressive as was that of Plato. But such a response is of course utterly unacceptable to the classical liberal.

In chapter seven, I offer a suggestion as to how such problems might be addressed. The fundamental idea is that one might do so by way of citizens being offered choices between more specific forms of life within the setting of an underlying political regime which would have a character close to that of Robert Nozick's liberal metautopia. Classical liberalism, it would seem to me, differs from 'modern' liberalism in that it sees no problem in people choosing to give up certain of their civil rights; for example, as one of the conditions of being on the property of other people. Just as, say, if one chooses to enter a theatre, or to visit Disney World, one becomes subject to regulations that are imposed by the owners of the theatre or of Disney World, so, I would suggest, we may think of people's being able to choose to enter regimes which impose upon them certain specific forms of conduct. Those entering Disney World may well not understand the rationale for specific rules being imposed, but they accept them as part of the conditions of being there, because they like the overall atmosphere that is created by people following them. I would suggest that we may think of specific rules and codes of conduct of the kind that Hayek advocates, as, similarly, being things that people may choose because they like their large-scale products, without being able to *understand* their overall rationale – which is, indeed, the situation that Hayek argues that we must, typically, be in. At the same time, the wider but minimalist liberal setting within which such arrangements would operate would imply that, in a sense, individual rights and individual choice are preserved, and are given priority over the specific demands of any particular social formation. However, the priority would involve not the individual's being able to demand that a specific social formation be changed to meet his or her demands, or, even, the free exercise of their 'civil rights' within it, but, instead, that they have the liberty to take themselves and their property elsewhere. The reader familiar with Hayek's work will spot that I am, here, offering a reinterpretation of some of the 'evolutionary' themes of Hayek's later work upon a somewhat more rationalistic basis. Such ideas would also offer a framework within which Hayek's own more specific ideas – including his arguments for certain forms of governmental intervention – could themselves be tried out, but in a situation in which people retain the right to exit.

In chapter seven I am able to discuss these ideas only in a programmatic manner; and they clearly raise many more problems than I can sensibly attempt to resolve in a context such as this. But they seem to me personally the most suggestive of the ideas that I discuss in this volume. For, despite the obvious problems to which they give rise, they suggest distinctive ways of approaching several other and difficult problems facing contemporary liberalism.

The first of these relates to an issue raised by communitarianism. This concerns the way in which individuals, families or groups of people may favour a specific social order, the generation of which depends upon the following – and if necessary the imposition – of specific codes of conduct or ways of life, to which the individual's insistence on the exercise of particular rights may be disruptive. I think that communitarians are completely correct in their view that specific ways of life may demand specific such disciplines (although there are also forms of moral accountability that may work perfectly well within a 'great society').[10] But I also think that communitarians are completely wrong-headed in looking to political solutions to these problems, not least as there may be genuine diversity as to what forms of life people within a specific *political* community want, or as to what their preferred trade-offs are between individual liberty and the imposition of such codes. My suggestion is that one might more usefully think of such issues as being addressed by way of voluntary membership of proprietorial communities; communities set up and run by entrepreneurs (although there is nothing to stop these communities being of a cooperative or a democratic character, if would-be members are particularly interested in such things). This would allow individuals in principle to choose the form, degree and substantive character of the social control to which they would wish to be subjected. Although, clearly, their choice would be limited by economies of scale, and by the wider liberal setting of the arrangements within which I am suggesting that such forms of organization should operate.

The second issue relates to problems of identity. These arise in a striking way for liberalism, for two reasons. First, liberalism is universalistic in its character, and so has no built-in concern for the preservation of any specific identity. Second, people's identities within a liberal political economy have, as a material basis, the specific arrangements under which people are living: their ways of life, culture, habits, language and so on. Yet all these things have, in their turn, an economic basis, and one which, within liberalism, is not sacrosanct. Rather, it is open to change in ways that may depend on the decisions of people who may be remote from the people in question, and who, more generally, may have no way of knowing what the consequences of their actions will be in this regard, and no special reason for caring.

These contingencies must be squarely faced: they are the other side of the freedoms of the countless other people with whom we are cooperating through the international division of labour. In the face of them, we seem to me to face a choice. We may decide to go with the flow, and to open ourselves and our characters up to how things may turn out. Alternatively, we may feel that this is unsatisfactory, and face the problem that what we want may have to be created artificially, by way of the creation of social arrangements which foster specific ideals, and forms of organization upon which specific identities may be sustained. This is something that, in my view, is again best addressed in entrepreneurial terms, rather than seeing it as something that can occur spontaneously,[11] or through democratic initiatives. There is also a particular advantage to looking at these issues in such a manner. For it would allow more easily[12] for the imposition, on the character of such arrangements, of the requirement that what they foster should not be at odds with the underlying liberal character of the wider setting within which they are operating. It may also – though this is a difficult business – be more easy to exercise moral pressure such that the rules that are imposed do not move too far from the discrimination that is needed to keep specific identities intact, towards discrimination in a more unlovely sense.

I will not explore these matters further in this volume. But it seemed to me worth indicating what this strand of the argument in the book is leading towards. These are issues for further research, rather than ones upon which I can here hope to contribute more than programmatic suggestions. At the same time, the broader approach within which I am working argues not only for the importance of the explication of such programmatic ideas, but also for their criticism – which I am, obviously, now happy to receive.

THE METHODOLOGY OF RESEARCH PROGRAMMES

As I have mentioned above, my approach to Hayek's political thought has been influenced by the criticism of foundationalism and of the programmes of justification that are associated with it, within epistemology and the philosophy of science.[13] These ideas do not necessarily bring with them relativism, or the end of philosophy.[14] For it is possible to make a comparative appraisal of competing theories on a basis that is not foundationalist in its character.[15] Such appraisal, however, brings a historical dimension into normative appraisal, as it is concerned with the assessment of a theory or a research programme as progressive in respect of its problem-solving powers, over time.

The ideas to which I am here referring were developed in the work of Karl Popper and of various writers associated with him, and have been elaborated upon by Imre Lakatos. My own views are closer to those of Popper, in a respect that is of some importance for the overall character of this volume, and which I should therefore explain.

Popper is well known for his ideas about the appraisal of scientific theories. Popper argued that if ideas are to be counted as scientific they must be an improvement upon our previous ideas, and also open to falsification. For something to be an improvement on previous ideas means that it must not diminish from the content of what we knew, previously. It must also say something new; either by way of resolving some problem that we had not been able to solve previously, or – perhaps even more challenging – saying that something that we had previously taken to be unproblematic is, in fact, false. Openness of theories to falsification involves it being possible to test them against a (revisable) intersubjective consensus as to what is the case. Accordingly, it is incumbent upon the proponent of a theory to explain how it can be put to such empirical tests, in terms of publicly accessible objects. In the event of such a test going against a theory, what happens? We need to make some change to our views. It may be the case that the new theory is incorrect; alternatively, it may be all right, but some other assumption that we had made may need to be revised. It is open to us to conjecture where an adjustment is to be made. But the same criteria to which I referred above – improvement on our previous knowledge, and testability – must again be brought into play. Popper also discussed the way in which, in science, we may also require that there be a simple and unifying idea behind the development of our theories, and he also discussed the way in which, at various times in science, untestable theories, such as atomism, formed research programmes for the development of scientific explanations.

Lakatos, in his writings on the 'methodology of scientific research programmes', offered what was, in effect, a generalization of these ideas. However, he suggested that one might be able to appraise the performance of research programmes in terms of their ability to generate progressive sequences of scientific theories. He also discussed the way in which elements of scientific theories themselves might be treated as programmatic ideas, by way of a methodological decision to direct criticism not to these theories, but to our other ideas.

Popper developed the ideas to which I have referred as an account of natural science. But he also offered a generalization of his ideas about falsifiability, so that they might be applied to ideas which are not testable, too. Essentially, he suggested that we might ask the proponents of theories which are not falsifiable, towards what problems the solution of which they are directed, and appraise them as such. This brings out an additional dimension to Popper's work; one which, in my judgement,[16] is lost sight of in Lakatos, whose ideas about the appraisal of programmatic ideas are largely restricted to the appraisal of their empirical success. Popper, by contrast, opens up the possibility that we may discuss programmatic ideas as such, and appraise them also in terms of their ability to resolve the problems to which they are addressed. Such an idea is of the greatest interest and importance; not least, as it points to the way in which we may gain through the discussion of programmatic ideas as such, and in broad terms, rather than having to restrict ourselves to the discussion of specific empirical or technical results.

It is this approach which underlies the overall procedure that I adopt in this book, in which I generalize Popper's approach to the study of normative political theory. For not only am I concerned – as were Popper and Lakatos – with historically based appraisal. But my discussion focuses upon Hayek's ideas as a research programme, and with the question of what would have to be done in order that we make progress in its development. In addition, the latter part of the book is concerned with the discussion of programmatic ideas. Not only – following Popper – do I believe that this is a legitimate activity, but I also believe that it is important. For one key respect in which Popper's approach differs from that of Kuhn, is that it allows us to ask: is the pursuit of normal science within some specific paradigm something that we *should* be doing? Does it make sense in terms of where we wish to go? And my concern, in the latter chapters of the book, will be to suggest that we should think again about some approaches that have been pursued by those interested in Hayek's work, while at the same time urging the importance of work on some issues that are not, to my knowledge, currently being pursued.

The approach that I am taking also involves the acceptance of Duhem's argument that our ideas face the world as a system.[17] From such a perspective, we cannot appraise a solution to a problem if it is offered in isolation, just because the relevant constraints on the solution are constituted by the other problems that we also wish to solve, and the kinds of solutions that we are proposing to adopt towards them.

I will now explain what all this amounts to in the context of the appraisal of normative political theory. I will set out these ideas by way of a systematic, yet self-contained, argument, rather than in a manner that depends on the further invocation of ideas from the philosophy of science.

APPRAISING NORMATIVE POLITICAL THEORY

How should we appraise the work of a normative political theorist?

First, we might ask whether what is being said is logically consistent. Consistency is obviously a virtue. If a work contains inconsistencies, then, on the basis of our most usual logical ideas, anything can be deduced from it. However, if little is being asserted, and an author is not offering us a solution to an interesting problem, it is no big deal that he is consistent in what he says. However, I would be surprised if any of the major works in the history of political thought were internally consistent. But this, while showing that such works are flawed, plainly does not show that they are worthless. Indeed, the existence of such inconsistencies may generate a research programme for those attracted to an author's main ideas, or to a particular tradition: the programme of showing how such inconsistencies can be removed in ways that do not diminish – and, ideally, improve – the attractiveness of the more general view.

Second, we might note that the author is advancing certain theses. Should we then appraise how his theses are justified? It will clearly be a point against an author if he claims that some consequence follows from particular premises and it does not in fact do so. At the same time, it is easy to overrate such matters. On a purely technical level, the fact that the argument that he has offered does not do what he had hoped does not, of itself, show that there is not some other argument that could do the trick. But more important, the idea that justificatory argument in political theory should be about such proofs and disproofs is, in my view, mistaken.

If we want to establish some thesis, it simply will not do to show that it can be deduced from something else. If such an argument is valid, all that this would tell us is that the premises from which we have deduced it are (at least) as contentious as the thesis that we wished to establish. If our thesis were itself contentious, all that we would have done is to show that our premises (which, presumably, we had taken to be unproblematic), in fact have hidden content to them which makes them contentious, too. The root of this problem – our desire for proof, and the belief that such proof can be obtained by reasoning from axioms, of the correctness of which we can be assured – is, I suspect, an old error, the role of which in recent times may well stem from a misunderstanding in the late sixteenth and early seventeenth centuries of the epistemological character of Euclidian geometry.[18] For it is this – and the attachment of Descartes and Newton to a generalization of mathematical reasoning, understood in such a way, as a method of argument – which left us with the epistemological project of the discovery of rational and empirical foundations of knowledge which dominated Western philosophy for so long.

This project, which has led us into many extremely interesting issues, also led us on a wild goose chase for subjective indicators of objective validity, and thence into an epistemology which was one-sidedly individualistic and subjectivistic. More striking still, it would seem that could 'foundations' be discovered that would satisfy the epistemic demands of this tradition – that we could know them to be true beyond the possibility of error – they would not be of much use to us as foundations. For they would be of little use to us in the process of justification for which they were destined, just because of the inevitable poverty of their content.

But does this mean that the project of discovering that something in which we are interested follows from particular premises must be dismissed as worthless? I think that if this is understood after the fashion of foundationalist justification, then indeed that is correct. Happily, however, this is not the only way in which such a 'proof' might be understood. To give these points some specificity, let us consider a concrete example.

Someone interested in political philosophy might ask: what is the point of

16

those sections of Nozick's *Anarchy, State, and Utopia* which explore what follows from premises about the rights of individuals that most readers would not themselves accept? Some might say that their value is technical. But while Nozick's argument is often ingenious, this is hardly adequate as an answer in itself. For there is no reason why we should be interested in technical sophistication *per se*. It is only if the argument has some bearing upon our problems and concerns – intellectual or practical – that the activity would have been worth undertaking in the first place.

A better response is that such work is clearly of interest to those people who are attracted to the particular normative ideas which Nozick discusses, and who are, perhaps, concerned about the compatibility of these ideas with others. Consider a radical individualist who believes that people have rights in the sense of something close to Nozick's reading of Locke. Suppose that such a person is repelled by the anarchistic conclusions which others have drawn from such views. Suppose that he wishes to be reassured that his radical individualism is compatible with a minimal state, but is concerned lest – as arguably in Locke – a state that is generated to defend individuals' rights seems, in the end, to threaten to devour them. In such a case, the strongest proof of compatibility is if the possibility of a minimal but no more than a minimal state can, in fact, be derived from these ideas, together with other innocuous premises. Thus, what gives such results their interest is a normative concern for the claims that are being made.

From such a perspective, the rationale of the first parts of *Anarchy, State, and Utopia* would be to reassure a radical, rights-based individualist who wants to accept a minimal, but not more than a minimal, state. Or, alternatively, to challenge another such individualist who wishes to claim that no state could be legitimated upon such a basis. And indeed, it is striking that much of the critical commentary upon those sections of Nozick's work has been written by individualist anarchists.[19]

Such argument would thus be read avidly by individualists. But it is not clear that, in itself, it would be found interesting by anyone else, other than because its perspective was – to many – novel, and also because Nozick is a brilliant and inventive philosopher, such that what he says on these issues may be suggestive of applications elsewhere. However, someone who is critical of such an individualistic perspective – perhaps the later Nozick? – might also be interested to see what can be done within the ambit of such an approach. Nozick's work, if understood in these latter terms, exemplifies a meta-level approach to philosophy which is attractive, and which is close to that set out in the Introduction to Nozick's *Philosophical Explanations*.[20] On such a view, the theorist would be judged not on the basis of whether he had justified some idea, but, rather, on the basis of whether he had shown some idea to be compossible with others to which he is also attracted. One task for the normative political philosopher is thus to show how it is possible to have what he wants – in the face of objections from others that he is trying to have his cake and eat it, too. This also allows for the possibility of someone's discovering that ideals which they had hoped to espouse are in conflict with one another.

Such an approach may seem to have little critical bite. And this is indeed the case if we consider our ideals just one by one. But it starts to become more interesting once we bring together more and more of our ideals, and also pertinent factual information, too (including, of course, ideas from social and economic theory).[21] It may prove much more difficult than we at first thought to have all the things that we want at the same time. And by exploring ideas – empirical and theoretical – which we had supposed to be compatible, we may make discoveries which surprise us. We may also discover that what we had taken to be the 'obvious' means to the realization of some ideal will not, in fact, be effective. Or we may discover that there may exist historical examples of things which we had assumed not to be possible.[22]

This marks a point of contrast with more usual 'analytical' approaches within moral and political philosophy. For, against them, it suggests that seeing our task as the explication of relationships between particular concepts is radically defective. It is defective, first, because such a view underspecifies the task upon which the theorist is engaged. It is only if *other* assumptions and desiderata are explicated that the theorist's task becomes properly formulated. Just as Duhem argued in respect of the empirical, so it is in respect of the normative: any specific element of our knowledge can be preserved in the face of difficulties, if we are willing to make appropriate adjustments elsewhere. Accordingly, when seen from a non-foundationalist perspective, it is the systematic philosopher who is *more* rigorous than the analytical particularist, committed to the analysis of particular concepts upon a piecemeal basis. It suggests, further, against the current practice of leading journals in moral philosophy, that work that situates itself within the theoretical perspective of a historical or current theorist is *more* rigorous than the 'analysis' of only isolated problems or concepts, because it is only the systematic approaches that explicate the constraints in relation to which their solutions to particular problems are to be evaluated.

Second, such an account is defective in so far as it presents itself as involving an appeal to, or an analysis of, 'our' concepts, or 'our' ways of using language. Two arguments are pertinent here.

The first is that the 'our' of 'our concepts' or 'our intuitions' may stand in need of critical scrutiny. For it may reflect a history of domination exercised by one class, sex or status group over another. Concepts and intuitions may, for this reason, be rooted in various kinds of domination, rather than representing a neutral tribunal to which issues can be brought for settlement. What had been assumed to be a consensual judgement on the acceptability of some theory – and thus for the preferability of certain concepts – may be questioned from the point of view of the epistemological acceptability of the social processes that served to form or to preserve the integrity of the judgement. To make such a point, however, is not to presume that there is some neutral perspective immediately available to us, or some key to our situation the possession of which will remove all prejudice and leave truth manifest to our inspection. Rather, such an approach should be understood as an extension of fallibilism, and its programme of the piecemeal improvement of our knowledge. In taking it up – and in thus suggesting that the way in which some consensus has been reached stands in need of a particular kind of critical scrutiny[23] – we should recognize that we will be involved in the messy business of the investigation of the interplay between the historical, the empirical and the theoretical. Further, any claim that our previous ideas have been defective due to the existence of some socially maintained barrier must be argued on the basis of our usual criteria for the acceptance of empirical and theoretical claims and their revision.

To maintain this is not to be unnecessarily conservative. For in our own day, powerful and illuminating criticism has been offered in such a manner of the work of some of the greatest figures in the history of political thought, from a feminist perspective. It is indeed striking, in retrospect, how it had been possible to overlook discrepancies between arguments conducted in purely general terms concerning the characteristics of human beings, and institutional arrangements which treated first slaves and then women in ways that were flatly at odds with such arguments. I suspect that we have a lot more yet to learn from feminist criticism of the assumptions of political theory, and I believe that we must always be open to the possibility that further such revisions may be necessary from other and as yet unsuspected directions. Further, for reasons to which I have already alluded in my discussion of disaggregation earlier in this chapter and which I will discuss in more detail later in this volume, the very idea that the analysis of social institutions is usefully to be conducted in terms of the analysis of shared concepts,[24] is open to criticism. There may be such concepts, which are even used by all parties to give an account of what they are doing. But to presume that this 'official' account actually illuminates what is going on runs the risk of serious misunderstanding. This will be the case notably in so far as the concepts pertain to what are, in fact, the emergent products of meaningful action, of negotiation or of coercion.

The second argument is that – to elaborate on a point of Karl Popper's – it is poor practice for the theorist to focus to too great an extent upon concepts. To be sure, we may need to do this, *ad hoc*, if it turns out that we seem to be arguing at cross purposes and we suspect that this might be a result of a term's being used in different ways (indeed, my brief discussion of different interpretations of socialism, earlier in this chapter, was a response to just such a problem). But beyond this, to focus upon concepts is counter-productive just because, faced with disagreements about concepts *per se*, there is little that can be said. In my view, the approaches both of those who talk about concepts being 'essentially contested', and the 'restrictivists' who oppose them,[25] are equally unhelpful (I also do not think that the distinction between 'concepts' and 'conceptions' helps things much, either). Rather, we should treat the theorist's choice of concepts as being akin to the choice of theoretical terms.[26] On such a view, the adoption of one rather than another concept would be given its point by our judgements about substantive theories and states of affairs, both factual and moral. The decision to use one rather than another concept is thus something that should depend on our comparative assessment of theoretical argument about matters of substance: what concepts we adopt should, in my view, be determined by what theories we find most telling.

To make all this a little more concrete, I would suggest that there is nothing much to be gained for the theorist by ruminating over different concepts of liberty or coercion. Rather, any theorist should simply say what he is proposing he thinks we should consider desirable, and why; giving us an argument at such point as one is needed. And this, clearly, will occur in part just at those points in which he is urging that we should depart from theories and judgements which are hitherto widely held. We can argue the merits of the idea that each individual should be entitled to positive assistance from others, should, say, they be in certain specified conditions of need. But nothing is gained by whether or not this entitlement is to be conceptualized as a right or, say, as related to the liberty of that individual, except in so far as this serves simply to explicate in more detail how it is being claimed that they should be treated. It is with respect to *this* issue that *arguments* can take place. How, *conceptually*, we handle matters is something that should be decided in light of what theories and what (consensually redeemed) intuitions in the end win the day, and also pragmatically in terms of what vocabulary comes most easily to those involved in such disputes.

If such ideas were accepted it would, in the first instance, leave the political theorist the task of showing that the various views that he wants to hold are consistent, and of investigating the trade-offs between the realization of one ideal and others. To this task, empirical material will clearly be relevant; and normative political theory will be clearly bound up with empirical investigation. Particular empirical results may be important for the assessment of the tenability of some combination of ideals. But normative theory will also generate research programmes or 'paradigms' for empirical study: we may be led by our normative ideas to try to show that a problem can in fact be solved in some particular way. (Thus, a socialist who is attracted to Marx's ideas about the overcoming of alienation in his early writings might be pressed into theoretical and empirical investigations as to how – or whether – a modern society could work in ways which realized Marx's ideals. Similarly, the classical liberal might be led into historical investigations of the strengths and weaknesses of the voluntary or cooperative provision of social services and of medicine, and into theoretical work as to how – or whether – such problems as were encountered historically could, in fact, be resolved in ways compatible with his view of the proper limits of state action.)

In so far as our concern is with compossibility – in the sense of showing the logical compatibility and the empirical co-realizability of different ideals – then it is worth noting that our normative concerns will properly play a major role in our empirical investigations (indeed, if an issue is unrelated to our normative concerns, we should ask ourselves why we are pursuing it). We will be concerned with what is compatible with them theoretically, or with whether they can be realized in what we take to be pertinent factual circumstances. They will thus quite properly play a leading role in the direction of empirical research. Such research, however, may serve not only to confirm the normative views that inspire it, but also to render them problematic. And one may see the success — or otherwise — of empirical and historical research inspired by normative ideals as one of the significant ways in which such ideals may be criticized.

So far, however, there has been something largely missing from our account; namely, other people. Our deliberations so far could well have been performed by Robinson Crusoe. Crusoe would come to his island already socialized, informed about the world, and with ready made ideas (such knowledge itself being the product of investigation that is, essentially, intersubjective in its character; but this need not concern us here). But (until Friday) he would not be concerned about the compatibility between his views and those of other people (except in so far as an implicit reference to the judgement of others is presupposed in the making of both factual and moral judgements), and with the issue of whether they would find his ideals and other constructions acceptable — except in so far as he had a carry over of ideas about the acceptability of his views from his previous life. Similarly, he would have no incentive to reappraise his ideals, other than on the grounds of their compossibility with his other ideals and pertinent matters of fact.

However, normative political theory is obviously concerned with other people, too: and not only in the obvious sense that we are involved in cooperation, competition and conflict with others. We are also concerned to show others that they ought to share the views that we favour, or at least to tolerate them. We may — and I think that we should — believe that we should hold certain views ourselves only if our holding them is also judged reasonable by others. Clearly, some of our concerns may be understood by us simply as matters of contingent taste and circumstance, such that we would not be disturbed should we have had preferences with respect to those things other than we do. But other preferences are only held by us because we believe that there is a compelling case for us to have such preferences; an idea that may usefully be cashed out by saying that, ideally, there should be an interpersonal consensus that we should hold them. Such judgements should ideally pass not only the scrutiny of other people in situations different from our own, but also that of our own self at different stages in our life. Suppose, in the end, the idea that there is only *one* approach which we should have taken is unrealizable, and that there is a pluralism of different competing approaches to moral and political life which people may wish to try out or to enjoy, between which no cognitive argument can help them decide. We will, at the very least, wish to discover the limits of such pluralism, and to offer cogent arguments as to why we – and others – are entitled to be left alone to pursue particular choices, within it.

In this task, in so far as it is part of normative political theory (as opposed to simply fighting off those who are not interested in argument, or coming to prudential compromises with rational economic men), we must start with things that our interlocutors accept – or which we can persuade them into accepting. Our task is then to show how the things that we favour follow from things which our interlocutors accept. (We may also, of course, be concerned to show our interlocutors that things that they had believed to be compossible are not, in fact, so.)

It might be thought: but such argument cannot work – for the very reasons that were advanced against the ideal of justification, above. If your interlocutor discovers that your ideals (which he never liked) follow from premises that he had previously accepted,[27] he may well then give that as grounds for rejecting those premises. But at that point, he faces a problem himself. Not only will he be reluctant to give up things which, presumably, are able to capture many things that he favours. But he, also, will be concerned with the acceptability and the plausibility of his ideas to others. And the fact that a proposed approach is not compossible with some quirk of his ('But it will still allow people to have dogs!') will cut no ice with anyone else. This will give him an incentive to couch his own arguments – and his own objections – in currency which is acceptable to others. (Where these may be matters in which they are in agreement with him, or in respect of which there is agreement that it is reasonable to differ.) One is not, here, appealing to things that are beyond question. For the 'foundations' of such arguments are matters in respect of which there is an open-ended, intersubjective consensus. And in the event of someone finding any element of this consensus to be unacceptable, it is open to them to argue that our judgements should, at this point, be revised (as is the case with respect to Popper's ideas about the 'foundations' of empirical knowledge). Such a consensus is not a matter of pure convention. For the consensus concerns the truth of a factual statement, or the moral acceptability of some normative statement. While it is only because that upon which there is agreement is not seen as purely conventional that argument is possible (that is, about such statements directly, rather than about them as a means to an end).

As I suggested above, such an approach allows for a new twist to be given to arguments about compossibility. For rather than compossibility's being restricted to the ideas and views about matters of fact of a single individual, this argument may be generalized to the attempt to show how particular ideals are compossible with (or to discover that they are not compossible with) ideas which are acceptable not only to oneself and a particular interlocutor, but to any interlocutor. (To emphasize this point again, this does not mean that they are conceived of as sharing the views in question, but merely as seeing these views as unexceptionable for someone in particular circumstances to hold.)[28]

Such a task may also generate a further problem for the political theorist, which is well illustrated by a challenge that Raymond Plant has made to the classical liberal.[29] Plant says, in effect: show me the basis on which you are suggesting that individuals are entitled to the kind of treatment that you favour, and I will show you that they are then also entitled to welfare rights of the kind that I favour.

What might such argument look like? The classical liberal may say that coercion is bad. His interlocutor may say: why? This should be understood not as a demand for a justification, but as a request for a further explication of features of the object in respect of which the judgement is being made, which serve to discriminate between it and other objects of judgement or – if the interlocutor is puzzled as to why the judgement has been made at all – which help to render it more comprehensible. Once this has been done, however, it may prove difficult to explain, say, why the judgement should not have been extended; say, from the respecting of negative rights to a duty to give positive assistance, against the classical liberal's initial intention. Thus, argument of the kind with which we are here dealing must show not only that one can get what one wants upon some suggested basis, but also that others can't use it to get more than one wants, too. (The 'too' here does not assume that the two sets of claims are consistent; rather, your critic may wish to claim that your argument, if pursued rigorously, leads to his conclusions rather than to yours.)

If someone is engaged in a task within normative political theory of the kind that I have described above, they may be involved with a particular set of problems that they wish to solve. They may, say, have taken on the task of showing that a market-based political economy will serve to realize certain values. But it is not enough just to see what some author is doing in a particular piece of work. For he may have lost sight of some larger task that he had set himself. Thus, in the task of the evaluation of the work of a political theorist, one may legitimately engage in the enterprise of discovering and then reminding him what it was that he was supposed to be doing. It may well be that some task on which he is currently engaged – which, in itself, may seem fine, plausible and well-argued – may be criticized on the grounds that it does not meet up with the standards set by his original task or concern.

Now, clearly, it is possible for someone to renounce some earlier attachment. But this may have implications for how their work is to be appraised. For while someone may change their views, they may also lose sight of the fact that their argument was originally addressed to other people who shared their earlier concerns. If, as a result of changing their views, they drop their earlier line of argument, the cost may be that their new argument is no longer telling to those other people. But this is something of which the theorist himself may lose track.

This is why, in studying Hayek's work, and in seeking to appraise it as normative theory, I believe that it is necessary to look at the history of his ideas. For only this, in my view, enables one to discover what the problems are to which his work is addressed, and also to whom he is making his claims. And this may be crucial. For someone may end up following the logic of some argument, and reaching a position that is consistent, but where the crucial point that must be made against them is that in the course of their argument they have – perhaps inadvertently – given up some claim that was vital for the larger enterprise in which they were engaged.

Such an approach may be extended beyond the individual, to the intellectual tradition within which he or she is working. Historical investigation may serve to disclose a problematic with which people working within some tradition may have lost contact. It may show them that what differentiated the tradition within which they are working was a claim that it could solve a certain group of problems – but where the latter-day spokesmen of this tradition may have lost track of the fact that it is important for them to accomplish this task. (As a concrete example here, one might consider what Marxian socialism was originally wishing to do, and contrast that with the views at which some theorists who still regard themselves as Marxists have now arrived.)[30]

Such historical investigation may also help us in the task of rendering commensurable theories and traditions which, as we currently encounter them, seem simply to be talking past one another. For if one looks at the historical origin of some theory, one can discover problems that existed prior to and external to that theory, to the solution or resolution of which the theory was being proffered. This may enable one to explain to the later proponent of that theory what it is that he or she is doing, to provide a basis on which their work can be fairly assessed, and also enable one to bring into contact diverse intellectual traditions.[31]

In approaching Hayek's work, therefore, my concern is not just with whether views that he is offering at some point are consistent. My concern, rather, is to disclose the broader argumentative structure within which he is operating. I have paid attention to the way in which he is – or is not – able to solve the problems that he set himself, or which are set for him by the tradition within which he is working. These are matters that can only be disclosed by historical investigation. And – as in Hayek's own particular case – the most serious criticism that one may have to make of a theorist is that, at some point in his work, he has forgotten what he was doing. He may, and I believe that this is the case with Hayek, introduce arguments into his work without assessing what consequences the use of these will have for his larger enterprise. Or he may, equally, follow an argument to its conclusion without stopping to assess what consequences this, in turn, has for his more general views.

In this volume, I only touch the surface of these matters. Even if the arguments offered in what follows should prove to be correct, more detailed investigation of Hayek's own intellectual history and its context will surely lead to revisions of the picture that I have painted. I am also all too conscious of having offered merely one side of – and a rather odd perspective upon – what is clearly a many sided conversation. Hayek, after all, was an Austrian; but I have been able to place him in that context only to a very limited extent. He was also a polymath. The proper appreciation of his problematic, and thus the real basis for the assessment of his work, would involve the reconstruction of the whole range of conversations to which he was party. In addition, he was a professional economist, and much of his work needs to be situated within the technical problem situations of that discipline before it can be properly assessed. In particular, I will not discuss Hayek's work on monetary and capital theory in the 1920s and 1930s, despite the fact that it was his major concern at the time, and that it clearly relates, in interesting ways, to his political ideas. I will also refer only in passing to his writings on methodological issues, although I have written about these elsewhere.[32] A more systematic engagement with his writings, however desirable, must in my view wait until further work has been undertaken on other aspects of Hayek's work, not least by others.

One final point. As I have indicated in the acknowledgements to this volume, and as will be clear to any reader of this work, I have benefited immensely from the work of Norman Barry and John Gray on these topics. However, the approach that I have taken to Hayek has differed from theirs, and in a manner that would make direct engagement with their writings somewhat counter-productive on this occasion. Later work – notably that of Kukathas – was published after the main lines of my interpretation of Hayek were developed, and it has proved useful to refer to it only on occasion, given the rather particular purposes of the present work. I would, though, wish to stress that the fact that I have not been concerned, on this occasion, with the major secondary literature on Hayek does not mean that I have found it uninteresting, only that coming to terms with it would be a task for another occasion. I would say, though, that what I would take to be the thrust of Kukathas's conclusion to his work – that Hayek's main contribution to liberalism is by way of his contributions to social theory – is a view with which I would strongly concur, and also that it is a viewpoint around which Roland Kley's approach to Hayek is structured, albeit in a volume that came to my notice too late to be discussed in this book.[33]

2

FROM SOCIALISM TO *THE ROAD TO SERFDOM*

HAYEK BEFORE LIBERALISM

Hayek was born into an academic family in Vienna in which the predominant intellectual interest was biology. As a young man, he became a socialist. In his Inaugural Address at the LSE in 1933, 'The Trend of Economic Thinking', Hayek said:[1]

> It is probably true that economic analysis has never been the product of detached intellectual curiosity about the why of social phenomena, but of an intense urge to reconstruct a world which gives rise to profound dissatisfaction. This . . . is as true of the phylogenesis of economics as of the ontogenesis of probably every economist.

He also quoted Pigou, thus:[2]

> It is not wonder, but the social enthusiasm which revolts from the sordidness of mean streets and the joylessness of withered lives, that is the beginning of economic science.

It is clear enough that, in referring to this practical and reformist impetus in the economist, Hayek also refers to himself. He has written of his generation in Vienna immediately after the First World War:[3]

> We felt that the civilization in which we had grown up had collapsed. We were determined to build a better world, and it was this desire to reconstruct society that led many of us to the study of economics. Socialism promised to fulfil our hopes for a more rational, more just world.

But what, more specifically, might this have meant? As a young man, Hayek was influenced by the writings of Walter Rathenau.[4] Rathenau was an industrialist and former director of war production who had turned social critic, and who offered a middle way between capitalism and socialism. Rathenau's ideas on social reform are set within a grander vision for the moral transformation of society. He described the existing pattern of social organization as a 'mechanism'. Under this head, he depicted the disadvantages of life in a factory, and expressed a concern for the cultureless and propertyless situation of the proletariat. All this, however, Rathenau believed could be transformed; the transformation to have, as its instrument, the activities of the state:[5]

> Mechanisation is capable of being morally permeated with spirit; the state, which is the highest and noblest part of the mechanistic system, has been thus permeated through a premature ordination, and could never fulfil its mission without this transformation.

Indeed, the purpose of the constructive part of Rathenau's book, *In Days to Come*, he tells us,[6] 'is to show that the spiritual guidance of life and the permeation of the mechanistic order with spirit, will transform the blind play of forces into a fully conscious and free cosmos worthy of mankind'.

In more practical terms, while Rathenau expressed some sympathy with socialism, he rejected the socialist movement, which he characterized as over-concerned with the material to the exclusion of the spiritual. Rathenau was critical of what he saw as its material egalitarianism:[7] 'It is not our aim to level the inequalities of human destiny and human pretension ... our ideal is the replacement of a blind and inexorable system of institutions by self-determination and self-responsibility'. And he rejected as irrelevant the ideal of the nationalization of the means of production, on the grounds that one needs to place capital where returns are highest, and thus to be guided by some notion of interest or a rate of return:[8]

> [Interest] will be inevitable even where all the means of production are concentrated into a single hand.... Thus the nationalization of the means of production has no economic significance.

Rathenau rejected competition as wasteful and he was critical of speculation. His positive programme involved the placing of restrictions on luxury spending, on the grounds that it represented a squandering of national wealth, and the advocacy of an inheritance tax.[9] He looked forward to a society in which production would be rationalized and idle hands would be put to work, all of which he expected would result in a vast increase in wealth. He also wished to encourage state-supervised monopolies. He argued that workers would do better under a monopolist than they would if they were counterpoised to a multiplicity of owners who would have class interests opposed to theirs.[10] He was also much concerned about power, which he saw as stemming from private monopolies. A 'spiritualized' state, however, was seen as a force for good. Rathenau wished that such a state should be unencumbered by material restrictions,[11] a condition that he thought would follow from the adoption of his economic ideas:[12]

> The state grows rich beyond imagination. All the tasks it has hitherto

performed, can be performed much better. The state can abolish poverty and unemployment: it can fulfil to an unprecedented degree all obligations of a generally useful character.

Rathenau favoured an economic order in which, while industrial enterprises would remain in private hands, the state would 'regulate and balance'. He was an advocate of a corporatist economy, in which industry in peacetime would be organized much like the war corporations that he had set up in 1914–15.[13]

I do not wish to attribute to the young Hayek any detailed commitment to the ideas of Rathenau. Not only is the evidence for any deep influence slight, but it is difficult to picture any serious-minded person finding Rathenau's work satisfying for very long. Felix has written that 'Rathenau wrote or dictated easily, and was said to send off his first drafts without corrections'.[14] And the reader of his work today is likely to appreciate Fuersteberg's remark about one of Rathenau's productions, to the effect that 'a book like that is easier to write than read'.[15] None the less, a comment that Felix has made about the general impact of Rathenau's work is much to the point:[16]

> [Rathenau's] ideas . . . had found the great opening between doctrinaire socialism and irresponsible capitalism. Many felt that he was correct in general, whatever error in the details.

My point in discussing Rathenau, and the young Hayek's interest in his work, is to try to convey something not only of the problems that he found pressing, but also of the kind of response to them with which he felt some sympathy, when as a young man Hayek returned to Vienna after the First World War. Like many of his generation, Hayek was profoundly affected by what seemed to be an end to an older social order; and this, together with a passionate concern to better the lot of the poor, led him towards what he later described as a form of Fabian socialism, and to the wish to study economics. All this drives home the fact that Hayek was not born a classical liberal. Rather, he became one. But how did this occur, under what circumstances, and why?

At the University of Vienna, Hayek was first attracted to study with Othmar Spann. Spann was an influential proponent of what he called 'universalism'. This was, in effect, a form of ethically directed corporatism, Spann's arguments for which included a strong dose of what would today be called 'communitarian' criticism of liberalism. Spann also accorded a positive, and moralizing, role to the state. Hayek's attraction to Spann quickly waned. Hayek and a friend were barred from Spann's seminars for voicing their dissent. Hayek chose instead to study with Friedrich von Wieser, a leading figure in the Austrian School of economics. Wieser also considered himself something of a socialist. Indeed, Hayek has written about his choice of a teacher of economics:[17]

> I was attracted to [Wieser] . . . because unlike most of the other members

of the Austrian School [of economics] he had a good deal of sympathy with [the] mild Fabian Socialism to which I was inclined as a young man. He in fact prided himself that his theory of marginal utility had provided the basis of progressive taxation, which then seemed to me one of the ideals of social justice.

The Austrian School of economics plays a major role in Hayek's work, and it might therefore be useful to say a little about it here. The school developed from the work of Carl Menger. While it can be regarded as the Austrian wing of the 'marginalist' revolution in economics, this is not a particularly helpful way in which to approach it. For the Austrian School had many character-istics which distanced it from other forms of marginalism, some of which will be of importance for our story. Menger's own work differed from that of the other founding fathers of 'marginalist' economists in various respects.[18] Menger took methodological ideas very seriously and wrote on them at considerable length. He championed a version of the resoluto-compositive method, in which a large-scale phenomenon was to be understood by breaking it down into its component parts. Menger characterized the way in which we understand these parts, however, as involving our grasping the essence of the phenomena in question. The Aristotelian overtones of this terminology have been linked by some commentators with Menger's resistance to the idea that marginalist economic analysis should be expressed in mathematical terms.[19]

Menger's social philosophy and his methodological views were developed in contrast to those of the German historical school.[20] While his relations with the older historical economists are a matter of some interpretative controversy, there is no question about the fact that Menger became embroiled with the leader of the younger branch of the historical school, Gustav Schmoller, in the *Methodenstreit*. This was a ponderous dispute about the methods of the social sciences, which generated more heat than light. However, out of it came Menger's own *Investigations into the Method of the Social Sciences* (of which more later), and the entire dispute also forms part of the background to Max Weber's methodological writings. Menger's economic writings also had several dis-tinctive features, the most notable of which were his historical approach to the understanding of money, and his analysis of capital.

At the time at which Hayek attended the University of Vienna, the Austrian School had, in effect, split into two parts.[21] On the one side there was Wieser, with whom Hayek chose to study. On the other there was Mises. Wieser, while he wrote extensively on methodological issues, and was influenced by distinctively Mengerian themes, was in some respects closer to non-Austrian marginalist writers – at least, by contrast with Mises. At the same time, Wieser was concerned not only with economic issues, but also with the analysis of power. All this led to a somewhat complex approach to issues in political economy. While Wieser argued that, for methodological reasons, one should start with idealized constructions, he wished progressively to qualify the picture that such an approach conveyed by taking note of institutional factors and disparities in power. All this forms the setting for his remarks on policy issues in his more explicitly economic writings.

Given the association, with which we are today familiar, between Austrian economics and a staunch economic liberalism, one might be surprised by the critical tone in which Wieser treats both liberal economists and capitalist institutions. The former, he believes, are the victims of an intellectual error. For, from his perspective, they have confused the *initial* stage of economic theorizing – a simplified intellectual construct – with reality. In Wieser's view, economics should operate first with over-simplifying models, and then, gradually, bring in social and institutional factors. Liberal economists, in his view, simply read economic lessons off the initial stage of economic investigation, forgetting that the picture that these ideas convey is the product of an over-simplifying methodological device.

Commenting on his own discussion of the impact of competition upon production, Wieser says:[22]

> Our exposition has given undue weight to the apparent effects of competition on the progress of production. This is because our discussion has rested upon the idealizing assumptions which, so far, we have adhered to in our work. To come back to every day standards, we must now, by decreasing abstraction, familiarise ourselves with typical conditions of reality. We shall have to consider more especially the social powers which largely rule the destinies of man. The exaggerations in the classical doctrine are due to the fact that its authors carried the idealizing approach into actual observations. They were possibly not even conscious of this and accepted the results of such idealized observation for unimpeachable truth.

But what did his differences with the classical economists amount to, in more specific terms? At various places in Wieser's *Social Economics* he can be found taking issue with the social policy of the classical economists – and especially with that of their less sagacious followers who, in his judgement,[23] 'accepted the rule of freedom word for word without noting any of its accompanying restrictions as set forth by the masters'. For Wieser:[24]

> The theory of the simple economy only explains the condition of the isolated and idealized individual economy that follows its laws of motion without constraint. But in the social economy these individual units meet from all directions. Indeed, they clash with great force. We must, therefore, ascertain whether their conjunction does not alter their law of motion and whether in particular the amount of power does not exercise a decisive control.

And indeed, when discussing capitalism in his *Social Economics*, Wieser writes of the 'tyranny' of large-scale capitalist institutions; of 'capitalist power ... not infrequently [verging] on a crushing despotism' and of 'disfigur[ing] capitalist forces', in respect of which action by the state is not only required, but is in harmony with 'the social spirit of the economy'.[25] He concludes a general discussion of such themes by writing:[26]

> For a sound modern economic policy, the safeguarding of the highest possible social benefit in the face of capitalistic despotism must be the paramount law. A completed theory of utility will be able to demonstrate to that policy under what conditions the law will meet with compliance, under what conditions it will miscarry.

As the end of the above quotation indicates (for he does not consider himself able to offer such a 'completed theory') Wieser is only tentative in his views as to what should be done. From some provisional conclusions which follow the quoted passage, it would seem as if, even in the area of large-scale industry, 'the private constitution is to be maintained'.[27] He appears to favour a system in which private ownership is to continue, but in which the private exercise of power is to be limited by legal controls: 'the constitution of large industries will have to be changed by law'. After mentioning 'workers' protective legislation and ... social insurance which restrict the private constitution as regards the contract of labour by certain prohibitions and by compulsory insurance',[28] he says that this 'probably does not exhaust the possibilities of social reform'. But Wieser's ideas for additional measures are vague, the following being about as specific as he gets:[29]

> Indications are not lacking, which suggest the methods according to which a new constitution of the large industries might be formulated, a constitution following the middle course between the despotism of the all-powerful entrepreneur and socialistic demands, in a manner resembling the attitude observed in a constitutional monarchy between absolutism and republicanism.

I have gone into some detail about the ideas of Rathenau and then of Wieser to emphasize the *kind* of ideas with which Hayek was familiar, and with which he showed some sympathy prior to his espousal of liberalism. Hayek would also, of course, have been familiar with many other forms of socialism – including Marxian Social Democracy – from the Vienna of this period.

But what led Hayek from his early and mildly socialist views and from sympathy with those of Wieser? Essentially, it was the influence of Ludwig von Mises, both in a personal capacity and through his writings on the problem of economic calculation under socialism.[30]

Hayek tells us that, when he was at the university, while he 'had looked in at one of [Mises'] lectures [he had] found that a man so conspicuously antipathetic to the kind of Fabian views which [he] then held was not the sort of person to whom [he] wanted to go [for instruction]'.[31] However, they were later brought

31

into contact when Hayek was seeking employment. Mises, as one of the directors of a new temporary government office concerned with settling certain problems arising out of the treaty of St Germain, was looking for young lawyers with some understanding of economics. Hayek fitted the bill: his studies at the university had included both law and economics. He also had a good grasp of foreign languages. For the next ten years Hayek worked with Mises: for five years in the government office (during which period Hayek spent some time on leave in the United States, doing some research for an economist at New York University)[32] and for the next five years as Vice-Director of an Institute of Business Cycle Research that he and Mises had set up together, on Hayek's prompting.[33]

THE IMPACT OF MISES

Mises' impact on Hayek was considerable, although it is worth noting what Hayek has said about its character:[34]

> I perhaps most profited from [Mises'] teaching because I was not initially his student at the university, an innocent young man who took his word for gospel, but came to him as a trained economist, trained in a parallel branch of Austrian economics from which he gradually, but never completely, won me over. Though I learned that he was usually right in his conclusions, I was not always satisfied by his arguments, and retained to the end a certain critical attitude which sometimes forced me to build different constructions.

Mises' views on socialism had a crucial impact on Hayek's personal development. In fact, they were the starting-point not only for Hayek's most distinctive ideas about economics, but also for many of his best-known ideas in political philosophy.

Hayek has told us that 'When [Mises'] *Socialism* first appeared in 1922, its impact was profound. It gradually, but fundamentally, altered the outlook of many of the young idealists returning to their studies after the First World War. I know, for I was one of them'.[35] Indeed, Hayek reports that the promise of socialism to fulfil the hopes of young idealists such as himself for a more rational, more just world, was dashed by this book: '*Socialism* told us that we had been looking for improvement in the wrong direction'.[36]

But who was Mises, and what were the views set out in that book? At university, Mises had studied law and political economy.[37] The economics that he was taught was influenced by the later German historical school. His initial work was on 'The History of the Landlord–Peasant Relationship in Galicia',[38] and 'Older Austrian Laws on the Limitation of Child Labour in Industry',[39] topics typical of the historical school's concern for economic history. Mises was also an economic interventionist.[40] In addition, as Hayek has commented,[41] '[Mises] even joined one of those organizations which prompted a German

32

satirical weekly to define economists as people who went round measuring working men's dwellings and saying they were too small'.

However, Mises eventually became interested in the views of Menger, reading his *Principles* in 1903. From 1906, Mises worked on problems of money and banking, and in 1912 he published his major work, *The Theory of Money and Credit*, which applied Austrian marginal utility theory to the analysis of money. In what Mises describes as the early years of his academic activity, he did some lecturing and gave a seminar on problems of economic theory. From 1920 onwards, however, his

> main teaching effort was focused on [his] *Privatseminar*. During the months of October to June, a number of young people gathered round [him] once every two weeks.... In these meetings [they] informally discussed ... problems of economics, social philosophy, sociology, logic, and the epistemology of the sciences of human action.[42]

These 'young people' included Hayek.

Mises' ideas about the problems of economic calculation under socialism, which grew out of his book on money, were first explored in a paper given to the *Nationaloekonomische Gesellschaft* in 1919.[43] They were then elaborated in his *Socialism*. This book deals at considerable length with a whole range of arguments for socialism – both with those claiming to show that it is an inevitable development from a system founded on private property, and with those founded on ethical considerations (which Mises discusses from an economic perspective). There is much of interest in this vast volume; but, as Mises himself has written, 'The doctrine of the impossibility of economic calculation in a socialist community constitutes the gist of [this] book'.[44] It is to a brief consideration of this central argument of Mises' that we must now turn.

Mises' argument was directed against Marxian socialism, and at other proposals (such as one by Otto Neurath) which would replace a market-based economy with a moneyless, centrally directed economy.[45] Mises took the views that he was criticizing as proposing a shift from capitalism to a form of socialism which would involve the abolition of private ownership and exchange in the means of production, and thus the abolition of a market, and prices, for capital goods. Mises argued that such a socialist economy would not, as socialists expected, be more productive than the capitalist economy that it replaced. Those taking decisions within it would face an insuperable problem. They would not be able to take rational *economic* (as opposed to technical) decisions with regard to investment in capital goods, as between the alternative possible uses of resources.

At its simplest, Mises' argument might be put in the following terms. Consider a problem that might face those taking decisions in such an economy. Should they make widgets by a process that, *ceteris paribus*, uses two units of steel and one of rubber, or two units of rubber and one of steel? Such decisions are taken, in a market economy, on the basis of prices which provide information in a highly abstract form about alternative ways in which the materials could otherwise usefully be used. But such prices – and hence such information – are not available to the socialist planner, because there is no market for capital goods. In so far as socialists had seen that there was such a problem, Mises argued that they had not understood its gravity, and had proposed answers – such as calculation in terms of units of labour time – which were grossly inadequate to the task.

Mises presented his argument in some detail. However, I will not discuss the details here, not least because the precise terms in which Mises was arguing have themselves become the subject of controversy. While this discussion is of great interest, and we will consider some aspects of it later in this volume, the points in dispute are not of immediate importance for understanding the impact that Mises' work made on Hayek at the time.[46]

It should be noted, however, that in addition to his central argument about economic calculation, Mises, in his *Socialism* and in many individual essays (for example, those subsequently collected in his *Critique of Interventionism* of 1929), conducted a dogged critique of economic interventionism in many forms that fell short of the adoption of a fully planned economy. Broadly speaking, Mises' line of argument was that such interventionism is counter-productive, largely because it ignores the consequences that will follow when individuals who have freedom of action within a market react to it. Indeed, Mises' argument was that interventionism creates its own dynamic towards centralized control of the economy, when those who have ordered the initial intervention are prompted to intervene once more, in the face of the new problems generated by other people's reactions to their initial intervention.

In the 'Foreword, 1978' to the Liberty Press edition of Mises' *Socialism*, Hayek does not write in much detail of his personal response to the volume. He does say, however, that '[*Socialism*] shocked our generation, and only slowly and painfully did we become persuaded of its central thesis'.[47] And, commenting on a re-reading of the book, he said that he 'was surprised . . . by how many of its arguments, which [he] had initially only half accepted, or regarded as exaggerated and one-sided, have since proved remarkably true'.[48]

Mises' impact on Hayek was profound. In my judgement, three related elements in Hayek's subsequent work can probably be attributed to the impact of Mises' argument (although, as with all such matters, it is difficult to argue such things in precise terms).

First, Hayek was convinced by Mises' broad argument against socialism. While Hayek was himself to become involved in the refinement and development of the argument, one thing stands out in his work from this point on: market prices, and decisions taken upon them, are seen as an essential rather than an accidental feature of societies such as those in which we live. The impact of this strand in Mises' argument stands out clearly from Hayek's Inaugural Address at the LSE, as we will see shortly. Second, there is what might be called a *functional* approach to the market that Mises' argument introduced. Mises focused upon a specific task performed by markets, and asked: How is this to be accomplished if there is not a market? A general lesson from this approach bears fruit in Hayek's subsequent concern for the various functions which markets perform, and with the problems that would be posed if markets were no longer there to perform such tasks. As we will see, Hayek also comes to a more general concern with the functions that may be performed by institutions that we have inherited, but the workings of which may not be transparent to us. Third, there is a point that is a little more difficult to express, but which is particularly challenging to someone with the kind of concerns for social reform that were shared by the young Hayek. It is that, after his encounter with Mises, Hayek starts to be concerned with the market, and more generally with social institutions, as *systems* in which the discharge of desirable functions may be ineliminably linked to other things which are unattractive.

HAYEK'S INAUGURAL ADDRESS

Perhaps the best way in which to appreciate the impact that Mises made upon Hayek is to consider Hayek's Inaugural Address at the London School of Economics in 1933. This address (which Hayek did not himself reprint in any of his collections of articles) contains one of the most significant statements of his ideas. Indeed, it is a key text for my discussion of Hayek's work. It is significant especially because from it one can see the kind of impact that Mises' argument had had upon Hayek, at a time when he still identified strongly with his own earlier concern for social reform. The Inaugural Address also exhibits the influence of another thinker, Carl Menger, whose *Collected Works* Hayek was editing at around the same time as he delivered the address.

Apart from some papers on rent control, Hayek's work up to 1933 was almost exclusively on topics in theoretical economics in the Austrian tradition. (His early writings are on such issues as money and imputation, and later, on capital theory and problems in the theory of trade cycles. He also, however, developed some striking ideas about intertemporal general equilibrium, of which more later.) However, in March 1933 he gave an Inaugural Address at the LSE,[49] to which he had been invited to take up a Chair after having given some lectures there on his theory of trade cycles.[50] As is customary in an Inaugural, Hayek reflected on his discipline and his approach to it. But his address also serves as a tract for his time, in which he sets out his social philosophy. In particular, Hayek explains what he sees as the opposition that exists between the knowledge offered by the discipline of which he is a spokesman, and widely accepted ideas about economic policy.

The best way into Hayek's address is to examine his view of the German historical school of economics, and what he considered its baneful influence.

The German historical economists, who claimed inspiration from the historical jurisprudence of Savigny, had criticized classical economics for its abstract and ahistorical character. There were, as we have already noted, two 'historical' schools: one associated with such figures as Roscher and Knies;[51] the other, the 'younger' historical school, with the economic historian Gustav Schmoller.

The older historical school offered some rather loose ideas about the course of a nation's development being explicable in terms of the realization of that nation's 'spirit'. This served as a framework within which they set out theoretical ideas drawn in part from classical economics together with historical and institutional information. Some historical economists, it appears, also anticipated features of marginalist economics.[52] Their views on economic policy differed from those of the classical economists, in that they allowed for a greater degree of historical relativity with respect to economic policy, and in some cases favoured protectionism. The younger historical school argued that economists should base their work upon empirical information obtained through the study of economic history (hence the topics of Mises' early work). Economists of the younger historical school were closely associated with the *Verein fuer Sozialpolitik*, and the social policy of 'Socialism of the Chair'.

It was against some aspects of the work of the older historical school that Menger had written his methodological work, *Investigations into the Method of the Social Sciences*,[53] and it was with Schmoller, the leader of the younger school, that he became embroiled in the *Methodenstreit*. In the account that follows, I will report Hayek's arguments against the historical school without pausing to consider the historical correctness or otherwise of his claims, for our concern is here to understand Hayek's views on social policy at this time, rather than to look at the history of the *Methodenstreit* itself.

In Hayek's view, the ideas on economic policy of the classical economists were challenged by the historical economists in two ways. First, there was the explicit teaching of the younger historical economists on issues of economic policy: 'many of the palliatives and quack remedies which, in the past, had been rejected . . . were introduced by the new generation of historical economists'.[54] But more important was the influence of their theoretical ideas upon popular opinion: 'Refusing to believe in general laws, the Historical School had the special attraction that its method was constitutionally unable to refute even the wildest of Utopias'.[55]

This was of special concern to Hayek because of his view of the advantages, and the vulnerability, of a market-based social system. As we saw above, the impetus behind Hayek's interest in economics and, in his opinion, behind the development of the discipline, was a dissatisfaction with society as it is. However, for Hayek:[56]

It was only when, because the economic system did not accomplish all we wanted, we prevented it from doing what it had been accomplishing, in an attempt to make it obey us in an arbitrary way, that we realized that there was anything to be understood. It was only incidentally, as a by product of the study of such isolated phenomena, that it was gradually realized that many things which had been taken for granted were, in fact, the product of a highly complicated organism which we could only hope to understand by the intense mental effort of systematic inquiry. Indeed, it is probably no exaggeration to say that economics developed mainly as the outcome of the investigation and refutation of successive Utopian proposals.

For the post-Mises Hayek, economics is particularly important because it informs us about limitations upon our ability to change social arrangements to fit in with our ideals. Economics consists in large part of information about constraints upon our actions: about the way in which there are limitations upon our ability to remedy society's ills while still enjoying benefits which we initially take for granted. More specifically – and it is here that the impact made by Mises' work on economic calculation is clear – it tells us how some of those things which we had taken for granted (such as the coordination of economic activity and the ability to make economic judgements about the use of resources) were the products of complicated mechanisms of which we may not be aware. The existence and character of these mechanisms was something that had to be discovered; but it seemed to Hayek that it was this very knowledge that the historical school was urging us to reject.

This abstract and theoretical argument may be seen as forming the background to some early work on a topic in applied economics: on rent control. In a paper, 'Repercussions of Rent Restrictions' (1930), Hayek had drawn out some of the systematic – and undesirable – consequences that followed from the government's getting involved in rent control. He wrote that while 'the immediate benefits of rent control . . . are obvious to everyone, theory is needed to uncover the unintentional consequences which intervention brings in its wake'.[57]

In his Inaugural Address, when talking about complicated, undesigned social mechanisms that we have inherited,[58] Hayek comments that

> when we begin to understand their working, we discover again and again that necessary functions are discharged by spontaneous institutions. If we tried to run the system by deliberate regulation, we should have to invent such institutions, and yet at first we did not even understand them when we saw them.

And a little later in the address he appeals specifically to a theme from the economic calculation debate:[59] 'The wisest thing [the intelligent planner] could do would be to bring about, by delicate regulation, what is accomplished spontaneously by competition ... [however] he would lack the most important guide to such action which the competitive system affords'.

In Hayek's view, economics also teaches that the inherited mechanisms which play such important functional roles rest upon aspects of human behaviour which, considered on their own, were unattractive:[60]

> From the time of Hume and Adam Smith, the effect of every attempt to understand economic phenomena – that is to say, of every theoretical analysis – has been to show that, in large part, the coordination of individual efforts in society is not the product of deliberate planning, but has been brought about ... by means which nobody wanted or understood, and which in isolation might be regarded as some of the most objectionable features of the system. It showed that changes implied, and made necessary, by changes in our wishes, or in the available means, were brought about without anybody realizing their necessity. In short, it showed that an immensely complicated mechanism existed, worked and solved problems, frequently by means which proved to be the only possible means by which the result could be accomplished [note again the influence of Mises' arguments about economic calculation] but which could not possibly be the result of deliberate regulation, because nobody understood them.

This passage hints at what becomes one of the most interesting themes in Hayek's work. It is that the *best* institutions that we can choose have ineliminable imperfections, which represent the negative side of institutions that are required if we are to realize goals of pressing moral importance. It is a theme to which Hayek returns in many places in his writings, as posing problems for views of which he is critical. In my view, the identification of this theme, the argument that such problems do not allow for utopian resolutions, and the elaboration of the significance of this point for normative political theory is one of Hayek's most important contributions to political thought. At the same time, this idea also generates problems for Hayek himself concerning how citizens are to handle such imperfections in their social institutions ... but here I am getting ahead of myself. Let us return to Hayek's Inaugural Address.

The significance for Hayek of the historical school of economics was that it called into question important lessons he thought we should learn from the theoretical achievements of economics. He had come to believe, as a result of his interaction with Mises, that the views on policy of the classical economists were broadly correct. And if Hayek was right, the 'organism' of the economic system, which we have inherited but whose workings we do not understand, will be damaged by what may seem the most obvious and humane efforts at social reform: efforts to deal with the problems of a market-based society through direct governmental intervention in the economy. Hayek is therefore concerned about the danger of an unholy alliance between popular sentiment and the anti-theoretical influences of the historical school. For in his view, these economists denied that there were constraints on our action of precisely the kind that had been emphasized in Mises' work. In the field of policy, they typically advocated direct remedies to social problems through state activity. In Hayek's view, these were just the kinds of policy that would have popular appeal, but would be damaging in their consequences.

However, it might seem strange that Hayek was attacking the views of the German historical school in his inaugural address. For that school of thought was by then in ruins. Hayek explained his concern in terms of 'its influence on popular thought at the present time'.[61]

Hayek's view of the importance of the historical school relates to an idea which he was later to discuss in *The Constitution of Liberty* with reference to J. S. Mill and J. M. Keynes. It is the view that popular opinion is ruled by ideas; but that the ideas which have such an influence are not so much those of contemporaries as those of the previous generation of economists and political theorists. At the time at which he was writing, Hayek believed that it was the ideas of the German historical school which had such a role.[62] That such a thing is the case was, in his judgement, ironic, as more recent developments in economic theory had often rehabilitated the ideas on policy of the classical economists.

This theme in Hayek's Inaugural Address also introduces a further concern that runs throughout his writings. It looms especially large in his later work, and it marks an important point of distinction between Hayek's views and those of other classical liberals of his generation in whose work economic issues play a major role. For Hayek, the problems of social and political order are not a matter just of individuals and their interests. Rather, Hayek offers us a complex picture of social systems as largely the undesigned products of human activity, and as depending on individuals following rules or patterns of conduct the rationale for which may not be clear to them. Just because such social and political institutions are imperfect even at their best, a difficult problem is posed concerning their stability, especially when citizens are offered the promise that a social order can be constructed that – from Hayek's perspective – allows them to have their cake and eat it, by enjoying the benefits of certain social institutions without suffering their intrinsic disadvantages.

In exploring these issues, Hayek was dealing with a problematic which would have been familiar to some of the political theorists of the mid to late eighteenth century. But their approach dropped from sight when, in the nineteenth century, it was suggested that the problems with which they were dealing were open to a relatively simple resolution. It is fitting that Hayek was later to make important points of his own by way of the critical exposition of ideas from Mandeville, Hume and some of the thinkers of the Scottish Enlightenment. For Hayek's work can in part be seen as a return to the problematic of this tradition; a tradition which largely disappeared from the scene with the French Revolution and its aftermath.

CONSERVATIVE ASPECTS OF HAYEK'S INAUGURAL

Hayek, despite his own protests, has sometimes been regarded as a conservative. He was even led to add an appendix to his *Constitution of Liberty* to explain 'Why I am not a Conservative'. However, themes which certainly *look* conservative play an increasing role in Hayek's thought with the passing of the years. And even in Hayek's Inaugural there are ideas which might seem to have a conservative character – at least if they are contrasted with Hayek's early socialism, with the more radical aspects of his own views, and with the liberalism of Mises.

First, by his endorsement of the ideas on social policy of the classical economists Hayek might seem to have turned his back on his earlier 'revulsion from the sordidness of mean streets' and the values that led him to wish to reconstruct society and to build a better world. Hayek, however, explains that it is not his values that have changed, but his ideas about how such values are best realized. He clearly feels some embarrassment about finding himself in the same bed as conservatives, and tries to explain what he is doing there in a way that does not besmirch his character. The passage in which he does this merits quotation at some length:[63]

> It seems to me to be almost inevitable that, on the basis of such economic ideas as are imbibed as part of the general education of the day, every warm-hearted person, as soon as he becomes conscious of the existing misery, should become a socialist. This has certainly been the experience of a great many economists of the younger generation to whom, when they took up their study, economics meant little else but more information about these deplorable facts which cried aloud for a remedy. But the conclusion to which the study of economics leads some of them seems so violently in contrast with the reasons which led them to embark upon their study of economics that most people conclude that their ethical standards must have undergone a complete change. It is, indeed, one of the interesting facts of the present time that a growing number of economists of the younger generation who have not the slightest sentimental attachment to conservatism – and many of whom began as socialists – feel more and more compelled by their reasoning to take a conservative attitude towards many problems.... And this happens with men who not only have all possible sympathy with the ethical motives from which economic radicalism springs, but who would be only too glad if they could believe that socialism or planning can do what they promise to do.

It is striking that, in an address 'On Being an Economist', which he delivered to the Students Union at the LSE in 1944 (the same year in which *The Road to Serfdom* was published), similar themes are to be found. Hayek refers to the way in which, as an officer in the Army in the First World War, he had borrowed –

and read right through – what turned out to be an exceedingly dull textbook on economics, seeking for an 'answer to the burning question of how to build [the] juster society for which [he] really cared'.[64] In this address Hayek also writes movingly, on lines similar to those of his Inaugural, about the way in which he wished that he were able to believe that socialism could achieve what its advocates promise:[65]

> If I could convince myself that they are right this would suddenly remove all the clouds which to me blacken all the prospects of the future. I should be free to share in the happy confidence of so many of my fellow men and join with them in the work for a common end.

All this strongly suggests that it is not initially Hayek's *values* that changed, so much that he came to doubt that they could be realized in the way that socialism suggested. The changes in Hayek's view can well be seen as the product of the impact upon a person whose sentiments were broadly socialist, of ideas in social theory. Indeed, in a striking passage at the end of his Inaugural,[66] Hayek indicates that his differences from his former socialist colleagues are about means rather than ends:

> The peculiar historical development which I have sketched has brought it about that the economist frequently finds himself in disagreement with regard to means with those with whom he is in agreement with regard to ends; and in agreement with regard to means with those whose views regarding ends are entirely antipathetic to him – men who have never felt the urge to reconstruct the world and who frequently support the forces of stability only for reasons of selfishness.

Two points, however, should be added. The first is that, during the period between which Hayek wrote the Inaugural and the Students Union Address, and certainly in the period thereafter, his values, or at least their formulation, undergo some changes. For he comes over time to place increasing emphasis upon freedom and the minimization of coercion, where these are expressed largely in terms of a 'negative' conception of liberty. There is also a shift in the language used to express the more economic side of his concerns – from misery, well-being and (as in the Students Union Address) social justice, to the satisfaction of preferences and the coordination of individuals' plans. All this raises issues which we will pursue later. Second, the 'conservative' aspects of Hayek's Inaugural, with which we have dealt so far, are conservative only in the sense of being at odds with his earlier socialism. The views to which Hayek had shifted, which we have discussed so far, are clearly compatible with a *radicalism* of a market-orientated character. And indeed, a streak of just such radicalism runs through much of Hayek's work which we will discuss later in this chapter, and in the light of which it is simply mistaken to try to make of him a conservative.

However, there are, even in his Inaugural, two other strands of thought that might be thought conservative in their character, and which we must also consider.

First, there is what might appear to be a more specifically conservative aspect to the impact of Mises' ideas on Hayek. Mises himself was a classical liberal, and his arguments against socialism are of a straightforwardly rationalistic character. How is it possible that their impact upon Hayek could have a conservative aspect? The reason is that Hayek interprets Mises' arguments about socialism as showing that there are mechanisms which accomplish desirable ends in ways of which we are not aware. As a result, Mises' argument about economic calculation leads Hayek to favour attitudes which are almost Burkean in their character. This may be illustrated by the following passage from the address, in which Hayek refers, in a footnote, to Mises' work:[67]

> We still refuse to recognize that the spontaneous interplay of the actions of individuals may produce something which is not the deliberate object of their actions but an organism in which every part performs a necessary function for the continuance of the whole, without any human mind having devised it . . . that . . . we are part of a 'higher' organized system which, without our knowledge, and long before we tried to understand it, solved problems the existence of which we did not even recognize.

Hayek argues that the view of the economist will be different from the view of the person who sees economic phenomena as just a number of independent events. And while telling us that the economist will not rule out all 'interference' with the economic system, in Hayek's view the economist's knowledge 'may, and very likely will, mean an almost consistently negative attitude towards those proposals for interference which are not based upon an understanding of the working of the system'.[68] And he even follows this by stating that 'in view of the incomplete nature of our knowledge, it will mean that, in all doubtful cases, there will exist a presumption against interference [with the working of the economic system]'.

However, while these ideas may perhaps be suggestive of a Burkean conservatism, there are two crucial differences. First, Hayek's argument is rooted in specific theoretical claims made as an economist, not in a general disposition to trust the products of history and experience. Second, Hayek not only contemplates, but even urges, radical reform of existing institutional arrangements in order that they may better play their role in a market-based social system (as we shall discuss in detail shortly). As a result, the 'conservative' aspects of Hayek's early views would seem to be less Burkean than functionalist,[69] where Hayek's functionalism is based on specific theoretical claims, 'an understanding of the working of the system', and can support radical reform.

At the same time, and as is evidenced by his 'presupposition against interference', there are signs that Hayek is disposed to generalize the lessons from Mises' work to cases for which he does not have theoretical arguments to back him up. Indeed, later in Hayek's work one can find an increasing proclivity to discern in markets, and other inherited institutions, valuable features of which he was not previously aware. And in what might be called the writings of Hayek's old age, he at times seems to offer a generalized defence of the wisdom of inherited institutions, backed up by only the sketchiest of theoretical accounts of an evolutionary process through which they are supposed to have developed their desirable characteristics.

The second conservative strand in Hayek's work I believe to come from Carl Menger.[70] In the material from Hayek's address which we examined above, he places emphasis upon the importance of organizational arrangements which are not the deliberate product of human design. I would conjecture that the presence of this theme is the result of Hayek's reading of the work of Carl Menger. During the period 1933–6, the LSE brought out a reprint of Menger's collected works under the editorship of Hayek. Hayek wrote a general introduction to the series, which was published in 1934, while the reprint of Menger's *Untersuchungen* (*Investigations into the Method of the Social Sciences*) appeared in 1933, the same year as his Inaugural Address. In the course of Hayek's Introduction to the collected Menger volumes, he discusses the historical school's attack on classical economics in terms close to those of the Inaugural.[71] He also suggests that Menger's treatment of their work is of contemporary significance. For example, when discussing Menger's *Untersuchungen*, Hayek says:[72]

> Discussions of somewhat obsolete views, as that of the organic or perhaps better physiological interpretation of social phenomena [i.e. the social theory of the older historical school of economics], give [Menger] an opportunity for an elucidation of the origin and character of social institutions which might, with advantage, be read by present-day economists and sociologists.

There are, in fact, two aspects to Menger's discussion. First, there is his treatment of the organic patterns and analogies in the development of institutions which were stressed in the work of the older historical school. These Menger did not dismiss as without value. But he did dismiss the historical school's organicist theoretical ideas, and he suggested that the patterns and analogies that they had highlighted stood in need of explanation in individualistic terms. Second, Menger noted that the largely reformist social policies of the followers of the historical schools of economics were very different from the conservatism of the historical legal jurists, by whose work these economists claimed to be inspired.

But what was Menger's own attitude towards the issue of conservatism and reform? This is a matter of current controversy, in which an article of Menger's somewhat critical of Adam Smith is being weighed against notes taken by

Crown Prince Rudolf from private lectures delivered to him by Menger, which contain strong statements of economic liberalism.[73] Menger does however offer, almost in passing, a most suggestive critical discussion of Savigny's work. In this, Menger tries to take a middle way between Savigny and what Menger presents as the 'one-sided rationalism' of Adam Smith, a rationalism which he took to be characterized by

> the not infrequently impetuous effort to do away with what exists, with what is not always sufficiently understood, [and] the just as impetuous urge to create something new in the realm of political institutions, often without sufficient knowledge and experience.[74]

Menger also criticizes the 'Smithian' approach as having 'in the main ... only an understanding for positive creations of public authority', claiming also that: 'It therefore did not know how to value the significance of "organic" social structures for society in general and economy in particular and therefore was nowhere concerned to preserve them'.

Menger argues this point, against 'the Smithian school', stating that our aim should be

> not ... simply [to] maintain ... what had organically developed as unassailable, as if it were the higher wisdom in human affairs as opposed to the intended ordering of social conditions. The aim ... [is], on the contrary, the full understanding of existing social institutions in general and of organically created institutions in particular, [and] the retention of what had proved its worth against the one-sidedly rationalistic mania for innovation in the field of economy. The object was to prevent the dissolution of the organically developed economy by means of a partially superficial pragmatism, a pragmatism that, contrary to the intention of its representatives, inexorably leads to socialism.[75]

Menger, however, also clearly dissociates himself from some of the more conservative views of the historical school of jurisprudence. He decries the assertion

> that common law, in spite of its not turning out to be the result of a social will aimed consciously at the common good, benefits the latter none the less to a higher degree than ... corresponding positive legislation could .... [C]ommon law has also proved harmful to the common good often enough, and on the contrary, legislation has just as often changed common law in a way benefiting the common good.[76]

The general character of the views which Menger favours may perhaps be indicated by the following passage:[77]

> If individual eras have failed to recognize the peculiar worth of common law and changed the law by immature or hasty reforms, instead of

44

bettering it, it was the duty of the historical school of jurists to avoid a similar procedure for the future – not by proclaiming the higher wisdom of common law, but by teaching the proper evaluation of the insight they gained in legislation. The fruit of their view was not to be the avoidance in principle of positive law development, however well stipulated. It had to be the purification of the latter by new insight gained from the thoughtful consideration of common law...[The] historical school of jurists had to make us understand the previously uncomprehended advantages of common law...but never...may science dispense with testing for their suitability these institutions which have come about 'organically'. It must, when careful investigation so requires, change and better them according to the measure of scientific insight and the practical experience at hand. No era may renounce this 'calling'.

And it is just this 'calling' – the 'calling' both to appreciate *and* to assess critically and improve inherited 'organic' institutions in the light of theoretical knowledge – which, as we will see shortly, is taken up by the younger Hayek.[78]

It may be useful to review this sketch of the history of Hayek's views. Hayek, I have suggested, started out with – and maintained – broadly humanitarian concerns, in the sense that he was concerned with the well-being of his fellow citizens, and, in particular, with social justice and the alleviation of the misery that he saw about him in post-First World War Vienna. As a young man returning from the war, he seems to have expected these aims to be realized through some form of Fabian socialism. However, as a result of his encounter with Mises, he became convinced that it was something closer to a classical liberal perspective – a social order based systematically upon the market – which would best realize those goals. Furthermore, as a result of his exposure to Menger's *Investigations*, Hayek was also confronted with an approach to social philosophy which contrasted with that of Mises. For Menger had a healthy but not uncritical respect for institutions which were, in a phrase from Adam Ferguson which Hayek was later to use extensively, the results of human action, but not of human design.

All this leaves Hayek with concerns that differ from those of other economists with inclinations towards classical liberalism. First, his views contrasted with those of – and were found puzzling by – British liberals like Roy Harrod and Lionel Robbins.[79] They found the Mengerian strand in Hayek's work difficult to take: it seemed to them to contain a streak of Burkean irrationalism that did not mix well with Hayek's arguments from economic theory. There is, indeed, something distinctive about Hayek's views – in his appreciation of unplanned institutions and the results of social experimentation, and in his view of us, including, especially in his later writings, our reason, as being the product rather than the director of cultural evolution. At the same time, these ideas are combined, in Hayek, with the view that we can criticize, and may need to redesign and replace, inherited social institutions.

(There are, however, also some tensions here, which we discuss later in this volume.)

Second, there is a contrast with the approach of liberal economists (such as, say, those of the Chicago and Virginia Schools) who understand the problems of political economy in terms of individuals and their interests as these are typically depicted in neoclassical economics and game theory. While there are many respects in which their work is complementary to that of Hayek – for example, in the critical analysis of the politics of interest-group democracy – there are important points of difference between Hayek and these writers, especially in terms of their understanding of the individual and of his motivation and behaviour.

So far, however, my account has largely been in terms of the way in which Hayek's ideas were modified as a result of an exposure to the views of other people; notably, of Mises and Menger. We will now move to a field in which Hayek is himself very much of an innovator: his contributions to the debate about economic calculation under socialism. While Hayek's involvement in this debate clearly takes off from the impact of Mises' work, Hayek adds to Mises' contributions a number of distinctive ideas of his own. These were important for that debate, and important also because it is from this material that emerge Hayek's ideas about the role of prices in the transmission of information in a market-based social order. These ideas have had an important influence within recent economic thought. As I will suggest, they also play an important role in the shaping of Hayek's political thought and, in the end, lead to some interesting problems for Hayek's approach. But this, again, is to anticipate.

THE SOCIALIST CALCULATION DEBATE

The debate about economic calculation under socialism inaugurated by Mises' work is of central importance for Hayek's political thought. We have already seen the impact that the encounter with Mises and his work had on Hayek's general orientation to social policy. In what follows, we will see how many of the most distinctive features of Hayek's own political thought emerge out of the debate about Mises' argument, and Hayek's contributions to it. Further, however, we will see how the implications of some of Hayek's own most powerful and suggestive ideas also pose problems for his own approach.

Mises' argument about economic calculation under socialism spurred a number of socialist writers to reply, including the American economist F. M. Taylor, and, most famously, Oskar Lange.[80] Lange took the point at issue (whether information about how to take economic decisions concerning capital expenditure could be made available to socialist planners) to relate to the goal of a distribution of resources such as would be found in a market in perfect equilibrium. This was a situation in which:

All individuals participating in the economic system must attain their maximum positions on the basis of equilibrium prices; and ... the equilibrium prices are determined by the condition that the demand for each commodity is equal to its supply.[81]

Lange argued against Mises that it was possible in principle for a socialist economy to aspire to this same goal. For the allocation of resources in accordance with individuals' preferences that is effected through the (idealized) workings of a market could, he argued, be simulated by the solving of sets of simultaneous equations – the very equations which Walras had offered as a representation of a market economy in general equilibrium. And F. M. Taylor, and subsequently Lange, argued that it was possible for planners in a socialist economy to try to approach this goal through a process of trial and error – in a way that would parallel the activities of a Walrasian auctioneer.

It is often suggested that Lange had not only correctly represented Mises' argument, but that he had also answered it.[82] Even if this were correct, the kind of response offered by Lange might leave open difficulties for a socialist. For socialists had often argued that there was something fundamentally wrong with capitalism's market solutions to problems of economic activity, in such a way as to suggest that a radically different way of doing things is open to us. (Consider, for example, the idea of production for need versus production for profit, and the moral problems that have been raised about making merely instrumental use of human labour power, to say nothing of issues connected with alienation.) Lange and Taylor, by taking up Mises' challenge directly, might seem to be endorsing the view that the *ideal* results of markets were ones to which a socialist planner can (and should) aspire.

The centralized planning envisaged by such a system would also seem to generate political problems for the socialist. For it would involve the existence of a planning board that would have immense power as a result of being responsible for the co-ordination of economic activity. It would have power of a kind that does not exist in a 'capitalist' economy, within which economic decision-making is disaggregated. Such central planning would also not seem easy to reconcile with ideas about the radically democratic procedures of a future socialist society as they are hinted at in, say, certain of Marx's works. The planning board would seem to require specialized knowledge. This would make it difficult for service on the board, or as its officers, to be rotated among all citizens. And there are obvious limitations to the idea of making such a board 'democratically accountable' to an electorate, or operating it by means of a system of recallable delegates.[83]

Thus, Lange's response (which will be discussed below) might make sense if the argument about socialist calculation were about the merits of central control of the economy as an instrument for economic efficiency, as a defence of the Fabians, or even as a defence of what Stalin was sometimes thought to be up to. (Although it is also worth noting that Dobb,[84] for example, had misgivings about an approach like that of Lange just because of the weight that it gave to consumer preferences as opposed to investment that central planners might decide that a society would need for economic growth.) But it would seem far removed from what many in the socialist tradition had led us to expect from socialism.

It has been contended (notably, by recent writers who have been influenced by Mises) that Lange misunderstood Mises' argument, and that the way in which the 'socialist calculation debate' has usually been understood misrepresents what in fact happened. The arguments offered here are, typically, along two lines. First, that it is incorrect to understand Mises as offering an argument that was successfully met by Lange and others, *after which* Hayek then introduced other themes which posed problems for Lange (for instance, about competition and the dispersal of knowledge). Second, that it is incorrect to see Mises as having challenged the socialist to replicate the results of general equilibrium theory, because he implicitly rejected that approach as inadequate himself.

These issues are, in fact, all rather complex. Mises was later to distinguish sharply between general equilibrium theory and the views of the Austrian School,[85] and it has been argued that these differences were relevant to the understanding of Mises' criticism of socialism.[86] Don Lavoie at one point argued that while it is 'now' clear that there is a 'basic [difference] between the "Austrian" and "neoclassical" paradigms' this was 'not yet evident to either side at the time of the debate'.[87] But Lavoie's later monograph on the economic calculation debate seems to suggest that most of the significant points that emerged later in the debate were already implicit in Mises' earlier work.[88] However this may be with regard to Mises, I would not have thought that the idea that there was, from the start, such a fundamental contrast can be sustained in respect of Hayek. For Roy McCloughry, the editor of a collection of Hayek's early economic papers, has argued that until 1937 '[Hayek's] thought was dominated by General Equilibrium Theory'.[89] And in unpublished work, Adam Klug has emphasized not only the importance of Hayek's early writings as developing a theory of intertemporal general equilibrium, but also that Hayek was explicitly developing Walrasian ideas.[90]

Whatever the rights and wrongs concerning the historical issue of the character of Mises' initial paper,[91] there are important developments in Hayek's work on the problem of socialist calculation which go beyond what is to be found in Mises, and play an important role in shaping the general character of Hayek's political thought.

In 1935 there was published a collection of essays, edited by Hayek, entitled *Collectivist Economic Planning*. This collection, in addition to containing in translation Mises' original paper and some pieces by other writers which, in various ways, anticipated or complemented Mises' account, contained two essays by Hayek, one on 'The Nature and History of the Problem' and the other on 'The State of the Debate (1935)'.[92] In the second of these pieces, Hayek reviewed the situation as it then seemed to him to stand. He noted arguments of Taylor, Roper and Dickinson, against Mises, to the effect that:

> on the assumption of a complete knowledge of all relevant data, the values and the quantities of the different commodities to be produced might be determined [in the absence of markets] by the application of the apparatus by which theoretical economics explains the formation of prices and the direction of production in a competitive system.[93]

However, Hayek argued that such a procedure was 'humanly impracticable and impossible'[94] and moved on to discuss the kind of approximation to such decision-taking that might actually be envisaged under socialism. He argued that certain kinds of information could not feasibly be made available to centralized decision-takers.[95] Hayek mentions that in a competitive economy, different agents will be the bearers of different knowledge, and that 'those that make the most appropriate use of... technical knowledge will succeed' (suggesting, albeit not too explicitly, that *which* knowledge is utilized by a market system will depend upon a competitive process, rather than on some process that aggregates all the judgements of all individuals). In addition, he argues that the knowledge that is utilized in a competitive system may include 'a technique of thought which enables the individual engineer to find new solutions rapidly as soon as he is confronted with new constellations of circumstances'.[96] Hayek – perhaps with a little hindsight – may here be understood to refer to knowledge that cannot in principle be centralized, since it is tacit in character. Such knowledge, however, can be utilized in the decentralized decision-taking processes of a market system. And in a later article on the theme of economic calculation under socialism,[97] Hayek argues explicitly, against Lange, that a competitive economy allows for the possibility of the utilization of tacit knowledge (knowledge how) on the part of those within it, of a kind that in principle cannot be centralized.

There are, in fact, two different theses about the utilization of knowledge in a market to be found in this material.[98] The first is that in a market there is a selective function rather than just an aggregative one being performed, such that it is, in some sense, the best knowledge that is being made use of within it. The second is that dispersed and even tacit knowledge can be utilized. Corresponding to each of these, there is a problem for the would-be centralizer: (1) how to select which knowledge is to be used; (2) what to do about knowledge that is dispersed through the economic system, and tacit knowledge. To such points, Hayek adds that the task of assembling the relevant 'data' and of solving the number of simultaneous equations that Mises' critics would allocate to their planners could hardly be accomplished; and that 'The essential thing about the present economic system is that it does react to some extent to all those small changes and differences which would have to be deliberately disregarded under the system we are discussing if the calculations were to be manageable'.[99]

These papers, and Hayek's later 'Competition as a Discovery Procedure',[100] strengthen Hayek's claim that markets can perform functions that cannot be undertaken by the central planner. And this, together with the sheer inaccessibility to the planner of the kind of knowledge that would be required to fulfil the kind of task that Lange allocated to him, might indeed suggest that there is no substitute for markets. If to this one adds the problems that Hayek was subsequently to raise about the character of the planners' task and their motivation (which are discussed below), the argument would seem conclusive.

At the same time, however, the reader might start to smell a rat. For once Hayek stresses the selective role of actual competition on knowledge that is utilized by an economic system, and once tacit knowledge is brought in, the reader might well wonder what Hayek's understanding is of the results of market decisions. With what are the problems of a centrally planned economy being compared? He might wonder, further, about the possibilities of a Wieser-like approach, in which political activity is seen not as an alternative to, but as a way of modifying what occurs in, markets. To these issues we will return.

PROBLEMS WITH HAYEK'S ARGUMENT

Hayek's 1935 paper also discusses difficulties facing the ideas of those socialists who had suggested that, while there should not be the private ownership of capital, there should be some 'competitive' features to the organization of socialism. Hayek refers to those who believe that there should be a consolidation of business into industry-wide monopolies which should then compete with one another, or that the managers of all state enterprises should compete for resources. Hayek criticizes such ideas as liable to lead to the misuse of resources, or as posing problems concerning the taking of risk. The situation is different, Hayek argues, when people are taking risks using their own resources, as opposed to a planning board's trying to decide how to allocate public resources between different managers wishing to undertake risky ventures. For our purposes, however, what is of importance is not so much his criticism as the basis upon which it is offered. For once one has moved from Mises' formal impossibility argument (if such it be), one is involved in the evaluation of the pros and cons of different, concrete, less than perfect, alternatives.

In this connection, two issues loom large which pose some problems for Hayek. First, one will wish to know something about the size of the effects to which Hayek is referring, not least because his discussion might lead one to think in terms of possible trade-offs between efficiency and other factors. Second, when Hayek makes claims about what markets will do – for example, in terms of the allocation of resources or the handling of risk – one will need to know something about the basis on which he is making such claims.

For example, Hayek says, in the course of an argument against the idea that an industry in a socialized economy could aim at prices 'which will just cover their (marginal) cost':

> It almost seems as if excessive preoccupation with the conditions of a hypothetical state of stationary equilibrium has led modern economists... to attribute to the notion of costs in general a much greater precision and definiteness than can be attached to any cost phenomenon in real life.[101]

This is an important point on which Hayek subsequently elaborated. However, what is sauce for the goose is sauce for the gander. Once this point has been made by Hayek, what is the socialist to understand when Hayek claims that

> we should anticipate... that output, where the use of the available resources was determined by some central authority, would be lower than if the price mechanism of a market operated freely under otherwise similar circumstances.[102]

The same issue may be raised when Hayek makes claims about a centralized system involving 'a misuse of resources'.[103] In each case, with exactly what is Hayek comparing it? Is Hayek himself using an idealized model; and if so what is it? What do we know about the utilization of resources within this model? Also, what relation has any such model to the actual competitive systems in which we are living, or to which we might aspire? Further, when Hayek argues that the market can make use of tacit knowledge and react 'to some extent' to small differences that planners must overlook, we might well ask how significant this is, and how it is to be weighed against the fact that there are, presumably, concerns that planners can pursue which cannot be pursued within an economy in which economic decision-taking is completely disaggregated.

Such questions are of added importance because of the direction in which Hayek's thought moves subsequent to this essay. In his lecture 'Economics and Knowledge', delivered in 1936,[104] Hayek emphasizes, against the general equilibrium model, the incompatibility of the plans of typical individuals in an economy, the 'division of knowledge' (which he develops with a reference to Mises' *Socialism*),[105] and the role of the market in bringing people's plans into co-ordination, through the transmission of knowledge by prices.[106] Hayek argues (implicitly, against Mises) that the achievement of equilibrium (understood in terms of the coordination of people's plans) depends on empirical matters concerning the 'conditions under which people are supposed to acquire... knowledge and the process by which they are supposed to acquire it'.[107] In consequence, economic analysis cannot be confined to the (largely analytic) Pure Logic of Choice, with which, in his view, Mises was concerned.

Hayek's ideas about economics and knowledge have opened up many important issues. His work in this area has been discussed extensively by mainstream neoclassical economists, and it has also inspired interesting work within the Austrian School.[108] However, those interested in the issues that

Hayek has discussed within political economy should, I believe, take note of another point that he makes in the course of this work:[109]

> It becomes exceedingly difficult to say what are exactly the assumptions on the basis of which we assert that there will be a tendency towards equilibrium and to claim that our analysis has an application to the real world.

For this opens up an issue of pressing importance for those who, like Hayek, wish to commend the market to us on consequentialist grounds. In so far as Hayek is arguing against those who wish to do without private ownership and markets, these points are, I believe, of little significance in comparison to the problems facing those who wish to champion such views. But they seem to me of much greater significance if Hayek's opponent is, instead, championing the market-wise interventionism within a market economy, of the kind suggested by the ideas of Wieser which we considered above.

The more general thrust of my argument here is as follows. The ideas which Hayek introduced during the course of the argument about socialist calculation seem to me important not only in their own right, but also in terms of the contribution that they made to Hayek's political views. However, I wish, also, to introduce a note of caution, in so far as they also relate to what Hayek can claim in respect of the welfare consequences of markets. For it seems to me problematic should he be arguing, against proponents of a market-wise interventionism on the basis of socialist values, that one must shift from a general equilibrium perspective to one which looks at markets as processes through which information is transmitted to agents with imperfect knowledge by means of prices while, at the same time, making claims about the utilization of resources within a market-based economy, which would *look* as if they could only be sustained on the basis of a general equilibrium theory. Or, to put this another way, Hayek's work seems to me to raise the question of just what one *can* say about the *welfare* characteristics of a market economy if one is modelling it as he suggests and, more particularly, about what one can say about the likely costs and benefits of market-wise intervention.

One other theme that emerges from Hayek's contributions to the socialist calculation debate plays an important role in his political philosophy. In his 'Economics and Knowledge', Hayek emphasized the disparate and inconsistent character of individuals' plans. But this suggests that there may be no natural social consensus about values, and thus about the way in which resources should be collectively disposed. This idea comes into prominence in a pamphlet which Hayek wrote under the title of 'Freedom and the Economic System'.[110] This essay (which I discuss more fully below) is the germ out of which grew *The Road to Serfdom*. In his pamphlet, Hayek argues that those who favour central planning appeal to the idea that there is some rational ordering of the nation's affairs and thus a rational distribution of resources between different ideals and projects. But, Hayek claims, no such thing exists; and a government committed to planning will therefore discover that there is no way in which a plan exemplifying such an ordering of resources can be arrived at democratically. As a result, the attempt to plan leads to certain priorities – the priorities and judgements of certain people – being imposed, perhaps in the name of reason, on the rest of the population.

Hayek used such an analysis as the central theme of his explanation of totalitarianism in *The Road to Serfdom*. But it also stands behind his criticism in his later work of the ideal of social justice, and of modern pluralist interest-group politics. It is in this way that ideas that Hayek developed in the context of the socialist calculation debate, and as reflections on the character of a well-functioning competitive market system, come to shape the main lines of his political philosophy. It is important that we understand where these ideas come from, when we seek to understand and to appraise them; not least, because in some of Hayek's work – notably his *Constitution of Liberty* and in parts of his *Law, Legislation and Liberty* – Hayek sets out essentially the same views, as if they were pieces of analytical philosophy. If we interpret them as such, we will misunderstand what Hayek is about, and will underestimate the strengths of his argument. (It is also worth noting that inconsistencies in plans, and the need for adjustment, raise important issues concerning the welfare characteristics of a market-based social order, too; an issue that I will discuss in chapter five.)

HAYEK'S RADICALISM AND THE ROLE OF GOVERNMENT

The most striking feature of Hayek's work at this period, however, is what might be termed its radicalism: Hayek's concern for the active improvement of institutions that we have inherited.

I have previously suggested that the early Hayek is at heart concerned with social reform of a humanitarian character, and that what became the characteristic features of his views, including their 'conservative' aspects, are a product of his (developing) ideas on social theory. I here wish to argue that this broad interpretation of Hayek is given added weight by the more radical, and even in a sense 'constructivist' aspects of Hayek's views of the same period. In the work that I have in mind, Hayek identifies the kind of social order that he favours as involving a framework that may be brought about through planning (of a sort), the character of which is largely dictated by his ideas about markets and the social division of knowledge. He also suggests that existing institutions should be made the object of critical scrutiny from what he explicitly identifies as a utilitarian perspective. A substantive but clearly delimited role is also given to government. And when, in a slightly later piece (his Cairo Lectures, of 1955), Hayek reflects on the development of the doctrine of the rule of law, he accords a positive role to rationalistic improvements made, on the Continent, to ideas and institutions which had originally been forged in Britain.

In his *Freedom and the Economic System* (1939) Hayek, after criticizing central economic planning, discusses a form of planning that, in his view, is legitimate.[111]

> We can 'plan' a system of general rules, equally applicable to all people . . . which provides an institutional framework within which the decisions as to what to do and how to earn a living are left to individuals . . . we can plan a system in which individual initiative is given the widest possible scope and the best opportunity to bring about effective co-ordination of individual effort.

He discusses 'the construction of a rational system of law',[112] and invokes the idea of 'planning for freedom' as opposed to 'planning for constant interference'; and then describes some of the features of the institutional framework that he favours:

> By the construction of a rational framework of general and permanent rules, a mechanism is created through which production is to be directed, but no decision is made about the ends to which it is directed. The rules aim mainly at the elimination of avoidable uncertainty by establishing principles from which it can be ascertained who at any moment has the disposition over particular resources, and of unnecessary error by the prevention of force and fraud.[113]

These rules Hayek further characterizes as 'general not only in the sense that they apply to all people, but also in the sense that they are instrumental in helping people to achieve their various individual ends'.[114] Hayek also argues that 'These rules are not made . . . in the expectation that A will be benefited and that B will be harmed by them', and claims that 'both will find themselves in a better position than would be the case if no law existed'.[115] And he states:

> The very fact that the incidence of their effects on different individuals cannot be foreseen, because these effects are spread far too widely and the rules themselves are intended to remain in force for a very long period, implies that in the formulation of such rules no deliberate choice between the relative need of different individuals or different groups need or can be made, and that the same set of rules is compatible with the most varied views about the relative importance of different things.[116]

We have here a view which considers rules and an institutional framework as something that may have to be constructed. The basis for such construction, however, may not at first seem altogether clear. In part, Hayek seems to be taking up the perspective of a benevolent legislator who is concerned to respect each individual as having preferences, but who is not concerned with their content (other, presumably, than to disallow preferences that don't respect the autonomy of other individuals). There is also a strand in Hayek's argument which is akin to recent thought in the contractarian tradition[117] which places emphasis upon rules that all would agree to, as under them each betters their own condition relative to what it would be if there were no such agreement. There is also – in the emphasis on effective co-ordination – a possible concern for the overall character of the products of individuals' agreement. In addition, when stating that inherited legal principles stand in need of theoretical scrutiny and reform, Hayek suggests that the basis on which this evaluation is to be made is utilitarian. In view of the fact that Hayek has often subsequently distanced himself from utilitarianism, it is worth quoting a further passage from this pamphlet, so as to indicate the sense in which Hayek there identifies with this view:

> This task of creating a rational framework of law has by no means been carried out consistently by the early liberals. After vindicating on utilitarian grounds the general principles of private property and the freedom of contract, they have stopped short of applying the same criterion of social expediency to the specific historic forms of the law of property and of contract. Yet it should have been obvious that the question of the exact content and the specific limitations of property rights, and how and when the state will enforce the fulfilment of contracts, require as much consideration on utilitarian grounds as the general principle. Unfortunately, however, many of the nineteenth-century liberals, after they had satisfied themselves about the justification of the general principle which they had rightly refused to accept as a dictate of the law of nature, were on the whole content to accept the law in its existing formulation, as if this was the only conceivable and natural one. A certain dogmatism in this respect, which often had the appearance of an unwillingness to reason on these problems, brought the development of this kind of planning to an early standstill and has tended to throw the whole liberal doctrine into discredit.[118]

This same theme of the deliberate creation of institutions is taken up again by Hayek in *The Road to Serfdom*. For example, he there claims:

> There is...all the difference between deliberately creating a system within which competition will work as beneficially as possible, and passively accepting institutions as they are.[119]

And later:

> The liberal argument is in favour of making the best possible use of the forces of competition as a means of coordinating human efforts, not an argument for leaving things just as they are. It is based on the conviction that where effective competition can be created, it is a better way of guiding human efforts than any other. It does not deny, but even

emphasizes, that, in order that competition should work beneficially, a carefully thought-out legal framework is required, and that neither the existing nor the past legal rules are free from grave defects.[120]

It is striking – and, indeed, somewhat ironic – that it is in Hayek's 'Individualism: True and False'[121] that there is perhaps the clearest statement as to the principles upon which such an appraisal of the inherited legal order is to be based. I suggest that this is ironic, as this essay also contains criticisms of 'rationalism', and an emphasis on the idea that 'the individual, in participating in the social processes, must be ready and willing to . . . submit to conventions which are not the result of intelligent design, whose justification in the particular instance may not be recognizable, and which to him will often appear unintelligible and irrational'.[122] Indeed, it was for just these ideas that Hayek was criticized by Roy Harrod, in a review of 'Individualism: True and False', for conflating the essentially rationalist case of Smithian economics with 'the emotional foundations of loyalty' on which, in his view, Burke builds.[123]

However, this essay of Hayek's also has a more radical side to it. For in 'Individualism: True and False', Hayek is critical of the slogan '*laissez-faire*', on the grounds that it does 'not tell us what [are] and what [are] not desirable or necessary fields of government activity'.[124] And in response to this very problem, Hayek claims that:

> If each man is to use *his* peculiar knowledge and skill with the aim of furthering the aims for which *he* cares, and if, in so doing, he is to make as large a contribution as possible to ends which are beyond his ken, it is clearly necessary, first, that he should have a clearly delimited area of responsibility and, second, that the relative importance to him of the different results he can achieve must correspond to the relative importance to others of the more remote and to him unknown effects of his action.

That is to say, Hayek's approach is to argue for the revision of the institutional and legal framework within which people will be acting, along lines indicated by his own economic and social theories. He then argues that 'an individualist order must rest on the enforcement of abstract principles rather than on the enforcement of specific orders',[125] but recognizes that this 'leaves open the question of the kind of general rules which we want'. And here, while allowing that 'the best solutions of the concrete problems will in most instances have to be discovered by experience',[126] he does think that some general guidelines can be extracted from 'the general principles of individualism'. But what are these guidelines?

First, 'the rules, because they are to serve as signposts to the individuals in making their own plans, should be designed to remain valid for long periods'.[127] Second, there is a point made in a passage that again deserves to be quoted at some length, so that the full character of Hayek's argument comes out, rather than just his conclusions:

> The endeavour to make man by the pursuit of his interests contribute as much as possible to the needs of other men leads not only to the general principle of 'private property'; it also assists us in determining what the contents of property rights ought to be with respect to different kinds of things. In order that the individual in his decisions should take account of all the physical effects caused by those decisions, it is necessary that the 'sphere of responsibility' . . . be made to comprise as fully as possible all the direct effects which his actions have on the satisfactions which other people derive from the things under his control. This is achieved on the whole by the simple conception of property as the exclusive right to use a particular thing where mobile effects, or what the lawyer calls 'chattels', are concerned. But it raises much more difficult problems in connection with land, where the recognition of the principle of private property helps us very little until we know precisely what rights and obligations ownership includes. And when we turn to such problems of more recent origin as the control of the air or of electric power, or of inventions and of literary or artistic creations, nothing short of going back to [the] rationale of property will help us to decide what should be in the particular instance the sphere of control or responsibility of the individual.

Hayek's views here seem to me very much in the spirit of the ideas of Menger, which we considered above. For Hayek is clearly claiming that inherited 'organic' institutions, such as our fundamental legal categories, stand in need of scrutiny and improvement in the light of theoretical ideas about the functional role that they can play in a market economy.

Hayek's views are different from those which one might more commonly associate with utilitarianism. But this is in part because of the character of the economic theories to which Hayek subscribes and in part because of his view of the role played within a well-ordered society by human ignorance and by institutions of a systematic character. Hayek is often critical of utilitarianism in his writings. But this is largely because of the way in which this doctrine has become identified with the attempt to appraise the utility of individual actions, or at best rules, whereas in Hayek's view the only basis on which one can sensibly make appraisals is of institutions as systems. Hayek's utilitarianism might therefore – to use a term that has sometimes been used of the thinkers of the Scottish Enlightenment – be called a 'system utilitarianism'.

At the same time (and this is an issue to which I will return), Hayek is far from clear when he is telling us about the values that the institutions that he favours are supposed to serve. In his work, we are offered many different formulations of such ideas, without it being made too clear whether they are in fact compatible with one another. And variations in formulation aside, it seems to me that he appeals to three themes which might seem to pull in rather different directions: the humanitarianism, concern for the the relief of suffering, and worries about a 'juster' society which concerned him as a young man; the concern that people be able to act on the basis of their preferences, and coordinate their behaviour (themes which might also be linked to the system utilitarianism which we have just discussed); and his concern for a (negative) conception of human freedom, and for the minimization of coercion. Or rather, and this is an issue that we will explore later, the second and third of these ideas are (arguably) compatible with one another, and they bear a close relationship to ideas which are familiar from the assumptions of the neoclassical economist. What is notable is the fact that they are different from the first idea, and that Hayek does not seem to me to offer anything much by way of argument as to why they are to be accorded priority. To this issue we will return in chapters three and five.

One further element of radicalism in Hayek's views may be seen in some of the accounts that he gives of the development of the kind of legal order that he favours. In particular, in his Cairo Lectures, *The Political Ideal of the Rule of Law,*[128] he offers an account of the development of this order that contrasts strongly with later accounts, in which Hayek places great emphasis upon mechanisms of group selection. In the Cairo Lectures Hayek suggests that, in seeking to 'trace the beginnings of English liberty', there is little point in going back further than the seventeenth century. For while there had been extensive guarantees of personal liberty in the Middle Ages, 'these had largely disappeared with the rise of absolute monarchy'.[129] Hayek acknowledges that earlier documents (such as the Magna Carta) were of importance in the 'struggle for liberty' that then took place, as was the Greek idea of Isonomy (or equality before the law). But Hayek depicts 'the further development of [the] Whig doctrine of the Rule of Law [as] closely connected with the . . . fight against government-conferred monopoly and particularly with the discussion around the Statute of Monopolies of 1624',[130] and its full establishment as 'the work of the eighteenth [century]'.[131] He argues that 'so far as England is concerned, this development is in the main complete with the end of the 18th century',[132] and comments further that 'although in some respects the results of this evolution were left curiously incomplete, what was achieved became a firmly accepted political tradition which was not again seriously challenged until our own time'.[133]

What is significant is that, while Hayek refers to these developments as an 'evolution', what is going on here on his own account consists of a political struggle, guided by economic interest, in which ideas, such as that of Isonomy, are brought into play. From this, there emerges a product – the idea of the rule of law – which becomes valued for itself and for the benefits which it confers. But there is an element of political conflict and a degree of self-consciousness about the ideas involved in the entire process which distances it from Hayek's later accounts of the 'evolution' of social institutions. The difference between this account of Hayek's and his later work is perhaps most strongly brought out by his comments about the subsequent development of these ideas. For, he tells us, 'the task of systematizing and completing this development was performed mainly by Continental, and in the first instance, French writers who endeavoured to interpret to the world what England had achieved'.[134] Indeed, given the fact that, in his 'Individualism: True and False', it is 'French and other Continental writers',[135] among whose 'outstanding representatives...are the Encyclopedists [and] Rousseau' who are held up for criticism as representing false, rationalistic individualism, it is perhaps worth quoting at some length what Hayek says about this development of the rule of law:[136]

> On its political side, the 'Enlightenment', from Voltaire downwards, was little else than a spreading of the ideal of freedom as its leaders saw it realized in England. The interpretation of a bundle of traditions which had grown up there through generations of political struggle inevitably involved some artificial schematization and idealization. However well the set of institutions which had grown up in England had worked in the environment of traditions and beliefs to which it belonged, its evolution had left some strange gaps. Any attempt at a 'rational reconstruction' of how it worked and what it achieved required that principles be made explicit which had never been stated, and that gaps be filled which would at once have made themselves felt if the institutions had been simply transplanted into a different atmosphere. Not only had the English tradition never explicitly drawn such obvious conclusions from its basic ideals as the formal recognition of the principle *nulla poena sine lege* [no punishment without law]; it had also failed, until quite recently, to give the citizen an effective remedy against wrongs done to him by the State (as distinguished from its individual agents), and it lacked almost any built-in safeguards against the infringement of the Rule of Law by routine legislation. These anomalies could not escape the Continental students who by deliberate legislation hoped to equal and improve upon what Britain had achieved by slow growth.

In more specific discussions which follow this, Hayek refers not only to Montesquieu, but also to Rousseau for his idea that the law must be general in the sense of not referring to named individuals – an idea which (strikingly enough in view of Hayek's oft-expressed disapproval of Rousseau) was to form the centre of Hayek's writings on the idea of liberty in his *Constitution of Liberty*. He further discusses the importance of the theoretical contribution to the development of the idea of the rule of law made by German liberal theorists, from Kant and the early Fichte onwards, noting that

> the German contribution to the ideal of the Rule of Law was indeed largely a theoretical one, and in some measure this remained so since it was never given to the Germans fully to realise the ideal which they had

elaborated. But we must not underrate the value of their theoretical contribution.[137]

Hayek also argues in favour of the Continental movement for the codification of law:

> This whole movement is one of the most important parts of the Continental endeavour to establish the Rule of Law and it determined both its peculiar character and whatever advances it achieved, at least in theory, over the prototype in the countries of the common law. Of course, the possession even of the most perfectly drawn up legal codes can be no adequate substitute for a deeply rooted tradition, and the advantages which the former may give may not outweigh those of the latter. But this should not blind us to the fact that there is some inherent conflict between a system of case law and the ideal of the Rule of Law. Since under case law the judge constantly creates law, the principle that he merely applies pre-existing rules can under that system be approached even less perfectly than where the law is codified. And although the much lauded flexibility of the common law may have been favourable to the rise of the Rule of Law so long as general opinion tended in that direction, the common law also shows, I am afraid, less resistance to its decay once that vigilance is relaxed which alone can keep liberty alive.[138]

On this point, however, Hayek's views were to change. For while here he clearly comes down in favour of a codified system of law and sees this as, in certain respects, in tension with the common law tradition, he was to change his mind. And in *Law, Legislation and Liberty* (volume 2), he offers an account of a common-law based jurisprudence which would, he there suggests, possess the features of a *Rechtsstaat* liberalism.[139]

THE ROAD TO SERFDOM

In 1944 Hayek published his *Road to Serfdom*. He has described this work as 'a political book',[140] but it contains one of the finest statements of his work as a political theorist. In it, Hayek puts in a systematic way some of the points that emerge from the material at which we have been looking so far. And he offers a restatement of classical liberalism, with emphasis placed upon the idea of the rule of law, which is interpreted in accordance with the Continental *Rechtsstaat* theory. Hayek's *Road to Serfdom* is clear and readable, but also very densely packed; our treatment here must, in consequence, be highly selective. It is, however, worth highlighting some of its features, as it provides a useful overview of Hayek's political thought of this period.

The Road to Serfdom exhibits the centrality in Hayek's political thought of ideas developed in response to Mises' discussion of the problems of economic calculation under socialism. It is not the argument about the impossibility of economic calculation under socialism that plays a major role, so much as arguments about the concentration of power in a planned economy, and the impossibility of reaching a rational consensus about goals and projects.[141] The argument about rational consensus, which comes to play a major role in Hayek's work, was, as we noted, first developed in his *Freedom and the Economic System*. There, Hayek argued that a planning authority will need to take decisions among various alternative ways in which resources could be utilized, and he claims that 'there are within wide limits no grounds on which one person could convince another that one decision is more reasonable than the other'.[142] What Hayek means by this is, in my view, best explained in another passage, in which he argues that:

> Agreement on a particular plan requires for society as a whole the same kind of complete quantitative scale of values as that which manifests itself in the decision of every individual, but on which, in an individualist society, agreement between the individuals is neither necessary nor present.[143]

It is, essentially, this claim of Hayek's – which is close to the misgivings that he expressed about general equilibrium in 'Economics and Knowledge' and *The Pure Theory of Capital* – which underlies his later critique of the idea of social justice. It is also used in *The Road to Serfdom* as part of an explanatory theory concerning the character of totalitarianism. If planning demands that there be a consensus about priorities, and agreement cannot be achieved rationally, the planner is pushed towards imposing a solution and presenting it as rational. This in turn, Hayek suggests, offers an explanation in principle for why it is that the ideal of planning is found to be incompatible with democratic procedures, and why regimes which undertake such planning find it necessary to make use of the apparatus of the state for propaganda purposes, to try to convince citizens that the plan has a rationale.

It might be asked, however, why there is more of a problem here for the socialist than there is for the proponent of a market-based economic order. For he, too, it might be thought, gives tacit assent to some procedure for the overall allocation of resources: through the preferences of individual citizens. Why could not the same source be used by the planner? There are a number of answers to this, all of which draw on Hayek's ideas about the problems of socialist calculation.

First, the market-based solution to the problem of resource allocation is one which, through the decentralizing of decision taking, allows for individuals to take decisions upon the basis of theories, or of value systems, which may be mutually incompatible. Indeed, Hayek argued in *The Pure Theory of Capital* that an equilibrium couched in terms of the mutual compatibility of individuals' plans, while useful, was purely 'fictitious'.[144] But a planned economy might appear, from its very rationale, to be committed to the idea that there should be some single, coherent design running through economic activities (i.e. for the 'rational' use of resources for the good of citizens), or that, say, priorities for the allocation of resources should be decided on the basis of some shared conception of social justice.

It would be possible, however, for the advocate of central planning to deny that he was committed to this. He might – given problems with the settling of disagreements about moral priorities (to say nothing of those that are grounded in metaphysical or religious beliefs) – wish to argue that the content of his 'plan' would be determined by the preferences and decisions of individual citizens. In that case, differences would not have to be rationally reconciled; the plan, rather, would simply take individuals' expressions of preferences as 'data'.[145] But here one would hit the problems of the availability and the aggregation of such data which we encountered in connection with the 'market socialist' solutions to the problem of economic calculation, and above all the problem of the mechanism through which the adjustment and reconciliation of individuals' plans are to be accomplished. This, in turn, also points to the fact that in making a choice for a system of social organization based upon markets and private property, one is also choosing a system through which individuals' plans are to be reconciled and adjusted. We will discuss this issue later.

At the same time, there is a sense in which Hayek's own views seem to me vulnerable to the criticism that he has made, here, of the socialist. For Hayek seems to be simply presuming that a market-based society, with the features that he highlights, will itself be something that each individual citizen should find valuable; indeed, valuable to the point where his concern for it overrules his other concerns. We will explore this issue in later chapters, too.

Another important theme of Hayek's *Road to Serfdom* is a statement of a positive case for liberalism. As might be expected from the ideas that we have looked at so far, Hayek centres his exposition on a discussion of the advantages of a market-based economic system and the links that he draws between economic and political freedom. Emphasis is still placed upon consequentialist arguments concerning preferences and well-being; but there is also a growing emphasis on the importance of individual freedom *per se*. Hayek contrasts individualism with 'socialism and all other forms of collectivism', and writes of individualism's

> respect for the individual man *qua* man, that is the recognition of his own views and tastes as supreme in his own sphere ... and the belief that it is desirable that men should develop their own individual gifts and bents.[146]

He describes the way in which, as a product of 'the general direction of social development [in modern European history being one] of freeing the individual from the ties which had bound him to the customary or prescribed ways in the pursuit of his ordinary activities',[147] individuals gained a greater degree of political freedom. And he argues that this, in turn, led to freedom in the pursuit of economic activities, which in turn gave rise to economic benefits, such that, *a posteriori*, it was possible to offer a plausible argument in favour of political freedom upon this basis.

Hayek also emphasizes strongly the importance for liberalism of the rule of law. As we noted earlier, Hayek's view of the rule of law is strongly influenced by the *Rechtsstaat* tradition. He builds into his view of the rule of law the idea that law should not be directly aimed at particular people and also that government itself and its agencies should be subject to the law. Hayek has been taken to task for his treatment of the rule of law, first by Finer[148] and then by Raz,[149] on the grounds that he was importing into an essentially formal idea substantive elements of classical liberal political philosophy. The criticism loses its thrust if it is the case (as might seem plausible from *The Political Idea of the Rule of Law*) that Hayek is concerned with the rule of law in an explicitly moral sense.[150] But this very defence of Hayek in its turn raises the question of how the moral ideals of a *Rechtsstaat*, in Hayek's sense, relate to his other values – an issue with which we will also be concerned later in this volume. (Indeed, there is a sense in which what they are objecting to could be described as a Rousseauian strand in Hayek's legal theory.)

As we have seen earlier, Hayek argues that existing institutional arrangements should not be left alone, but instead should be remoulded so as better to fit the functional needs of a liberal economic system. Hayek is not an advocate of *laissez-faire*: he is not averse to government playing a considerable role; for example, in the area of the provision of public goods, in assisting with the smooth-running of the market order, and also in meeting welfare needs. Hayek's concern, rather, is that this should be done in ways that are compatible with, rather than serving to undermine, a liberal social and economic order. Much of Hayek's *Constitution of Liberty* is concerned with suggestions concerning how this might be achieved. His discussion combines specific suggestions about issues of public policy with the idea that government should be restricted primarily to measures that satisfy his own requirements concerning the rule of law.

One final question – to which I have already alluded in chapter one – might usefully be raised at this point. It concerns the political character of the views at which Hayek had arrived by the time at which he wrote *The Road to Serfdom*. We have already seen the way in which, in various of his writings, Hayek stressed that his values had not changed from when he was a socialist. Further, as I have argued, while Hayek had good arguments against certain kinds of socialism, it is not clear the extent to which he had arguments for adopting a classical liberal perspective, as against a view more like that of Wieser.[151] In the light of the active role that he gives to government in *The Road to Serfdom*, one might wonder about the extent to which he can be described as a classical liberal there[152] – as distinct from having set out some ideas by which the policy of anyone should be guided, if they were, as he thought essential, to preserve a market economy and to avoid measures which would have an adverse impact on individual liberty.[153] At the same time, there is clearly a strand in Hayek which is much more distinctively classical liberal in its character; something that, thereafter, becomes stronger with the passage of time.

A full investigation of this issue would take us far beyond tasks proper to the present volume. But it is worth noting the unease, in this regard, that was exhibited by Karl Popper on reading Hayek's *Road to Serfdom*. In some ways, Hayek seemed to him to have come, from a very different starting-point, to ideas which were astonishingly close to his own.[154] Yet Popper nevertheless privately expressed some unease as to whether Hayek's views were not more conservative than his own; at the way in which – as distinct from the thrust of his own *Open Society* – Hayek did not seem to show as much concern for the protection of the weak, and at the way in which Hayek's work was warmly received by conservatives.[155]

One possible explanation for what may seem to us the lack of clarity about these issues, relates to a change in the political problem-situation since the time at which Hayek wrote. That is, the divisions between liberals and those who held such forms of socialism as are compatible with Hayek's views, may have looked relatively minor as compared with the division between them, and those who favoured central planning, or explicitly favoured some kind of illiberal politics. This, certainly, was Popper's view at the time,[156] and it is striking that, in response to Hayek's invitation to him to join the Mont Pelerin Society, Popper wrote to Hayek urging that it was important that democratic socialists should be invited to join, the initial membership list being too closely identified with an anti-socialist perspective,[157] Popper expressing concern that the (to him) vital alliance of liberals and democratic socialists against those who favoured totalitarianism, might be broken.

In an interesting, unpublished paper on Hayek's political philosophy,[158] Chandran Kukathas has suggested that this division was a concern of Hayek's, too, and indeed that this opposition to totalitarianism is an important feature of Hayek's work that distinguishes it from that of more recent liberal writers, such as Rawls. In so far as this is the case, it would suggest that Hayek had good reason for not drawing too sharply the lines with which I have been concerned. Be this as it may, it is certainly true that, in Hayek's later writings, his views become more and more clearly identified with classical liberalism. But this faces him, ever more starkly, with the problem of how he would respond to the person who wishes to use the state in order to try to realize socialist values within a market economy, and who knows enough about markets to be able to avoid the more obvious problems of interventionism. There are, however, also some other important problems posed by Hayek's later views themselves, to which we will now turn.

3

HAYEK'S LATER THOUGHT

INTRODUCTION

In the period following *The Road to Serfdom* much of Hayek's work consisted of the elaboration and development of ideas we have already met. But there were also some new developments, and in addition some minor themes from Hayek's earlier writings took on a life of their own. In this chapter, we will look at some of this work. My treatment cannot be comprehensive. Rather, I will select themes which complement, or pose problems for, the ideas we considered earlier. In addition, I will be concerned with those themes in Hayek's later work which might help address the challenges posed by socialists and New Liberals who do *not* advocate central planning but, instead, advocate market-wise intervention within a market economy, in pursuit of their favoured values. My treatment of Hayek's later work falls into five broad sections.

My initial discussion relates to the topics of freedom and coercion. Hayek discusses these topics, notably, in his *Constitution of Liberty*. They are an important issue both in their own right, as they play a central role in his later work, but also in the light of problems that I have raised earlier. In so far as, in his writings, an account is offered as to why the freedom of others should stand as a barrier against the *direct* relief of suffering, and in so far as he has arguments concerning Wieser's problem of the exercise of power within formally voluntary arrangements of markets, this is where they are to be found.

Next, I discuss some of Hayek's work on political economy. This is broadly complementary to his earlier discussions. It includes some suggestive, if highly programmatic, ideas of which Hayek has urgent need if his wider argument is to be successful, and also his critique of the operation of modern Western unlimited democracies. These writings are not only of interest in themselves, but also as providing something that is needed for, but missing from, Hayek's earlier argument. For they suggest a basis for a critique of the views of Wieser or of those modern socialists who would *use*, rather than attempt to *simulate*, markets. We will also here look at the more positive aspects of the 'evolutionary' themes of *Law, Legislation and Liberty*.

From there, however, we turn gradually to themes which pose problems for his earlier views. We trace the way in which Hayek's legal ideas shifted from a *Rechtsstaat* approach, which was in some ways quite rationalistic in its character, to ideas which draw to a much greater extent on the common law tradition. While there is much of interest and of value in this work, there also seem to me respects in which it does not accord well with Hayek's earlier ideas, and must be found wanting. The move within Hayek's legal ideas, however, is symptomatic of a wider current within his work. For in his later writings, Hayek places increasing stress upon evolutionary and conservative themes, which start to displace some of the more radical ideas from his earlier writings. These developments are not without precedent. For in his Inaugural and in 'Individualism: True and False' we already met themes of this character. However, in Hayek's later writings, they come to take pride of place. In addition, there is a tendency within this work to downplay the role of reason, and to stress its limitations and its character as the product of, rather than as something that can give direction to, a process of cultural evolution. Hayek is by no means clear-cut in what he says on this theme; and there were also criticisms of 'rationalism' in his earlier work. In part Hayek also stresses that his concern is not to criticize reason, but its abuse, and he makes explicit links between his ideas and Karl Popper's critical rationalism. At the same time, however, there is a strand of argument in Hayek's later work which might seem incompatible with even a *critical* rationalist approach. This we identify and discuss in some detail. For if Hayek's later thought genuinely calls into question the ability of reason to play the critical role allocated to it by Menger and Popper, it would seem to me that Hayek's earlier analysis, which I have described and which I would wish to champion, would be damaged.

By way of contrast with all this, there is also, in Hayek's later work, an oddly optimistic and utopian strand. At the very same time as he is concerned to counsel us on the weakness of human reason, and on the need to hold fast to what we have inherited, making improvements to it only upon the basis of internal criteria, Hayek also launches into a striking exercise in constitution-making. One major theme of his *Law, Legislation and Liberty* is the idea that an older tradition of limits to the powers of government has become moribund, and is now no longer even fully understood. Hayek urges us to take a bold step, and to adopt a new constitution which would restore limits upon government. He is, in this work, utopian. But he is also – in what becomes an important Hayekian theme – also in a sense conservative. For in offering to us radical ideas for a new constitution, he seeks to draw lessons from institutions that have worked in the past.

FREEDOM AND COERCION

One issue that Hayek addresses in his later work is his conception of freedom; notably, in *The Constitution of Liberty*. Hayek has much to say that is of interest, but I do not think that his account can be considered satisfactory. He works with two related but in the end somewhat different conceptions of freedom, as if they were one. I do not think that they are fully compatible, or that either of them is adequate in itself.

Hayek initially spells out the idea of freedom that he will be defending as 'the state in which a man is not subject to coercion by the arbitrary will of another or others'.[1] He takes some pains to distinguish between this and other notions of freedom, emphasizing that freedom, as he is discussing it, is to be distinguished from political liberty, power or inner liberty. Clearly, one can raise no objection to Hayek's being concerned with freedom in this sense; but the reader will wish to know *why* he thinks it important. It is here that the trouble starts. For Hayek offers what in the end amounts to two rather different accounts of this.

The first is to be found when Hayek discusses coercion. He explains this as

> such control of the environment or circumstances of a person by another that, in order to avoid greater evil, he is forced to act not according to a coherent plan of his own but to serve the ends of another.[2]

He comments, further, that coercion

> is evil precisely because it . . . eliminates an individual as a thinking and valuing person and makes him a bare tool in the achievement of the ends of another.[3]

Hayek suggests that coercion can only be minimized, not abolished, because 'the only way to prevent it is by the threat of coercion'.[4] This task of preventing coercion is allocated to the state. A sceptical reader might here, naturally, be led to think of Locke's famous comment on Filmer:[5]

> This is to think that Men are so foolish that they take care to avoid what Mischiefs may be done to them by *Pole-Cats* or *Foxes*, but are content, nay think it Safety, to be devoured by *Lions*.

But Hayek is well aware of the problem, and argues, with an eye to it, that the state itself should act on the basis of known and general rules, in order to remove its actions as far as possible from behaviour which fits more directly his definition of coercion (not least, as people can frame their plans such that they are not imposed upon adversely by such rules). As might be expected, he also reviews certain unlovely features of a market-based society, arguing that they are not to be understood as coercive – at least on his explication of that term – and, more generally, argues for the compatibility between his ideas about freedom and a liberal market order. In this connection, Hayek urges that coercion is to be distinguished from the general 'conditions or terms in which our fellow men are willing to render us specific services or benefits',[6] suggesting that 'as long as the services of a particular person are not crucial to my existence or the preservation of what I most value, the conditions he exacts for rendering these services cannot properly be called "coercion" '.[7] He commends the law for 'not recogniz[ing] contracts for the permanent sale of a person's labour or . . . even enforc[ing] contracts for specific performance'.[8] And while he recognizes that close relationships (including those within the family) might offer the opportunity for coercion in his sense, he argues that while it is essential to make sure that such relationships are 'truly voluntary', measures beyond this − which would include state-run programmes to promote autonomy in some more positive sense − are ruled out, because he fears that this would lead to restrictions on choice and conduct such 'as to produce even greater coercion'.[9]

Hayek is well aware − and is concerned − that occurrences which fit his definition of coercion might occur as the product of voluntary agreements within a society of the kind that he favours. (In this respect, Hayek's approach is to be distinguished from one in which what is or is not morally in order can simply be read off from ideas about individual rights. Rather, from Hayek's perspective, if one is going to use the idea of individual rights, they would have to be reinterpreted quite dramatically; for what gets a right-like status is that which is expected to minimize the occurrence of certain kinds of morally undesirable consequences.) Such cases as the power exercised by an owner of a spring in an oasis, that exercised by an employer over the person in ordinary employment in situations of acute unemployment, and the discretion of the manager of a mine in an (isolated) mining town might indeed, Hayek suggests, be coercive in their character, on the basis of his own definition. And in the face of this problem he suggests that 'the most expedient and effective method [of preventing a monopolist acquiring coercive power] is probably to require him to treat all customers alike',[10] in which connection he draws a parallel with his own treatment of the exercise of coercive powers by the state; i.e. that the state should be constrained so as to act only on the basis of general rules. (Is this, perhaps, a ghost of Wieser's suggestions about constitutional monarchy as a model for economic relations?) Hayek believes, however, that in the normal course of events, if there is freedom of entry into markets, such situations will not be a major problem in the kind of market-based society that he favours.

Two points, however, should be made about all this. The first is that Hayek's account of what is wrong with coercion does not cohere too well with this account of freedom. It is intuitively plausible that there is something *prima facie* objectionable about someone being 'forced to act not according to a coherent plan of their own, but to serve the ends of another'. But it is not clear that Hayek is, in fact, entitled to his point here about 'a coherent plan'. For, as I mentioned at the outset of this discussion, in setting out his account of liberty, Hayek distances his view from an account which places emphasis upon 'inner freedom'. Hayek's account certainly does not preclude people's acting on the basis of coherent plans; but there is no special reason why they should be doing so − as distinct from acting on mere whim or impulse. Indeed, Hayek may here have cheated slightly. It is not − I hasten to add − that I am suggesting that there is something desirable about the coercion of action, even where what we are concerned with is all that Hayek is in fact entitled to by way of his description of what is being coerced. Rather, my point is that it becomes less clear why this – the frustration of a particular subjective wish – is to be singled out as particularly important. Or, to put this another way, the point of emphasizing an individual's freedom is, essentially, to explain why this should be a moral constraint upon others.[11] But while freedom to act on the basis of a subjective impulse may count for something, it is not clear why it should count for very much. In particular, why should such freedom outweigh, say, our ability to give assistance to others who are suffering? Other aspects of Hayek's discussion, however, seem to veer in the opposite direction. In the case of coercion coming about within a market-based society (e.g. when he was distinguishing it from the conditions under which people are willing to supply goods and services) it was only things that were 'crucial to my existence or the preservation of what I most value' that were to count. But these are, clearly, only a small subset of what makes an individual 'a thinking and valuing person', or are involved in his being 'forced to act not according to a coherent plan of [his] own'.

The second point addresses this issue from the other side. In so far as a defender of Hayek's view *does* spell out why such coercion is wrong, it would seem to me that they would be drawn into saying something about the relation between the particular action and the concerns, personality and so on, of the individual in question. It is in such settings that even an impulse, perhaps, may seem to us to have a moral gravity, such that it should not lightly be frustrated. It is in that context that it counts, in the way in which that of, say, a cat or a baby does not, in the same way. But once this is done, Hayek's just singling out coercion as he defines it as being problematic, starts to look idiosyncratic. For the very things that give weight to the idea that the arbitrary frustration of an individual's considered plans is morally problematic, would seem to point in other directions, too. Why, in particular, does it not point us towards something closer to the agenda of the New Liberalism, and to obligations to assist other people with those things needed to furnish them with autonomy (or whatever), if they cannot furnish them for themselves?

But what of coercion itself? Hayek, in the course of his discussion, stresses the intentional character of coercion, in the sense in which he is dealing with it:[12]

> Even if the threat of starvation to me and perhaps to my family impels me to accept a distasteful job at a very low wage, even if I am 'at the mercy' of the only man willing to employ me, I am not coerced by him or anybody else. So long as the act that has placed me in my predicament is not aimed at making me do or not do specific things, so long as the intent of the act that harms me is not to make me serve another person's ends, its effect on my freedom is not different from that of any natural calamity – a fire or a flood that destroys my house or an accident that harms my health.

While Hayek is right that this does not seem to involve coercion in his sense, it is not clear why it should not seem equally regrettable, and its avoidance of equal moral importance. Hayek has suggested that certain specific kinds of conduct – action on the basis of certain kinds of general rules which will obviate the undesirable consequences of the occurrence of coercion – can be imposed on those who happen to find themselves in the position of the owner of the desert oasis (the constraints upon whom do not, as far as I can see, depend upon his having deliberately brought about the situation which places him at an advantage). It is not immediately clear why similar requirements should not be imposed upon other people, so that unfortunate occurrences like those described in the quotation from Hayek, above, will not take place – *if*, indeed, this can be done without unacceptable cost. It is certainly not something to which Hayek can object on the grounds that it violates people's rights. No objection of that kind was entered in the case of the owner of the oasis; and anyway, Hayek's argument is consequentialist in character, rather than being based on rights in the more usual sense. We will, however, explore a strand of consequentialist argument that may be of relevance here, in our treatment of social justice in the next chapter.[13]

There is, however, another strand to Hayek's account of liberty; one in which he discusses the importance of freedom in relation to what he calls 'civilization'. Here, Hayek offers us a broad-brush sketch of the conditions required for the flourishing of Western civilization. This is a picture of his market-based society, writ large, in which our behaviour is coordinated with that of others through markets, traditions and evolved systems of rules. Hayek stresses the way in which we, and our tastes, are formed and moulded by this process. However, while he describes what takes place within it as progress, it is not clear that this means more than change made in response to what we want to undertake at any one moment.[14]

In chapter five I will discuss some aspects of this general account, in connection with its conception of what is valuable. For now, my concern is with the relation between this account, and what Hayek says about freedom. After giving us a sketch of these ideas, Hayek writes:[15]

What is essential to the functioning of the process [that he has described] is that each individual be able to act on his particular knowledge, always unique, at least so far as it refers to some particular circumstances, and that he be able to use his individual skills and opportunities within the limits known to him and for his own individual purpose.

He then adds:

The case for individual freedom rests chiefly on the recognition of the inevitable ignorance of all of us concerning a great many of the factors on which the achievement of our ends and welfare depends.

These themes are echoed in his other discussions of freedom and coercion. For example, in considering J. S. Mill's problem of what it is that merits protection, Hayek writes that our

> aim cannot be to protect people against all actions by others that may be harmful to them but only to keep certain of the data of their actions from the control of others.[16]

There are many other respects in which Hayek writes of what is protected, when he is dealing with an individual's freedom, as being what enables them to make a contribution to this wider social process. It is an interesting line of argument, and is clearly suggestive of a way in which a consequentialist – even someone whose views are broadly utilitarian in character – might be led to admit the importance of according rights-like autonomy to each individual, because of the contribution that that individual's knowledge will make towards the utilitarian's overall concerns.

Here, I have four comments. The first is that what is being protected – in terms of the individual's unique contribution to the development of civilization as Hayek depicts it – is not necessarily the same thing as is protected in Hayek's previous account. It is not clear why someone's being prevented from certain kinds of participation in civilization as a result of coercion is any different from their being prevented by other occurrences which would not be coercive in Hayek's sense. If what is important is that each individual's knowledge, what is unique to their perspective, etc., be somehow fed into our decision-making processes, then this would seem to be frustrated if, say, they starve to death or in some way or another fall under the domination of others as a result of processes which do not count as coercive in Hayek's sense. It might be the case that the rules that Hayek suggests will best foster the possibility that each individual can contribute to civilization; but this, on the face of it, would seem to stand in need of support from a broadly empirical argument which we are not offered.

Second, Hayek's account of what is involved in 'civilization' is not very specific. While what he writes is in some ways highly suggestive, it would seem – at the very least – an exaggeration to suggest that each input by *every* person has an important role to play in fostering civilization, in his sense. But if that is not the case, the argument from such considerations to the freedom of *each* individual would seem to be undermined. I will explore this issue further, when considering a possible argumentative basis for the universalistic aspects of Hayek's legal ideas in chapter six.

Third, if *everyone's* contribution does count, then does Hayek not inadvertently suggest the basis for an argument for positive freedom – that everyone should have, at the very least, their bare needs met, such that they can indeed then contribute what is unique and distinctive? It is, thus, difficult to see how, if Hayek's argument works, it remains an argument for his views, rather than, again, being one for something closer to the New Liberal agenda. (Or, rather, we would seem, once again, to require empirical argument about the likely

71

consequences of each approach, in order to assess their merits – something that it is difficult to imagine anyone's being able to provide.)

Fourth, we may ask: just how much clout does this argument of Hayek's have? Civilization, someone might agree, is a wonderful thing. But is the contribution that *this* person would make, if I were not to coerce them, of any *real* importance? Surely, the answer is yes if the person in question were Beethoven just before penning his Ninth Symphony; I am fairly sure that the answer would be no, if it were Jeremy Shearmur, just before penning the present volume. But *most* of what even Beethoven did – in the sense of each particular action – is of little import, in the sense that it is not clear what would have been lost to others had he been prevented from undertaking it. And, beyond that, if it were of importance, is it of any real importance to *each* particular one of us? If someone was hungry, and others have what they need; if they could get it, but would have to coerce them or even to kill them to do so – is what those being coerced would contribute to civilization anything that should give the possible coercers pause? I am not asking here whether it would be in their self-interest, so much as whether what Hayek is offering here has any *moral* clout.

Let me try to sum all this up. Hayek faces a difficult problem. What he ideally needs to do is to show that there are ideas of freedom and coercion which command our moral attention, and which he can argue are fostered, on consequentialist grounds, by the kind of liberal market order that he favours. In so far as the backdrop is that of a choice between a free society and a planned economy, the argument is not that difficult to make. The work that is done by the axiological part of the argument need only be very limited, if all the weight is carried by consequentialist argument about *The Road to Serfdom*. Once, however, our concern shifts from socialism in the sense of economic planning and instead becomes concerned with what should be the scope and agenda of a non-market welfare state, things get much more messy. There is a sense in which, if the agenda has shifted to this discussion, one could say that Hayek has won the argument. But as I have indicated, it would seem clear that Hayek's concerns came to extend beyond this, to an espousal of classical liberalism. That, however, leads to the problem of what balance between axiological and consequentialist argument is to be offered for a specifically classical liberal view of freedom and coercion. Here, what would seem to be needed is an argument about what it is that is valuable about the individual, such that individuals should be valued by other individuals; that they should not be coerced, but that the positive entitlements that they should be able to claim from others should be limited to Hayek's (modest) agenda, and that the whole package should cohere with the characteristics and products of an extended market order, as Hayek understands it.

This task is a tough one; but it is not one that Hayek really comes even close to accomplishing, for reasons that I have indicated. One additional difficulty that faces the classical liberal is that ever since Adam Smith's discussion of these issues in the *Wealth of Nations* and *Lectures on Jurisprudence*,[17] it should have been clear (*pace* John Stuart Mill on individuality) that there is a tension between the civic humanist ideas about well-rounded individuals, or Romantic ideas about individuality, and the advanced division of labour in a market-based society. Whatever else one can say about the merits of such societies, and the freedoms that they accord to their members, it would seem clear that they cannot hold out much hope to most of their members, in respect of the autonomous realization of plans, or the cultivation of individuality. Rather, we have to earn our living, and to make our other various choices, within the options that are left open to us by our need to coordinate our activities with those of other members of such societies.

This whole issue poses an important problem for Hayek's approach. There is a danger that, when looking at the first, or axiological, issue, one may reassure oneself that any problems will be overcome by virtue of the fact that Hayek also has an interesting line in consequentialist argument. While, when one is considering the latter, one may always feel that one can obtain reassurance from the former. The fact that I have been critical of Hayek's account should not, however, be misinterpreted, for he has important things to say about some very difficult problems. But as I believe that his discussion is not satisfactory, and because these issues seem to me in need of resolution if a Hayekian approach is to be viable, I hope that the reader will forgive me for returning to them, at some length, later; even though I am far from sure that, in the end, I will have more to show by way of positive achievements in the face of them than does Hayek.

ON GOVERNMENT AND MARKET

I have argued in the previous chapter that in so far as one takes the problem that Hayek is addressing to be that posed by the advocates of central economic planning, his arguments look very strong. But what happens when our focus shifts to the case for classical liberalism, as compared to that for market-wise interventionism on the basis of socialist or New Liberal ideas? Or, as I put the issue earlier, what does Hayek have to say to Wieser, if one considers those aspects of Hayek's writings which relate not primarily to values, but to the workings of government and markets?

In the final volume of *Law, Legislation and Liberty*, Hayek sums up some of his views on these topics, in two discussions upon which we can usefully focus. The first is a striking overview of his understanding of the workings of the market. The second is a critique of the workings of modern pluralist democracy, and an exposition of the constitutional ideas that he hopes might overcome this problem. This is of especial importance to Hayek, not only in relation to his general concern about the working of a market-based social order and its erosion by an interest-group based politics, but also because of his (uneasy) endorsement of a more than minimal state. Together, they offer a possible answer to Wieser – to a market-wise interventionist concerned with issues of power – of a kind which, as far as I can see, the younger Hayek was not himself able to provide. Hayek also proposes institutional arrangements which he hopes would safeguard liberalism from the problems of unlimited democracy, while themselves being democratic in character.

The third volume of Hayek's *Law, Legislation and Liberty* contains what is possibly Hayek's most suggestive piece of work on political economy addressed to these issues. In chapter fifteen of that volume (which is in part a revised version of his 'Competition as a Discovery Procedure') he draws together a variety of themes from his work on the functions of markets, and integrates them into an account that provides – albeit in a highly programmatic form – something that is implicit in, but missing from, the rest of his work. Hayek offers an account of the working of markets in which pride of place is given to actual competition and discovery, rather than to an idealized picture of perfect competition in the production of some known good. His account differs somewhat from that of most neoclassical market-orientated economists,[18] in a number of respects. He argues that we are not in a position to demand that a government-run monopoly behave as if it were a competitive enterprise, just because what a competitive enterprise should do is something that has to be discovered through actual competition. He further argues that there is not anything wrong with industrial concentration as such – but that what is important is to make sure that there are no barriers to entry. In a manner that parallels, in an informal but extended manner, the theory of contestable markets,[19] he stresses that the possibility that other large companies might enter a particular field exercises a constraint upon those who are already in it, even if they are by far the largest, or even the only, company currently there. Further, Hayek goes on to spell out just what is wrong with corporatism, and with schemes for the government-led consolidation of industry into monopolies. It is that such arrangements, even if they were able to accommodate fairly all the interests that are currently present,[20] serve to erect formidable barriers to the entry of others; barriers which, in effect, are manned by those already in the field (one could clearly reinforce his point here, by reference to the political lobbying power that such groups would possess). This serves to cut off innovation, and what Hayek argues to be a vitally important source of checks to the power of large companies.

Hayek's account is important, both in its own right and because it suggests – at the level of political economy – arguments on the basis of which Hayek the liberal could respond to the pre-liberal Hayek, and to the market-orientated socialist and corporatist thinkers by whom he was influenced. It is complemented by his critical account of the workings of interest-group democracy, which we will discuss in the next section. Together they offer a programme which it might be possible to develop, so as to meet the arguments of Hayek's latter-day 'market socialist' critics.

At the same time, we should not overlook just how programmatic these views of Hayek's are. His work, and related work by others in the Austrian tradition, provides a much-needed corrective to the view, held by many people, that those in the classical liberal tradition are committed to a political economy that is centred upon a model of perfect competition. At the same time, Hayek's ideas are more of the character of explanatory sketches than of detailed analysis. They suggest interesting possibilities for empirical and theoretical work in economics and political economy. But they will not fully serve Hayek's argumentative purposes until such work has actually – and successfully – been undertaken. In particular, we stand in need of some broad, but reasonably specific, argument about the efficiency and welfare characteristics of an economic system of the kind that he favours. I am not suggesting that we need argument of a highly technical character, after the fashion of modern welfare economics, but instead something of a more concrete – and empirical – character.

In the material which we have been discussing, Hayek also returns to the issue of power as it occurs in markets which had been raised in such a trenchant manner in Wieser's work. Hayek addresses both the issue of the monopolization of resources and coercion (which, as we have seen, he had earlier addressed in *The Constitution of Liberty*) and also discusses the problem of the exercise of power within the setting of a market in more general terms. He does not take the view that the mere existence of monopoly – and even of monopoly that obtains extraordinary profits – is necessarily bad. He argues, for example, that if it is the case that a company is able to make such profits because of its efficiency or foresight, this may be perfectly legitimate. But he is concerned about the power that may be exercised by such a company if it can withhold resources that are essential to others and of which it has the only source of supply (as in the case of a well in the desert, which he had discussed in *The Constitution of Liberty*, and which we have discussed from an axiological perspective, above).

In *Law, Legislation and Liberty*, Hayek suggests that almost all the really harmful power of a monopoly relates to its power to discriminate between customers, but that this poses particular problems just because certain kinds of discrimination between customers may enable a company to exercise a better service. Hayek argues, after a survey of different possibilities, that a law against the enforceability of contracts that serve to restrain trade is the best kind of option available to us. For while, he suggests, it may be unsophisticated, it would be less likely to generate exceptions than would a more complex law. Hayek argues further against the objection that such restrictions should not be allowed because they would constitute a breach of freedom of contract, that other contracts – such as those for immoral purposes, for life-long service or for gambling debts – have long been held unenforceable, and thus that there is not an issue of binding principle here. Given, however, that this is Hayek's approach, and that, for example, he is *not* arguing on the basis of rights, or, say, from ideas about the inviolability of the freedom of contract, it would seem to me that Hayek's broad argument might be capable of being extended in directions of which he might not have approved.

Let us here consider a specific example that has been discussed in some detail by a writer whose theoretical approach contrasts in a striking way with that of Hayek. John Gaventa, in his *Power and Powerlessness*, discusses the situation of miners and other residents in an isolated Appalachian valley. His discussion raises issues which relate in an interesting manner to Hayek's work.[21]

First, over and over again, it seems that what actually counted, in relation to the situation of these miners, was less what their formal rights were, than what rights they could, as a practical matter, actually exercise. Yet this, on the face of it, might seem to require that there be at least a measure of *material* equality between the various parties in question. For example, when coal deposits were discovered on the land of various independent-minded farmers, many of the farmers sold their land cheaply, not knowing what its value now amounted to. From Hayek's perspective, this is presumably sad, but not something in respect of which it would be realistic to suggest that changes be made, either to the law or to other institutions. However, it also appeared that, where people did not wish to sell, a combination of intimidation and legal sharp practice was used to dispossess them. The key problem here seems to have been that those who were administering the law had strong (although in some cases indirect) financial interests in development taking place, and thus in furthering the concerns of the mining company which was developing the entire area, while the independent farmers were poor and relatively unsophisticated. Essentially the same pattern seems to have recurred later, in respect of the discouragement of union activity.

The heart of the problem here would seem to be that if there is not a measure of material equality – in respect of resources or of knowledge – it is difficult to see how one avoids what certainly looks like coercion, by way of a combination of law and sharp practice. For citizens to enjoy their formal rights, they need to know what these are, and to be able to take effective remedy should others transgress against those rights. It is not clear, in this situation, that the farmers had, or could have had, any effective remedy. If they wanted simply to farm, their situation seems to have been hopeless. And while, in principle, if their interest was in selling out at the best possible price to a mining company, 'contestable markets'-like considerations could have come into play; in this case, and one imagines in many other real-world cases, they did not, not least because the isolated character of the situation in which they were operating meant that there were no other potential purchasers of their farms.

We are dealing here with examples within an isolated mining area, a situation which Hayek himself saw as offering possibilities for coercion. Given the information available, it is difficult to tell whether or not these cases fell precisely into Hayek's category of coercion. But it is clear that Hayek should be concerned about them, given both that and why he thinks individual freedom important. There would seem, on the face of it, no formal obstacle (in terms of his general approach) to his taking the view that such cases do call out for remedy. However, his own ideas about action on the basis of general rules would not seem to be of much help. While the problems – also relating to what have been discussed as the 'second' and 'third' dimensions of power (the latter relating, in Gaventa's interpretation, to the internalization, by those with little power, of restricted conceptions of the alternatives open to them)[22] – would seem to pose some particular difficulties for Hayek's more general approach. For if we can, from Hayek's argument, draw out the conclusion that it would be desirable if something could be done to remedy such cases, it is simply not clear to what extent one could inject the kind of measures that would be needed into a broadly classical liberal approach to political economy, and to a conception of governmental action that sees it as limited by general rules.

A second issue relates to whether, in fact, the miners had any real alternative to employment in the mines in that area. From Hayek's perspective, this is important if we are to judge whether or not coercion is taking place. Hayek has argued that

> as long as the services of a particular person are not crucial to my existence or the preservation of what I most value, the conditions he exacts for rendering these services cannot properly be called 'coercion'.[23]

In the case of the miners whom Gaventa studied, whether or not there was an alternative raises an interesting issue. The miners were living in company towns, and in company-owned houses; indeed, the only institutions not owned by the company were the churches, and they were built on land granted to them by the company. In the event of people being in dispute with the company, other local employment seems to have been closed to them. (Gaventa cites a case in which some men lost their jobs for suing the mining company for damages in respect of an industrial accident, and could then not even obtain work in the sawmill belonging to the brother-in-law of one of them, because he feared for his contracts with the company.) Gaventa also cites a survey, from which it appears that the preferred alternative form of employment was farming, but also notes that the mining corporations owned all the farming land in the region.[24]

I do not know whether, in the period in question, work was obtainable elsewhere. If it was not, the case would seem to fall into Hayek's own category of the conditions for coercion having been met because of the unobtainability of other work. But it is again not clear what remedy is feasible which would be compatible with Hayek's general approach. If work was available, there is still a problem. On one level, one might say: but in the United States, people have been very mobile, and have made moves which, in some respects, must have been much more difficult (consider, for example, the movement of highly disadvantaged black agricultural workers from the South to Northern industrial towns). At the same time, the restricted horizons of the Appalachian 'mountain men' are surely the other side of a phenomenon that Hayek himself

77

emphasizes when he stresses the important social role played in the societies that he favours by specific customs, rules and habits. Further, the restricted perspectives of these particular people are, surely, not unconnected with the circumstances in which they are living, and their almost total dependence upon the company for whom they worked. I will not here take this issue any further, other than to say that Hayek cannot, on this score, have his cake and eat it. If, in relation to issues of what alternatives are available, he wishes to operate with an objective conception of alternatives (such that these people were not subject to coercion, as they could have taken up other options), then it would seem to me that he should use the same basis for his analysis elsewhere. If, alternatively, he makes positive use of subjective opportunities and the following of particular rules, he needs to take seriously the restrictions that these place upon what people see as alternatives open to them, and also the problem that the character of such rules may not always be beneficent, if it occurs in conditions like those of the mineworkers.

The only saving grace, from Hayek's perspective, might be that, within a market-based society of the kind that he favours, the occurrence of the concatenation of circumstances that arose in the location studied by Gaventa may be rare. However, similar conditions could be created spontaneously within such societies, by the migration of the relatively able and advantaged from undesirable inner-city locations; while they might seem to arise very easily if, say, large companies from industrialized countries are in interaction with people in non-industrialized countries.

Hayek's views about coercion might thus seem to provide a basis for more governmental intervention than he may have intended and, certainly, than would be found acceptable by most classical liberals. However, as I have suggested before, it is not obvious what response would be appropriate within a broadly classical liberal approach to political economy, for the desirability of which Hayek has other, strong arguments. All that one could say is that, from Hayek's perspective, one might consider if there are any actions which could be taken on the basis of general rules by government, or constraints that might be placed upon individual agents of a kind that parallel Hayek's treatment of persons who possesses monopoly power. One might also say that, from the perspective of the people who are suffering in such situations, it might be useful to look to see if there are ways in which they can improve their situation by encouraging freedom of entry. If others can be persuaded to enter the market for their services or possessions, things may not look as grim as when they are up against a single company.

POLITICS, MARKET SOCIALISM AND SOCIAL EVOLUTION

Hayek's critical reflections on the politics of modern Western societies are in some ways less striking than are his ideas about political economy. To say this is not to say that they are not interesting and powerful. It is, rather, to note the extent to which Hayek comes to conclusions which are similar to those made by public choice economists, although Hayek stresses different issues because of his somewhat different view of the political vulnerability of a desirable political and economic order.

There are three ways in which we can approach Hayek's argument. First, and in the most general of terms, one might see Hayek as arguing, with Leoni (see below) and public choice theory, that in considering an agenda for government action, we need to bear in mind how government will *actually* behave, rather than simply allocating to it powers under the assumption that it will act in the public interest. Second, Hayek takes seriously the problems that occur when government is influenced by interest groups. He refers especially in this connection to the work of Mancur Olson.[25] These ideas are given a particular twist in Hayek's work, however, because of his fears about the consequences of the actions of politicians influenced by such groups in the field of economic policy. Hayek is concerned about the way in which, in the face of economic problems, interest groups may request economic support rather than readjusting their activities so as to coordinate with those of other economic agents. Particular benefits are then offered by politicians at the expense of the interests of the wider population. The result may be a situation in which people's expectations concerning the economic system are greater than the system can deliver, and the only way in which the government can meet its obligations is through inflation. This Hayek views as disastrous, in that it delays and compounds problems of economic adjustment, and at the same time weakens the ability of the system of relative prices to convey reliable information about the economy. Indeed, it was in the face of such an analysis that Hayek concluded that government cannot be trusted with responsibility for money, and in which he was led to advocate its 'denationalization'.[26]

There is also a third strand of argument in Hayek's work which is distinctive, but which has not been made fully explicit. It is that the problems about planning discussed in his *Road to Serfdom* re-emerge as problems facing interest-group democracies. It will be recalled that, in his early work, Hayek placed emphasis upon the fact that there is no social consensus which can form the basis of comprehensive planning. Now, once we move from full-scale planning to the pursuit of group interests through political pluralism, in some respects things are better. For there is no suggestion that markets should be *replaced*; rather, the political system is seen as an alternative path through which people's interests are pursued, within a market-based economic system. However, there are two respects in which a *planned* system may, in principle, have *advantages* over an interventionist system of such a character. The first is that one might hope that the planned system is, at least in aspiration, coherent – while there is no reason why, *a priori*, the various demands made upon a pluralistic system should make any overall sense at all. For a pluralist system may admit as legitimate (and in so far as the activities of government are themselves disaggregated, may in some sense attempt to meet) demands which are in fact incompatible. Second, one would assume that a planned system has, at least in principle, the aspiration of meeting morally pressing goals. In an interest-group based political system, there is no reason to suppose that the results – not least, of muscle-flexing by the strong – will have *any* morally redeeming features whatever. Indeed, it was striking that, in Britain, when attempts were made to conduct wage policy through a so-called 'social contract' within which it was argued that demands for wage increases should be moderated with an eye to social justice, trades unions with strong bargaining positions who were used to the traditions of interest-group pluralism became extremely restive.

My argument here (and the argument is mine, not Hayek's) is not for centralized planning or for corporatism, against both of which Hayek has given us good arguments. It is, rather, that political pluralism does not even have the merits to which these approaches can lay claim. It is a dog-eat-dog system, in which the destructive pursuit of self-interest at the expense of others is accorded a spurious respectability. As we have noted earlier, Hayek is no admirer of the self-interested behaviour which people may exhibit in the market-place. But *there* he, and a long tradition in economics, offers us arguments which relate such behaviour, in appropriate institutional settings, to the general well-being of others. In addition, some may take satisfaction that the behaviour in question can take place such that no harm is done to others, when harm is understood in terms of a negative conception of human freedom, and of freedom from coercion. By contrast, political pluralism in Western democracies would seem clearly to work to the advantage of the strong.[27] Indeed, the entire system of begging politicians for favours paid for with resources to be extracted by coercion from the weaker or less astute members of the political community seems to me an evil that I am surprised that we tolerate, let alone feel comfortable about participating in, still less uphold as a social ideal. In so far as such activities are themselves a product of the extension of the scope of government – such that a government, so extended, stands in need of input from such groups – these considerations constitute an argument against using government to solve our problems.

The reader may feel that my judgement here is intemperate, and also that it misses a key feature of much contemporary interest-group activity; namely, that such people typically claim that they are morally justified in pressing their claims. But it is against exactly this point that, in my view, Hayek has raised important issues. In part – as we will see in more detail later, when I discuss his arguments concerning social justice – he has argued that there are good reasons against the idea that a market-based society with a high degree of individual liberty, while itself morally defensible, *can* exhibit certain other kinds of moral order; order on the basis of the perceived defects of which such groups are urging that actions should be taken. In part, there is the problem that there may be necessary connections between certain morally unlovely features of a society, and its other, highly morally desirable, features. How these issues are to be dealt with poses a difficult issue, which we will address later. But one thing is clear from Hayek's argument: that the fact that their lot seems undesirable to a particular group of people does not, in itself, show that they have a legitimate call on others for its redress. Yet it is exactly this that lies at the heart of the organization of interest groups within pluralism, and some of today's 'new social movements'.

From this, let us now return to Hayek's own views. A reader of the first two chapters of this volume might well feel that there was an oddity concerning Hayek's intellectual progress – at least in so far as I have been able to reconstruct it. Hayek, in his development of Mises' argument about economic calculation under socialism, produced arguments which seem to me to highlight insuperable problems for the proponent of central planning. But, our critic could say, is there not something odd about what took place, given that those who influenced the pre-liberal Hayek, and thus, presumably, the pre-liberal Hayek himself, were not in fact proponents of the views that he criticized. It seems almost as if those non-liberal views with which Hayek was himself most familiar – what one might call the pursuit of socialist or corporatist values by means of a market-wise interventionism – simply disappear from the story. In so far as they are addressed (as in his arguments about the inefficiency of government action to promote industrial concentration), Hayek makes use of ideas the underpinnings of which become less than secure as Hayek moves away from a general equilibrium perspective.

Now it could be argued that there are strong contextual reasons why Hayek's arguments take the form that they do. For Hayek was concerned with ideas which were of political importance at the time at which he was writing. Wieser placed himself beyond the pale, politically, in his later publications, through his support for charismatic leadership.[28] And throughout the period during which Hayek produced his main work, there was a general revulsion from markets and an enthusiasm for planning and for the idea that discretionary power should be placed in government's hands. Indeed, those who did not share such perspectives seem to have formed a relatively small group, who found that they had more pressing issues on their hands than to explore their disagreements with one another. (It is striking, for example, that Karl Popper – who in his *Open Society* is no friend of economic liberalism[29] – was a member of Hayek's Mont Pelerin Society.) I also explored some other aspects of the political context of *The Road to Serfdom*, at the end of chapter two.

Indeed, it is only in the last few years, with the widespread acceptance of the case for markets and the (temporary?) demise of Marxism, that this issue has become pressing. However, as 'market socialism' – in various interpretations which envisage recourse to *actual* markets – becomes popular, the gap that we have discerned in Hayek's argument looms larger. It is striking, for example, to find David Miller, in a review of Hayek's *Fatal Conceit*,[30] concluding:

Hayek chooses to ignore... recent developments in social thought [Miller has discussed ways in which socialist goals might be pursued by means to which Hayek might not have objections]. He opts for a depiction of socialism which precludes by definition any creative synthesis of the kind sketched above. This seems to me a missed opportunity: as an advocate of market socialism I regret in particular that Hayek did not undertake a critical examination of such a system.

However, while detailed argument would have to be developed in respect of each specific proposal (and this, clearly, is not a task that can be attempted here) the ideas from the later work of Hayek, which we have just discussed, do suggest the lines along which a response might be offered. The challenge that they suggest to the market socialist (understood, here, as the devotee of the ideas to which I have just referred) has two aspects. First, the market socialist has to sketch out what he is proposing, in terms of a mixture between markets, legislation and governmental activity. He then has to argue that it can indeed be expected to generate desirable consequences. The relevant point is: can one expect from it consequences that are better than those of a market-based system such as Hayek's, given a realistic picture of how people will act in the situations in which they will find themselves in such a system? Second, however, he must offer us an account of how his favoured system is to come into being, and to sustain itself.

Such requirements seem to me to face the market socialist with some difficult problems, given the ideas that we have reviewed in this chapter so far. However, he might well insist that what is sauce for the goose is sauce for the gander, and ask if Hayek's own proposals can withstand the same challenge. Here, again, Hayek has a case to answer, especially, as we will see later, when we consider his ideas about the construction of a new constitution.

However, in Hayek's later work, there are also some ideas which are not constructivist in their character. Rather, they offer an account of the kind of social order that Hayek favours as the product of a form of social evolution. We will turn now to a brief discussion of them.

The appendix to volume three of Hayek's *Law, Legislation and Liberty*, and his *Fatal Conceit*, offer an account of his ideas that is distinctive, because of his stress on the theme of the evolution of the institutions that he cherishes. His argument is important and interesting, in so far as it serves to remind us of the role of the unplanned and the inherited, and of the limits upon our ability to rebuild our institutions from their foundations. However, in so far as Hayek's account goes beyond Menger's and becomes closer to those of the German theorists whom Menger criticized – in so far as he seems to say that institutions must be worthwhile *because* they are inherited, and discounts Menger's concern that we scrutinize them critically – he runs into problems.

The central theme of this work of Hayek's is our old friend, the market order, together with its associated institutions, and their vulnerability to certain kinds of moral criticism. In his *Fatal Conceit*, Hayek offers a striking overview of the development of civilization, in which traders and private property play a key role. Hayek's account, for which he provides a number of interesting historical references, is essentially the story of the development of a market-based social order which is sustained by its citizens following rules the rationale for which was not clear to them at the time. It was at odds, on his account, both with instinctively based moral reactions, and with many moral and religious teachings. His account of the development of the institutions with which he is concerned is, essentially, one of group selection. Those who followed rules of certain kinds prospered, sometimes at the expense of those who did not; they also grew in numbers and were imitated. Such, Hayek tells us, is our heritage; one that has made possible our civilization, and which is, literally, responsible for the fact that so many people can be alive today. Hayek's problem, as one might expect, is to defend such a social order from those – constructivist rationalists, and socialists – who are critical of it and wish to replace it. He is also concerned as to how it may be preserved from its citizens in their role as participants in politics.

Hayek's account of the development of a market-based social order is suggestive, and it makes important points about the human situation which are not adequately taken into account by much moral theory. For Hayek's argument is, essentially, that we benefit from institutions the character of which is not transparent to us as citizens. Not only may our moral ideals be at odds with the effective operation of such institutions, but our compliance with what enables such institutions to function may have been the result of all kinds of uncritically held traditions and taboos. Hayek is scathing in his comments upon those who would turn their back upon this achievement and condemn received institutions simply because, in some respects, they fall foul of our moral intuitions or because the rationale that we have for them is defective. His points are often well taken. However, his views also face problems, some of which we have also encountered elsewhere.

First, there is perhaps a false generality to his account. When one really comes down to it, Hayek is concerned primarily with a property-based social order in which individuals have freedom to act, subject to laws of a general character. One can grant to Hayek that the historical development of such a social order was not a creation of deliberate human ratiocination. But, at the same time, in the development of such institutions we are hardly dealing with a general process of human social evolution, unless this term is used so loosely as to cover almost anything. For – as Hayek has himself argued elsewhere – the story of the development of the kinds of institution that he favours is an odd mix of practice and its reflective improvement; of dogma, force, happenstance, reflective articulation, theoretical understanding and criticism. While Hayek makes a good point in his insistence that our institutions and the habits that sustain them are not a deliberate, rational creation *ex nihilo*, it is not clear that there is a *general* 'evolutionary' process at work of the kind that he depicts.

This is important in a negative sense, too. For Hayek's account runs the risk of being too general – in the sense of failing to single out that which is good from his own perspective from that which is not. Indeed, Hayek himself refers, in *The Fatal Conceit*, to work on the economics of law which suggests ways in which inherited property rights may be improved.[31] Hayek also suggests that in certain areas we should be more free to experiment than governments have allowed,[32] and he refers, in the same vein, to his own work on *The Denationalization of Money*. This raises the problem, familiar elsewhere from Hayek's work, that *despite* Hayek's account of social evolution, inherited institutions, on Hayek's own account, stand in need of critical appraisal and improvement. But how, if people were to take seriously what Hayek writes in *The Fatal Conceit*, is such appraisal to take place?

One further problem, which we have met before in our discussion of Hayek's 'Individualism: True and False', is that in so far as the lesson that we are to learn from Hayek's later work is one of social conservatism, and that we should be reluctant to discard inherited institutions, it would seem to run the risk of leading us to preserve things that are not of value along with ones that are. Hayek refers to the positive role of religion in preserving some of the institutions that he favours. But his account also contains references to religious doctrines which have served to undermine these very institutions.[33] It is not clear how the conservative citizen is to choose what it is that he should accept, and what he should be critical of. And critical he must be. For the very developments of which Hayek is so full of praise were themselves, presumably, at times taken against moral pressure exercised by the communities of which individuals are members. (Hayek does offer us, in *Law, Legislation and Liberty*, an account of how some standards can be revised on the basis of others. But it is not clear why the products of such a revision should possess any particular functional properties; and especially the ones that Hayek favours.)

Indeed, there is a sense in which Hayek's argument in *The Fatal Conceit* is not fully appropriate to the situation which he is addressing. For the problems with which he is dealing only arise once we have come to a certain degree of critical awareness about issues in social policy. But if that is the case, then to endorse – to say nothing of improving – our existing institutions requires that we can offer some rationale for so doing. (The problem, further, is that in so far as Hayek does offer such a rationale, it is one that is accessible to the social theorist, but not to the ordinary citizen.) To put the issue in such terms might seem to run foul of a point that Hayek makes in the very writings that I am discussing: that we are not in a position to appraise all our traditions and institutions at once. But what of more piecemeal reform? And how should we assess the utopian strand and concern with constitution-making in Hayek's own work in the light of his own off-expressed reservations concerning the powers of human reason?

In *The Fatal Conceit*, Hayek lists various criteria which, in his view, have been widely canvassed by modern intellectuals as the basis upon which choices should be made. They include such things as:

> that it is unreasonable to follow what one cannot justify scientifically...that it is unreasonable to follow what one does not understand...that it is unreasonable to follow a particular course [of action] unless its *purpose* is fully specified in advance...[and] that it is unreasonable [to act] unless [the] *effects* [of that act] are not only fully known in advance but are also fully observable and seen to be beneficial.[34]

Hayek finds such ideas wanting. But on what basis are we to appraise – and thus to cherish, and perhaps also to improve upon – the institutions with which he is concerned? This is left exceedingly unclear in Hayek's later writings. At one point, after referring to Popper and Bartley's anti-justificationism, Hayek seems to suggest that an understanding of the basis upon which these institutions developed can itself offer us a rationale for their appraisal:[35]

> and in so doing [offering a conjectural history of such institutions] we can to some degree understand the needs that they serve. To the extent we succeed in this, we are indeed called upon to improve and revise our moral traditions by remedying recognizable defects by piecemeal improvement based upon immanent criticism.

But in *The Fatal Conceit*, Hayek pictures the rationale of the institutions that he favours as being the survival and growth in numbers of the group of which one is a member; and if, as Hayek remarks,

> There is no reason to suppose that the selection by evolution of such habitual practises as enabled men to nourish larger numbers had much if anything to do with the production of happiness.[36]

the problem is raised: why should the individual care about the basis upon which such institutions have been selected, once he is aware of it, if it is to his personal disadvantage? Hayek has written:[37]

> Although this morality [the kind of rationale that sustains his favoured institutions] is not 'justified' by the fact that it enables us . . . to survive, it does enable us to survive, and there is something perhaps to be said for that.

This might be taken in two ways. On the one hand, it might be read as suggesting that the survival of the individual himself is placed in jeopardy by changes to the institutions that Hayek favours. But this, while a telling criticism of *some* changes, will hardly apply to most proposals for change. On the other hand, Hayek is arguing against the adoption of policies on the grounds that they would have bad effects upon the market order, and would thus bring misery and death to other people. This is certainly a powerful thesis;

85

and it would indeed be telling against certain proposals for large-scale social engineering – as we can learn from the history of our own century. However, to rule out policies which will have such consequences, while very important, again does not restrict our options all that much.

Two kinds of problem are particularly pressing. The first concerns the individual's conduct: suppose that some form of traditional practice poses a problem for an individual's well-being; and suppose that it is indeed related to the mechanisms that sustain Hayek's favoured social order. In what terms should that individual make an appraisal as to how he should act? While he will wish to avoid conduct that would bring starvation and death to his fellows, it is not clear that he should be interested in the multiplication of his own species as such, or place it above his own well-being or that of other individuals who are alive now. Indeed, in so far as Hayek is correct and the true story underlying much of our inherited morality is its role in the propagation of our species, we may well be that much more ready to reject it in favour of something more important, should we become conscious of this connection! (I will, however, suggest a way in which Hayek's argument may be reinterpreted, in a manner which I believe to be immune to these criticisms, in the next chapter.)

Second, there is our old problem of the market-wise socialist. Suppose that he grants Hayek's point – that there is a fragile social order based upon the market and related institutions which is at odds with some of the historic goals of socialism. He can still ask: but what about actions which may be taken in the pursuit of socialist ethical concerns, and which will not disturb market mechanisms? And what, also, about trade-offs? What, say, of the costs to the things that Hayek favours of introducing a somewhat more generous welfare non-market safety net than Hayek would allow for?

Here, Hayek faces a problem. For while he would wish to weigh against measures proposed by such a socialist the well-being of individuals, their ability to pursue their own concerns, and the minimization of coercion, the generality of his argument, and the very open-endedness of his view of human concerns, makes it difficult to assess trade-offs. The same would seem true of the policy of the improvement of inherited institutions that Hayek favours; not least because of Hayek's own important point that the best of institutions are likely to suffer ineliminable defects.

One final point, however, needs to be added here.[38] It might be objected to my discussion that I have displayed undue hostility towards *The Fatal Conceit* and towards Hayek's later work more generally. For given that, in *The Constitution of Liberty* and in some parts of *Law, Legislation and Liberty*, Hayek has already offered extensive and radical programmes for institutional change, why have I been so critical of *The Fatal Conceit* for not offering positive suggestions? Hayek can't do, and can't be expected to do, everything at once. This objection is useful, as I hope that it will help me to clarify the basis of my criticism. Hayek's earlier work is challenging, but it requires that we produce theories in the light of which we can evaluate and improve on our existing institutions, and – if we are so inclined – argue the merits of a classical liberal social order, against, say, various kinds of market socialism. Hayek's later work loses sight of these issues. Further, while it contains many interesting and suggestive ideas, it leads him into a position that seems to me a disaster.

For, first, it offers us developments of the conservative strand within Hayek's work which, as I have already argued, do not themselves offer a resolution of the intellectual problems that his views face. Second, and more important, the terms in which Hayek argues threaten to cast doubt upon our ability to undertake those very tasks which must be accomplished if Hayek's ideas are to be defended successfully against contemporary critics. Thus, in my view, not only is much of what is distinctive about Hayek's later work beside the point, but if it were sustainable it would damage what, in my judgement, are some of his own more telling ideas. If I am right about all this, one other question becomes pressing. Just why was it that Hayek moved towards the views that are to be found in his later work? In my opinion, to understand this we need to pay attention to some changes in his views about law.

FROM *RECHTSSTAAT* TO COMMON LAW

One of the most striking things about the development of Hayek's work is the transition between his earlier and his later writings on legal topics. It is not that his ideals change, so much as that there is a shift with respect to the way in which Hayek seems to understand their institutional realization. In his earlier writings, as we have seen, Hayek makes an explicit connection between the institutions required if markets are to function adequately and the ideas of *Rechtsstaat* liberalism. He tells a story of the development of such ideas, in which Continental writers learn from, but improve upon, views that had been worked out in more practical terms within British common law and the development of Britain's unwritten constitution. He identifies the ideal of the rule of law with the characteristics of law as described by Continental liberal theorists. And, as we have seen, he suggests his own programme for the critical improvement of law, such that it will better serve its functional role in a market-based social order.

If, in contrast with this, one looks at Hayek's later writings on legal issues – for example, in his *Law, Legislation and Liberty* – one finds something rather different. There is still a concern with the broad characteristics of the legal order of a liberal society, and much that is to be found there is familiar from Hayek's earlier writings. But Hayek's account of this system, and of its development, now places stress on common law and on the idea that law is there to be discovered by the judge. Parallels are also drawn between law and language. And Hayek pictures law as developing by way of the discovery of, and removal of, incoherencies. In this section, I offer a hypothesis as to what is going on, and discuss some of the intellectual issues involved in this transition.

LEONI'S *FREEDOM AND THE LAW*

The change in Hayek's views can in my view be best seen as a result of the impact of Bruno Leoni. This suggestion is not original,[39] but to my knowledge the aspects of Leoni's work in question have not been the subject of extended discussion, perhaps because Leoni's interesting work has itself been neglected.

Leoni, in *Freedom and the Law*, argued against Hayek's assimilation in his Cairo Lectures of British ideas on the rule of law to the Continental *Rechtsstaat* tradition. At the centre of Leoni's argument was the idea that there is a difference between the notion of certainty in the Continental tradition and that which was important in common law. The Continental tradition, on his account, identified certainty with law being explicit and available to the citizen. Leoni does not suggest that this is without value. But he argues that this in itself is insufficient to ensure freedom from coercion (as Hayek might perhaps be read as suggesting in *The Constitution of Liberty*); and that, more important, it diverts us from something that in Leoni's view is of greater import: certainty in the law in the sense of stability from revision.

At the heart of Leoni's approach there is a critique of law as legislation – of law as the product of a sovereign body – with which the *Rechtsstaat* ideal of codified law is associated. What is wrong with this – and thus, on Leoni's view, with Hayek's earlier account – is that it does not pay appropriate attention to the actual character of legislative bodies, in depicting which Leoni anticipates later work in public choice and law and economics.[40] Essentially, Leoni's argument is that a system in which legislative bodies are seen as the sources of law will not generate stability over time. He is especially concerned that such legal regimes will not give people the chance to order their affairs without the risk that the legal procedures under which they do so will subsequently be changed.

Leoni also offers his own more positive account of law. He draws parallels between law, language and the workings of a market-based social order. Law, in his view, is to be discovered by lawyers – not by some kind of Platonic intuition of natural law, but, rather, through the discovery of the people's will, in the sense of the rules by which they live. As Leoni puts it,

> the whole process can be described as a sort of vast, continuous, and chiefly spontaneous collaboration between the judges and the judged in order to discover what the people's will is in a series of definite instances.[41]

Leoni refers approvingly to Savigny and his critique of codification,[42] and it is in terms similar to Savigny's that Leoni's own more positive views are best understood. It might be mentioned, however, that Leoni does not think that legislation could be completely superseded by a common-law system of the kind that he favours.[43]

Leoni's work is important to our understanding of Hayek. For he has identified a tension in Hayek's work: the appeal, at the same time, to historical or common-law approaches to law and its development, and to law as it is understood in the *Rechtsstaat* tradition. That there is a tension here is evidenced by the fact that Hayek is drawing upon both sides in a historic dispute – as is made clear, for example, by Hegel's critical reaction to Savigny. Hegel – in this respect on the side of the *Rechtsstaat* theorists – is critical of Savigny's historical approach to the law, just because it does not seem compatible with the requirement that law be publicly accessible.[44]

Put in simple terms, for the historical or common lawyer law may be determinate. But its determinacy rests upon the tacit knowledge of legal practitioners, who – when a specific case comes up – will be able to draw upon their knowledge of other cases and the kinds of analogical reasoning in which they are skilled, and bring it and, as it were, their experience as craftspersons, to bear upon the concrete materials of that case so as to produce a determinate judgement. All this may be argued to give determinacy to the law (although legal realists would have some harsh things to say about such claims). But it is clear that this kind of determinacy contrasts sharply with the *Rechtsstaat* ideal, under which how the law will apply to a citizen's prospective action is something that he can determine in advance. Someone skilled in the common law can clearly offer his client guidance as to how his action may be treated. But the real determinacy of the law only comes in with the concrete judgement. It was to the historical lawyers' opposition to codification that Hegel objected, not least because of the connection between codification and the ability of citizens to know the law. Hegel is here on the side of the angels; and it is worth noting the connection between the ideals in terms of which Hegel is critical of the historical lawyers, and Hayek's own discussion of the relation of freedom to our ability to know the content of law.

As far as I know, there is no direct evidence from Hayek's published writings that he changed his views under the impact of Leoni's work. But in a letter to Leoni, written on 4 April 1962, Hayek says that he has not only enjoyed *Freedom and the Law*, but that it has given him new ideas. After a brief discussion of these, he indicates that he hopes to address these issues in 'a little pamphlet' on Law, Legislation and Liberty.[45] Before turning to Hayek's work, it might be useful to survey some problems that arise in respect of Leoni's own approach.

First, there is his concern for the long-term stability of law, and his link between this and a realistic theory of legislation (i.e. one that pays attention to the actual processes through which legislation takes place, rather than simply allocating a function to legislators which they are supposed to fulfil, without showing why they would have knowledge of what to do, or reason to do it). This seems a most important development, and one which will apply, equally, to those theorists who make extensive demands upon the actions of the legislature, and those who, like Hayek (and to a degree Leoni himself), give it a significant but lesser role.

Second, however, there are aspects of Leoni's views which are not acceptable

89

as they stand, but which seem to me to raise some interesting problems both for his own views and for those of Hayek. The first is that the dichotomy with which Leoni works – short-term versus long-term certainty – seems to me false. I would not endorse Hegel's views on legal issues as a whole. But he is surely correct that what is at issue, in legal codification, is not the construction of a new system of law *de novo*, but the making explicit in a general form of the content of existing laws.[46] Such work is important if citizens are to know what the law is (although, as Hegel also noted, it cannot be absolutely complete). However, when such codification is attempted, it will typically be discovered that the historical material is incoherent, or that particular decisions seem clearly mistaken. It may also turn out that there are problems as to how the law is to be applied to some new field. Citizens may also come up with problems as to how the law will apply to what they wish to do, which they will wish to resolve *prior* to taking the action in question. If we are concerned not only that citizens can discover in advance how the law will apply to their actions, but also that the law be as coherent as possible, some institution is needed to clarify such matters. However, there is no reason why codification and reform of the law may not be undertaken by something that falls short of the kind of legislative activity of which Leoni was, justly, so critical. I have some ideas of my own as to how such matters might be handled institutionally, but it would not be appropriate to discuss them here.

Leoni's views also seem to me to run into a problem akin to those encountered by Savigny himself. In his *Of the Vocation of our Age for Legislation and Jurisprudence*, Savigny took the view that law initially exists 'in the consciousness of the community'. But he suggests that, as society develops, law assumes a twofold life – first as a continuation of its initial form, which he refers to as the 'political', and second as a science of jurisprudence, the 'technical'.[47] But as far as I can see, he leaves us completely in the dark as to the relationship between the two. A problem arises here that may be put in the following way. While in some sense or other the lawyer or judge may be depending, initially, on citizens' intuitive feelings about custom, law and justice, a body of law will swiftly grow up which has an existence independent of the knowledge of individual citizens. What is more, in order to resolve difficult cases, the judge will have to come to decisions which will not carry with them any intuitive sense as far as citizens are concerned. Further, all kinds of decisions have to be made on a basis which must be called conventional in the strong sense of being undetermined by any form of natural law or moral argument (e.g. how many people are needed to witness a document, such as a will).[48]

All this presents three difficulties for Leoni's account. The first is that, once law has started to take on some kind of complexity, it is not clear how useful his account is to us. For law in the sense of a complex body of doctrine, involving conventions, is not something that, in itself, can be produced by individual citizens interacting with one another. They, rather, will wish to go to the lawyer and discover what the law says as it pertains to their concerns. And while lawyers may wish that, in some sense, the law should keep up with changes in social customs, how it should do so may itself pose an interesting technical problem for the lawyers. I am not claiming that such problems cannot be solved. I do think that in order to solve them we will have to move away from Leoni's account of the process through which law is made.

A second difficulty is posed by Hayek's argument, following Hume, that the legal system required by a market-based society will be morally imperfect in its character, in the sense that we are not likely to be able to find a functional legal system the consequences of which are intuitively satisfying in all respects. This also suggests a further problem as to how law, as a technical body, is supposed to relate to the political choices of citizens made, presumably, on the basis of their judgements as to whether or not legal decisions *are* intuitively satisfying.

Third, there is the difficulty – raised by Hayek in his earlier writings – that our existing system of law may in certain respects be inadequate for our purposes. For example, it may be, or become, dysfunctional for our economic system. This raises an important point in its own right: how, given the concerns of Hayek and of Leoni about legislation, are such problems to be handled? It also points to a difficulty concerning Leoni's more general views. For Leoni, when stressing the parallels between a legal system and individual decision-taking in a market, sometimes puts his point in such a way as to suggest a parallel with subjectivist views of economic welfare: that is to say, as if all that we could ask of a system is that it was the result of the uncoerced decisions of individuals. But in fact this is not all we can ask (see, on this, the discussion in chapter five, below), as Hayek's question about the functional character of the legal system *vis-à-vis* the market makes clear. To put the matter bluntly, we do not want our legal system to be an undesigned order merely in the sense of being the product of uncoerced decisions. Rather, we will wish it to be functional with respect to our concerns. (In making this point, I do not wish to claim that the products of uncoerced decisions cannot have such a character. My point, rather, is that they do not necessarily have such a character, and that the task facing those such as Leoni and Hayek – and, indeed, myself – who emphasize individual choice is to explain how we can enjoy both of these things together.)

Now, one reaction to such a point might be to suggest – taking a lead from some of Hayek's other ideas – that what we should seek for is a legal order that can be of use to us, whatever our (non-coercive) concerns may be. This is an attractive ideal. But for a legal system to have such a character, or to come as close to it as may be obtainable, is surely for it to have certain very specific properties. To take such a view of our requirements concerning the legal system is surely not to make *less* of a demand upon it than might be made if we were concerned just with economic efficiency. It faces us not only with the theoretical problem as to what the characteristics of such a system should be, but also with the more practical problem as to how knowledge of such things is to be accorded social recognition, and given institutional form. Let us now turn from this to the characteristics of Hayek's own later jurisprudence.

HAYEK'S LATER JURISPRUDENCE

The account of the development of law that is given in 'The Confusion of Language in Political Thought', and at greater length in volume two of Hayek's *Law, Legislation and Liberty*, differs from that offered in his earlier work. Hayek's account is of the development of a system of law of the same character as we have met before. However, the way in which he writes about it suggests a shift from viewing law after the fashion of Continental, codified law, to seeing it after the fashion of the common law. And the account that he now offers of its development is very different – and not as rationalistic.

If someone were to turn from Hayek's earlier writings to his later jurisprudence, they might well wonder about Hayek's understanding, in his later work, of the overall aims or concerns of such a system. As we have noted, in his earlier work Hayek seemed willing to identify his perspective with that of a utilitarian appraisal of the legal system. In *The Constitution of Liberty*, Hayek also expresses a strong concern for the minimization of coercion. From his later writings, it might at times seem as if Hayek is critical of the very idea that a legal system might be treated as having *any* aim or purpose. For example, in 'The Confusion of Language in Political Thought', Hayek argued that having such an aim or purpose is a characteristic of a designed order, a *taxis*, rather than a *cosmos*: a spontaneous order of the kind that he now considers the legal system to be.[49]

However, Hayek does nevertheless believe that a legal system of the kind that he favours serves two broad functions. On the one side, as he argued in *The Constitution of Liberty*, Hayek sees such a legal order as a system in which coercion is minimized. In 'The Confusion of Language in Political Thought', a *nomos* – the kind of rule or norm corresponding to a *cosmos* – is *defined* as 'a universal rule of just conduct applying to an unknown number of future instances and equally to all persons',[50] where this is the characteristic that Hayek had argued, in *The Constitution of Liberty*, would characterize a social order in which coercion was minimized. It would certainly seem as if these are characteristics that Hayek believes will be possessed by the kind of laws produced by the kind of legal system that he describes in the writings that we will here discuss.

Second, in Hayek's earlier writings there was a concern for the well-being of citizens; and, as we have seen, he endorsed changes that had been made in the legal system that had a broadly utilitarian rationale, and argued that further such changes are desirable. In his later writings, there is a shift towards referring to individuals being able to coordinate their plans, whatever these may be, such that the connection between Hayek's views and utilitarianism becomes less obvious.[51] And in *Law, Legislation and Liberty* – not to mention

The Fatal Conceit – Hayek is at times explicitly critical of utilitarianism. (Although his views might still be described as an attenuated version of utilitarianism, but one within which individuals are – as we have seen – restricted and also protected by the requirement that the legal system should minimize coercion. Indeed, this mixture is suggestive of the Pareto criterion.)[52] In the first few pages of volume two of *Law, Legislation and Liberty*, while criticizing the constructivist aspects of utilitarianism, Hayek somewhat grudgingly agrees that his discussion of the function of rules of conduct might be called utilitarian – provided that this term is taken in such a wide sense that it would also apply to the ideas of David Hume, Aristotle and Thomas Aquinas.[53] Hayek indicates that he is concerned with rules that will enable citizens to best pursue their particular ends (between which one will not expect there to be agreement) in a situation of ignorance, and which will enable them to make use of the 'widely dispersed factual knowledge on which the affluence and adaptability of the Great Society rests'.[54]

From all this, one might expect that what would follow would be a (generalized) version of the same kind of argument that we have encountered in Hayek's earlier writings, and which is presented in *The Constitution of Liberty*, i.e. an account of the liberal ideal of the rule of law, as satisfying these requirements. But this is not the case. For while Hayek takes issue with legal positivism[55] – as would any clear-headed utilitarian (as the fact that a law has been commanded by a sovereign does not imply that it is acceptable on utilitarian grounds) – the basis on which he does so is perhaps unexpected, as we shall see from the following.

In volume two of *Law, Legislation and Liberty*, Hayek sets out an account of the legal order of a free society for which he argues in terms that differ from what we have met so far. Rather than the market-orientated functionalism and reasonably explicit system utilitarianism of his earlier writings, we are offered what looks more like a common-law derived view of the character of law. Hayek starts from a situation in which people already have a body of inherited general rules of conduct,[56] and also a 'general sense of justice'. The task of those making law is pictured as consisting, initially, of the articulation and development of these rules, in ways that fit in with this sense of justice:[57]

> Those who are entrusted with the task of articulating, interpreting, and developing the existing body of rules of just conduct will . . . always have to find answers to definite problems, and not to impose their unfettered will. They may originally have been chosen because they were believed to be most likely to formulate rules that would satisfy the general sense of justice and fit into the whole system of existing rules.

Innovation and revision are possible. Innovation is to be judged acceptable by the criterion of whether a maxim that is introduced can be universalized in such a way that it does not conflict with other rules. Universalization, however, is to be taken in some sense that goes beyond mere logical form, and to apply to an

unknown number of future instances, not just to a set with one member.[58]
However, as our subsequent discussion will suggest, we cannot necessarily
discover at the time a rule is introduced whether or not it has this property.[59]

Revision is somewhat more complicated. Hayek suggests that such a system
of law initially arose

> from the process of gradual extension of rules of just conduct to circles of
> persons who neither share, nor are aware of, the same particular ends.[60]

Once we have a system of such laws, revision would seem to take place at two
levels. We may come to discover that some rule which we had accepted cannot
be maintained in a universal form without coming into conflict with other
rules. Hayek writes, for example, of

> a negative test that enables us progressively to eliminate rules which
> prove to be unjust because they are not universalizable within the system
> of other rules whose validity is not questioned.[61]

And in such a situation, preference would seem to be accorded to the more
general principles:

> It will occasionally be necessary to reject some accepted rules in the light
> of more general principles. The guiding principle will always be that
> justice, i.e. the generally applicable rule, must prevail over the particular
> (though perhaps also generally felt) desire.[62]

The second level at which revision takes place is that of a judgement – to the
effect that some rule is unjust – in respect of a particular case. Thus, Hayek says:

> Though our sense of justice will generally provide the starting-point,
> what it tells us about the particular case is not an infallible or ultimate
> test. It may be and can be proved to be wrong. Though the justification of
> our subjective feeling that some rule is just must be that we are prepared
> to commit ourselves to apply it universally, this does not exclude the
> possibility that we may later discover cases to which, if we had not
> committed ourselves, we should wish not to apply the rule, and where we
> discover that what we had thought to be quite just is in fact not so; in
> which event we may be forced to alter the rule for the future. Such a
> demonstration of a conflict between the intuitive feeling of justice and
> rules we wish also to preserve may often force us to review our opinion.[63]

Concerning what results from such a process of development and revision
Hayek says that

> It is irrelevant (and, of course, normally unknown) from which initial
> system of rules this evolution started; and it is quite possible that one
> kind of system of such rules is so much more effective than all others in
> producing a comprehensive order for a Great Society that, as a result of

the advantages from all changes in the direction towards it, there may occur in systems with very different beginnings a process corresponding to what biologists call 'convergent evolution'.[64]

And Hayek refers, in this connection, to David Hume's 'three fundamental laws of nature' (stability of possession, transference by consent and performance of promises). At the same time, he also says that 'It is at least conceivable that several different systems of rules of just conduct may survive this test [of universalizability]'.[65]

Now there is, in all this, a certain parallel, of which Hayek is well aware, with Popper's ideas about the development of scientific knowledge. For in Popper's account there is an interplay between statements concerning particular matters of fact (here the parallel in Hayek is with statements asserting the injustice[66] of some particular action); some generalization about the conditions under which the events reported can be reproduced (which in Hayek parallels the requirement that the initial assertion be related to some universalizable principle); and other theories (which in Hayek parallel other principles of law). The parallel is not far from Hayek's own thoughts. For after giving an account of Kant's ideas about law,[67] he refers to 'a negative test which enables us progressively to eliminate what is unjust, namely the test of universalizability'. He then refers to Popper's idea of falsification, calling it 'a test which, in the last resort, also proves to be a test of internal inconsistency of the whole system'.[68]

The enterprise upon which Hayek is here engaged looks most striking. For he would appear to be offering us a path to a liberal system of law[69] that can start from anything, and depends only on judgements that something is unjust, the introduction of rules subject to the requirement of universalizability, and judgements of the consistency of some rule with others.

But all this is, perhaps, not what it might seem. For while Hayek would seem to be offering us a strikingly minimalist path to liberalism, it is not clear that his ideas actually get us there. My critical points here must be somewhat tentative, just because Hayek's own positive views are set out in such general terms that it must be easy to misunderstand exactly what he means. But these criticisms are, I think, worth making, even if they should turn out to relate more to my reconstruction of Hayek's ideas than to what he, perhaps, intended. Let me start with two problems internal to his ideas, and then move to some issues relating to the overall character of the legal system which he seems to expect to result from them.

First, one must look carefully at the role played by the requirement of universality. For there is the world of difference between the requirement that laws be universal in form, and that they be universal in the sense of applying equally to all persons – the sense required by the ideal of *Isonomy* in liberal theory.[70] Not only is there the issue of *who* counts as a person, but the formal requirement of a law's applying to an unknown quantity of future instances does not entail that there may not be an illiberal discrimination between different classes of persons built into the law.

It is possible to argue that this point may be adequately met by our sense of injustice. There is something attractive about Hayek's fallibilistic consensual intuitionism as an account of the foundations of law (I certainly find it attractive as an account of the foundations of knowledge and of morality). But it would seem to me highly optimistic to believe that such a thing will generate an easy consensus on judgements of a liberal character. And it would, surely, be unreasonable to allow blank cheques drawn on the supposed character of such a consensus to do all the work in a theory such as the one that Hayek is presenting – not least as we are living in a world which is hardly full of Hayekian liberals, and which has not been so for most of its history, either. Indeed, Hayek himself has made much of people's instinctive reactions often being hostile to liberal ideas.

Hayek could possibly claim that it was the earlier 'gradual extension of rules of just conduct to [new] circles' that did this work. But we can here ask: why should such gradual extension have been made on the basis of treating all members of such groups equally? To this, Hayek could further respond: but to ask such a question is to put the cart before the horse. His argument, rather, is that groups who behaved in such a way were more successful, and multiplied and were imitated by others. But this argument – which is very much the view to be found in Hayek's later writings[71] – presents a problem for the internalist view of the development of law that we are here discussing. For such a view is, in effect, making claims in external or functional terms, in a situation in which, on Hayek's account, the people in question are not themselves aware of the functions in question, and so are not explicitly guided by them. But why should systems that pass these tests also have the internal characteristics that feature in Hayek's account? (In addition, for reasons that we will discuss in chapter six, below, there seems reason to question whether there is this neat link between survival – and self-interest – and liberal universalism.)

Second, Hayek writes in passing of 'the pursuit of the ideal of justice (like the pursuit of the ideal of truth)'.[72] This parallel may also be important. For it is possible that to get the conclusions that Hayek is after, a role must be played by substantive views concerning the ideal of justice; for example, by the idea that a desirable system of law is highly general in its character. In order that the process that Hayek has described leads to the results that he favours, Hayek may have to assume that his lawyers are themselves guided by the idea that the law, in an adequate legal system, must be bold in the sense of consisting of a few, powerful principles, rather than something that simply copes, *ad hoc*, with issues as they arise.

There is in fact a parallel here to what Landes and Posner should have argued, in their well-known article on the disadvantages of private arbitration systems.[73] The idea here is that legal systems have two different functions, the resolution of disputes, and the production of coordination rules. There seems no special reason why there should always be a 1 : 1 correspondence between what is required in respect of the discharging of each function, such that one could well imagine that, if – as would seem to be the case in a completely private system – the system were to depend for its living upon arbitration, on occasion it would be found to the advantage of the parties in question to come to agreements which, while adequate for those parties, would not serve to produce clear coordination rules which would be useful for other citizens. In particular – as indeed happens within the existing system of private law – the parties may settle, rather than bearing the risks and expense involved in taking the case to the point where the coordination rule, important for others but not for them, is clarified.

That such an assumption – the pursuit of the ideal of justice – may be needed is suggested by the parallel that Hayek draws with Popper. For in the philosophy of science, Hattiangadi and Briskman,[74] have developed approaches which, while in some ways closely akin to Popper's ideas, by way of contrast with his view avoid postulating an aim or goal for science. Briskman and Hattiangadi offer an account which closely parallels the ideas in Hayek's work which we have just discussed; not least, as it depends upon the internalist resolution of problems, and there is no aim of science postulated externally to the system. But it would seem to me that their views do not explain why science has, typically, gone beyond *ad hoc* adjustments in the face of problems, to the development of a few simple and powerful theories. Accordingly, in so far as the parallel holds good, and if I am right about what seem to me to be the problems facing these ideas in the philosophy of science, then to get the results which Hayek favours lawyers would need explicitly to invoke the idea that a system of law should have a general character.

To this it might be objected that law would have to have a general character, because those who use the law would need to have principles available in a form that was easy to use. It might, further, be argued that in the early development of legal systems, when law was unwritten, it had to be simple such that it could be memorized.[75] All this is true. But again, considerations from the philosophy of science are of some relevance here, in that pragmatic requirements such as those reviewed above would lead to the selection of general principles along instrumentalist or conventionalist lines that parallel the ideas of Ernst Mach or Pierre Duhem,[76] rather than the truth-directed approach to which Hayek appeals in drawing his parallel with justice and which would also be suggested by the parallel that he draws between his work and that of Popper.

If I am right about all this, Hayek's ideas will not work quite as he suggests. Rather than a system of law with the general character required by Hayek's liberalism arising on the minimalist basis which he suggests, generality can only come out if a specific requirement for generality (something over and above mere universality of form) is introduced as a condition on solutions to legal problems. And this, in turn, poses the question: why should there be such a requirement, and what is its relation to the humanitarian concerns from which the young Hayek started, and in terms of which much of his initial argument was developed?

There is, however, also a problem of a different kind facing Hayek's account. He is engaged, throughout this section of his book, in a running polemic against legal positivism. He criticizes legal positivism for the fact that it does not necessarily deliver a system of law that is 'inseparable from private property and at the same time the indispensable condition of individual freedom'.[77] But we can ask Hayek, equally, just what is the relation between the account that he offers us in his later work and the kind of characteristics that he takes the legal system of a free society to possess?[78] Is it the case that a system of law that satisfies the formal requirements spelled out in Hayek's later work must have the functional characteristics that he favours? Hayek's account in his later work is, clearly, one of the development of a legal system largely through immanent criticism.[79] This would seem to give a relatively privileged position to those customs and rules from which we happen to start. But what if they were illiberal in character? Clearly, one could postulate that there develops a consensus to the effect that the illiberal features are unjust. But this seems like cheating, if no account is given as to why it is just these features of the legal system that will come to be judged unacceptable. Similarly, we may question why there is supposed to be a preference for universality. And here we should note that this issue is of especial importance, given that Hayek offers an account of freedom from coercion which relates freedom to exactly this feature of the legal institutions of a liberal society.

Perhaps the best that can be done for Hayek's argument would be to say that it is the intuitive judgements made within those systems that prove successful that have this character. But if this is the case, the connection between the internal development of legal criteria and the success of the system – in terms of well-being and the absence of coercion – would seem to be contingent. Indeed, Hayek may be right about the initial stages in the development of a legal system (although his earlier accounts in which sheer contingency, issues of power politics and the explicit appeal to ideals like *Isonomy* played an important role, look to me more realistic). But once we have – or come to desire – a system which is protective of individuals from coercion and which is attuned to the functional needs of the market, I think that we would need to identify these goals explicitly, and guide decisions in matters of law upon such a basis, if our legal system is to possess such features.

Indeed, we should here recall the way in which, earlier, Hayek was urging that the inherited legal order stood in need of deliberate reshaping so as to bring it better into line with the functional requirements of the market. There was – as far as I can see – no suggestion there that there was anything *formally* defective which stood in need of reform, or, indeed, that the legal arrangements that he was criticizing were unjust or that Hayek's functional concerns would be met by purely internal criticism. Of course, one might try to reinterpret Hayek's earlier demands as resting on the discovery of injustice, but that would seem to me to be very far-fetched. For it was there, surely, with certain rather general and abstract characteristics of the legal system, with which he was concerned. And rather than to particular instances of injustice, his critical appraisal appealed to specific claims in economic theory and to their relation to a humanitarian view of the good society. After all, when talking about legal reform he seemed in broad terms to identify his ideas about reform with those of the utilitarians.

Let me sum up. Hayek's more recent views about jurisprudence, while containing much that is of value, would seem to me not to stand on their own as an account of the legal foundations of a liberal social and economic order. The issues raised by the reformist and more explicitly utilitarian younger Hayek still remain of relevance. Accordingly, Hayek's later work on law, despite its interest, does not supersede his earlier discussion. The problems raised by that earlier work still remain. To them, however, we may now add a further issue. How are the ideas about universality of Hayek's legal theory – which are so important for his ideas about freedom – related to the terms of his earlier discussion?

I would, however, like to raise one more radical point concerning the character of the legal system of a liberal order itself. For the turn, in Hayek's work, towards a common-law style rationale for the development of law raises a further question. May the conflict between such a view and a *Rechtsstaat* conception of a liberal legal order relate not just to our understanding of the origins and the maintenance of such a system, but also to its character? It is striking that, in *The Fatal Conceit*, Hayek is critical of the association that is often made of the relationship between development and a 'modern' rationalized state. This, together with the ideas discussed in this chapter, raises an interesting question: is a *Rechtsstaat* conception of the character of a liberal legal order, and, more generally, a Weberian conception of a modern liberal society, correct? Hayek's work should, I think, lead us to consider this issue anew. And I have recently been struck that this point has also been raised in the work of other scholars who are themselves sympathetic to classical liberalism.[80] All this raises an issue of the greatest importance, in that it would be of considerable significance if both liberals and their critics were *incorrect* in their characterization of some important features of liberalism, and more generally of modernity.

I find the issue pressing, personally, just because my own discussion has come down *against* the later Hayek here. But what if he is right? After all, one phenomenon that should haunt the intellectual concerned with social reform is that the proposals of people like him for the rationalization of our social order have served, all too often, to place power into the hands of people who *he* supposed would be enlightened despots, but who turn out merely to be despots. There is, to say the least, something worrying to find oneself relating liberty to a centrally administered legal code; one, furthermore, which might seem to be the product of the (supposedly benevolent) rationalizing activities of the state!

99

I cannot pursue this issue here. Accordingly, for the moment, worries about these matters are simply something which I must face alone, when my conscience wakes me in the middle of the night, and I try to console myself that it will hardly be the case that my arguments here about Hayek will make that much of a difference ....

In conclusion, I would like to raise one further issue. For immediately prior to my discussion of Hayek's ideas about law, I raised the question of why Hayek moved towards these interesting but highly problematic ideas. I would conjecture that, under the impact of Leoni's argument, Hayek comes to question two aspects of his own earlier views. That he should do so, however, serves more to raise tensions implicit within his own earlier ideas than to introduce totally new themes.

The first aspect relates to what one can expect of government. Here, Leoni's concern with what legislatures *actually* do seems to me to raise a key problem for Hayek's earlier work. For in his *Road to Serfdom* and in various subsequent writings, Hayek allocates tasks to government without also offering us an explanation as to why we should expect government to behave in the manner that he is indicating that they should. The second issue concerns Hayek's views about reason. There is, running through much of Hayek's work, a significant line of criticism of the ideas of social planners, on the basis that they are engaged in a kind of rationalistic hubris. As I will describe, shortly, his criticism of this – and of the notion of reason that is involved – is heightened in his later writings, to the point where his argument calls into question not only the kind of rationalism of which he has previously been critical, but also the critical rationalism – and the Mengerian approach – which he had often espoused.

Together, these ideas might suggest that what he felt was wrong about his earlier views was that he was himself expecting government at times to act as a rational, benevolent despot, when, on the basis of the ideas to which he had now come, it had neither the motivation nor the capacity to do anything of the kind. And I would suggest that we might try to make sense of some of the ideas in his later work as attempts to deal with problems that his other writings had raised, but without what, in his earlier work, was an unrealistic optimism about what one can expect of government, and also without the rationalism of which, with the passing of time, he seemed to be increasingly critical. In my view, the problems are real, in the sense that a normative political theorist needs not only to offer us ideas about what might be desirable, but also to show *how* a society could run, so as to realize the ideals that he is commending to us. I also think that Hayek's misgivings about government are to be taken very seriously although, for reasons that I will explain, I am not in agreement with his criticism of rationalism. I also do not think that the ideas that he offered in his later writings, to deal with these problems, are very satisfactory, either.

It is, though, difficult to generalize concerning Hayek's later thought, as, along with the ideas to which I have referred, are also to be found not only reaffirmations of his older views, notably by way of his espousal of critical rationalism, but also ideas about a new ideal constitution, an enterprise which might seem to exemplify the large-scale, rationalistic social engineering of which he is elsewhere critical.

HAYEK'S IDEAL CONSTITUTION

Hayek should not be understood as a critic of democracy. He emphatically favours democracy as a system in which government can be removed by popular election rather than by force only. Hayek's worry, rather, is with what democratic government can do when it is unrestricted in its scope. But, lest the reader draw incorrect conclusions from this point,[81] Hayek's concern is not to restrict the scope of democracy by giving power to someone else, but rather to suggest a system of democratic institutions in which the scope of government will be restricted by another democratically elected body – a second chamber of a bicameral system. This second body would set the rules within which government operates. The relevant parallel here is with the steps that an individual might take to constrain himself in the face of his recognition of his own weakness of will: of our choosing to impose a system of constraints upon the activities of government because of a concern for what an unrestricted government may do. (What would here correspond to a knowledge of the weakness of his will on the part of the individual, would be our knowledge of how modern democracies actually function.)

Central to Hayek's proposal is, thus, an analysis of the workings of contemporary Western democracies. Interest groups gain special privileges or advantages for their members. Others then seek for these privileges to be extended to themselves. However, such privileges cannot be granted to everyone, and the attempt by people to acquire them may be damaging to the society as a whole. Yet, Hayek thinks, people would be willing to renounce their claim to such privileges if they could be sure that they would be granted to no one. Hayek's constitutional proposal seeks to suggest how this wish might be satisfied. He proposes that a division be made between the functions of government (in something like the sense in which we are used to it in Western democracies, today) and a legislative body, the task of which will be to set the general rules within which the former body operates. This latter body would thus, on his account, be concerned with such matters as the proper scope of health and safety legislation; and it would seem that it would also, where necessary, make changes to common law, should it go astray. (However, as a different body would be responsible for the original drawing up of a constitution, and there would also be a judicial body with responsibility for handling disputes between government and its legislature, it is possible that certain of these functions might be allocated on a different basis.)

Hayek has offered some suggestions as to how all this would work. The functions of government would be conducted within rules set by a legislative chamber, along lines with which we are already familiar from Western democracies. There would be political parties and interest groups. The legislative chamber would be elected. Hayek has suggested that it might consist of people of the age-range from 45 to 60, elected by those, as it were, of the same vintage. Hayek would expect the members of the legislative body to be people who had already made their mark in some other profession.

In order to assess such ideas, it is important that we keep in view several features of Hayek's work.

First, Hayek is not a proponent of a Nozick-style minimal state. Not only does he accord to government a much larger range of duties than does Nozick, but these clearly go beyond that upon which one could imagine that there would be unanimous agreement. Indeed, Hayek has referred to the discharge of governmental functions as providing a basis for coercion:[82]

> Far from advocating ... a 'minimal state', we find it unquestionable that in an advanced society government ought to use its power of raising funds by taxation to provide a number of services which for various reasons cannot be provided, or cannot be provided adequately, by the market ... *even if there were no other need for coercion* ... there would still exist an overwhelming case for giving the territorial authority power to make the inhabitants contribute to a common fund from which such services could be financed [emphasis mine].

But are the constitutional ideas that Hayek has advanced, for example in *Law, Legislation and Liberty*, adequate to the tasks that he would have government perform?

Hayek's ideas are an imaginative response to the problem with which he opens *Law, Legislation and Liberty*: the breakdown of limited government. And they provide an interesting development of his thesis that the problem with unlimited democracy is that we are forced, for the sake of self-defence, to make political demands that we would not make if we could be assured that no one would receive these things for themselves. However, Hayek's proposals seem to me defective in themselves, and inadequate to his wider concerns – specifically, to the discharge of the functions (and nothing more than the functions) that he allocates to government.

Hayek's constitutional ideas are inadequate in themselves just because those electing representatives to his legislative body are already socially situated, and will have specific interests which will affect their preferences for rules and, thus, for the choosers of rules. Any general rule will impinge differently upon people in different social positions. This may make it difficult for people to make the kind of separation between general rules and their particular interests that Hayek calls for. And even if they could make such a separation, they may not be motivated to do so, when they discern that some rule may operate to their personal disadvantage. (All this will be the more pressing, just because regular governmental activity, with political parties, is envisaged as taking place in Hayek's governmental body.)

When weighed against this, Hayek's appeal to what there is in common between different age groups seems very limited in its force. If there were a system of uniform institutions that everyone of a particular age would have gone through – say, a single system of state schooling, and a system of peacetime conscription – it is possible that there might be a common perspective to which appeal could be made. Much the same might be true in a small country, with a population that was culturally homogeneous, and which exhibited relatively narrow differences in respect of wealth or forms of occupation. But such things would hardly be expected to arise in a society of the kind that Hayek favours, in which individual freedom and experimentation are at a premium.

To put this point another way, one problem with Hayek's suggestions, as with all suggestions about new constitutions, is that decisions about such things are not made by citizens from behind a veil of ignorance. And this generates problems about the basis upon which people will make choices. To have *some* rules is to the advantage of everyone. But it is not clear, on Hayek's account, why each person should choose a constitution on the basis of what would be in the general interest, or in the interest of a person chosen at random, as opposed to what is in their own interests (including within this the interests of those for whom they care) as they actually are. And it is by no means clear that, if people choose on the basis of what is in their interest, that they will choose a system, such as Hayek's, which accords *each* individual equal protection under the law.

This problem also arises in a more concrete way, too. Hayek's own account of the scope of government gives it a more than minimal character. As a result, *what* government does will hardly be equally in the interest of everybody. It may therefore be important to people to make sure that the functions of government, and the coercive powers which it holds, are those which *they* would wish to have exercised. There is, as a result, a risk that people would spend their time fighting for personally advantageous rules, rather than settling on minimal rules under the sway of which they can then pursue their affairs in peace.

More telling, however, is the inadequacy of Hayek's constitution to the tasks that are allocated to government in his own work.

First, there is the problem of the improvement of our inherited institutions, such that they will better perform their role in a market-based system. Related to this is the role that Hayek allocates to a governmental body to correct undesirable developments in common law. Hayek's second chamber is totally unsuited to such a task, because such revisions need to be made on the basis of expert knowledge: they are technical rather than consensual in their character. Even if one were to grant to Hayek the idea that there is – or could come to be – some deep-seated agreement about the rules upon which a particular society functions of the kind that Hayek seems to envisage his legislative body as articulating, there seems to be no reason why this will capture the *functional* requirements of a liberal economic system. In addition, while – for the sake of argument – we might envisage Hayek's legislature as coming to a consensus about the general character of the rules that government should follow, it is not clear why this should be expected to be a *liberal* consensus, or why, say, their rules should have the characteristics of Hayek's view of the rule of law. A similar problem is posed by the fact that Hayek believes that government should sometimes play an interventionist role in the economy.[83]

A second problem is posed by Hayek's important arguments about the disadvantages of a market order and of its concomitant institutions. Those who are members of a legislative body – prompted, no doubt, by those in government or those who have expectations about what government might achieve – would presumably be concerned to choose rules which would constitute the best social order attainable. But how will they weigh some of the difficult choices posed by the imperfections of even the best of our institutions, and people's differing reactions to them? The problem here, again, is one of *knowledge* – in this case, theoretical knowledge as to what the alternatives are, and that, say, the best attainable system *has* some disadvantages. In respect of both these problems, the key issue is that Hayek has offered a constitutional system that rests upon consensus, and which does not give an appropriate role to expert knowledge. At the same time, any system that allows for the exercise of expert knowledge faces a problem of the selection and control of the experts. In my view, the best model here is one in which individuals are able to exercise a choice between – and are free to exit from – competing systems that lay claim to such knowledge, and offer specific packages of costs and benefits. This is a theme to which we will return in the final chapter of this book.

A separate consideration that points in the same direction concerns what Hayek says about government. Hayek, as we have noted, is not a proponent of a minimal state. He expects that government would function much as governments do now (although subject, of course, to the rules set down by his legislative body). Hayek is less than enthusiastic in his case for government, and is well-disposed towards attempts to deal with welfare issues through voluntaristic means. But he is unambiguous in his view that government is needed to handle externalities and public goods, a list of which he furnishes.[84] Within this category are included not only such obvious examples as protection against violence, epidemics and such natural forces as floods or avalanches, but also many of the amenities which make life in a modern city tolerable – most roads (other than long-distance highways on which tolls can be charged); and the provision of standards of measure and of many kinds of information ranging from land registers, maps and statistics, to the certification of the quality of some goods or services offered in the market.

I have no doubt that government might perform these – and other – functions (such as welfare and the discharge of such control of the economy as Hayek thinks needed), financed by taxation. What is not so clear is why we should believe that it is desirable that it should do this. There are two aspects to this argument.

First, it may be argued that there are non-governmental means through which most such services can be provided – including markets, cooperative or charitable activity or through entrepreneurs offering bundles of services on the market. (Consider, for example, the ability of a developer to package streets, utilities, police and a code of conduct in 'public' places along with a housing development, and to set up a holding company to administer it.)[85] It need not be claimed that such provision is ideal; and there may be some things which are, *prima facie*, desirable which cannot be provided by such means. The advantages that they offer, however, include diversity and (relative) freedom from political capture.

This brings us to the second argument: the problems posed by governmental provision. This, in turn, has two parts.

First, there is the question of efficiency. We may ask here both about what is provided and how it is provided. Under governmental provision, what is provided is decided in part through the ballot box, but more importantly through the discretionary decisions of various officials (and the influence of those who lobby them). It is striking that, in practical terms, consumers of governmental services have virtually no initial say in what it is that is provided to them, that there are few mechanisms for the revision of such decisions, and other providers are typically prevented by law from offering competing services – and thus, innovation.[86] To all this, one can add, further, the fact that government is not likely to wish to take risks, just because it is not in the interests of a politician to have been responsible for something that goes wrong. Governmental provision is thus about the most effective check that one can imagine to the learning by experiment that Hayek favours. (And indeed, given the problems of subjecting government to critical scrutiny, the last thing we would want is an experimenting government.) Similarly, governmental provision typically removes the possibility of clear assessment of the efficiency of the provision, and, for example, the possibility of assets being put to better use, by others being able to take over control of the enterprise through the stock market.

Second, there are Hayek's old points about collective decision-taking in the absence of consensus, and the disadvantages of interest-group democracy. There is also the threat that the activities of government operating in circumstances of imperfection pose to the institutions of a Hayekian society. If government has a popular mandate, and it would appear as if some general rule upheld by his legislative body stands in the way of what is presented as an effective solution to a problem, it is not difficult to see what would give. (One should not underrate the fact that government would be staffed by professional politicians; the legislative body, on Hayek's account, by distinguished amateurs.)

Indeed, it seems to me that Hayek draws the wrong conclusions from his own argument. His critique of pluralistic politics is telling. But this raises problems for his own ideal of a limited but active state; problems which his own constitutional proposals do not meet. As a result, I think that the appropriate lesson to draw from Hayek's work is that the proper scope of governmental activity should be minimal. But this is not to preclude the possibility of voluntaristic associations being set up within the scope of such a minimal state, which offer a richer programme for collective activity to those that want it – such, indeed, as Hayek's own.

THE MANTLE OF MENGER

We encountered earlier Hayek's interest in 'organic' institutions, which we discussed in connection with Carl Menger. Menger, with Savigny and the 'historical' jurists, was critical of those for whom an institution was only considered functional if it had been deliberately designed to fulfil a certain purpose. But Menger was also critical of Savigny and his colleagues in so far as they seemed to suggest that any 'organic' institution must be better than institutions which have been designed. Menger argued, further, that 'organic' institutions stand in need of critical assessment and improvement.

I earlier suggested that Hayek's views on this matter – at least in his earlier writings – were close to Menger's. But this is by no means the whole story. For there are strands in Hayek's political philosophy – and especially in his later writings – that do not seem readily compatible with the picture that I have painted.

In particular, there is Hayek's theory of social evolution – of the development of cultural practices and institutions as the products of individual action but not of individual design – which is a theory of group selection. Hayek offers us an account of individuals being led to join – or to mimic the behaviour of – certain groups that prove successful, but where, typically, the relation between the rules and conventions in question and the 'success' is not theoretically understood (as it may include rules concerning the content of which the people in question do not have a conscious awareness)[87]. All this, in turn, might be used as a point round which could be integrated three other themes in Hayek's work.

(1) It may be linked to Hayek's plea for conservatism in respect of certain social conventions. We have already encountered Hayek's view that if certain useful social institutions are to be sustained, it is necessary that citizens comply with various rules and conventions the rationale for which they do not understand. Such a view is given added point if the institutions and practices are themselves understood to be the products of an 'evolutionary' process.

(2) A link may be made with Hayek's account of human behaviour at a deeper level. Hayek's *Sensory Order* emerged from his critical reworking of Machian concerns – although Hayek worked on a realist as opposed to a neutral monist basis.[88] In this work, Hayek pictures human perception as structured by various rules and classificatory procedures. These, while in some sense themselves the products of experience, come to play a role in the constitution of future experience. This, in turn, leads Hayek to a picture of human beings as under the sway of cognitive rules which cannot be brought to human conscious awareness except in a piecemeal fashion. In his subsequent work, Hayek developed links between the themes of *The Sensory Order* and his 'evolutionary' writings – through the idea that human behaviour is governed by rules, of some of which we may not be aware.[89]

One might well think that these ideas call into question the interpretation of Hayek's work offered in the first two chapters. Our account there gave a significant role to human reason in the assessment and improvement of institutions. But consider the account of human reason, and of our cognitive faculties, that emerges from those writings of Hayek's which we are now discussing. Hayek pictures human beings as following various rules and procedures which are the product of their past experience. Indeed, we have no option but to follow such rules, as they are constitutive of us – of our rationality and of the way in which we perceive the world. Hayek's account might also seem to downgrade the status of human reason. Not only is human reason, as we usually consider it, depicted in *The Sensory Order* as being something like the conscious tip of a largely unconscious iceberg of classificatory activities. But Hayek, in subsequent work on the same theme, depicts even our conscious awareness as subject to rules which we cannot comprehend and communicate. And in some of his later work, he tied reason ever more closely to particular products of cultural evolution:

> The mind is embedded in a traditional impersonal structure of learned rules, and its capacity to order experience is an acquired replica of [a] cultural pattern which every individual mind finds given.[90]

And:

> If we are to understand [mind], we must direct our attention to that process of sifting of practices which sociobiology neglects [i.e. Hayek's account of cultural evolution].[91]

And later still:

> It is less accurate to suppose that thinking man creates and controls his cultural evolution than it is to say that cultural evolution created his reason.[92]

But if human reason is seen in such terms (and it is useful to remember here that Hayek's account of cultural evolution is not a rationalistic process), is reason capable of playing the role in the critical scrutiny and improvement of our institutions that it is accorded in the account of Hayek's work that we have presented, above?

(3) Next, there are Hayek's ideas about 'spontaneous orders'. There are several ambiguities about Hayek's writings on this theme.[93]

First, Hayek is sometimes concerned with the working of certain kinds of large-scale institution, such as the market and its associated legal order, or with human language, and with the way in which such institutions allow a whole variety of other human activities – including innovation and the use of socially dispersed knowledge – to take place within them. However, when Hayek writes of 'spontaneous orders' he sometimes seems to be concerned, rather, to assert that such large-scale institutions have themselves 'evolved' through a process of group selection. But the fact of such evolution is clearly not a necessary feature of the history of such institutions, as Hayek's own suggestions about the design of institutions which would function in this way – such as his constitutional proposals and ideas about the denationalization of money – make plain.

There is also a second ambiguity, concerning what Hayek means by 'evolved'. Sometimes he means the product of some specific (evolutionary) process. In this connection, he uses the term to refer both to the products of his own theory of cultural evolution and to law when it has developed in accordance with the ideas he has generalized from common-law procedures. Sometimes, however, he uses the term simply as an antithesis of 'deliberately designed'. This difference is important, for where there is a specific evolutionary process at work, then its products can be expected to possess certain specific features, relating to the characteristics of the process which produced them. And if it is the case that these features are desirable, then it is appropriate for us to value these products for possessing them.

It is such considerations that, presumably, underlie Hayek's enthusiasm for evolved institutions in his *Law, Legislation and Liberty* and *The Fatal Conceit*. Indeed, this enthusiasm at times seems to verge on a Panglossian conservatism to the effect that, whatever is, is good – provided it was not designed.[94] But this is clearly not an attitude that Hayek sustains. For *Law, Legislation and Liberty* starts from the problem that older institutions which divided and limited constitutional powers have broken down – something which, in Hayek's view, was clearly neither designed nor desirable. And, as we have seen, throughout his work Hayek exhibits a concern for the improvement of inherited institutions.

At a theoretical level, it is also clear that Hayek's conservative enthusiasm for things evolved cannot be sustained. First, there is the important point that if something has evolved simply in the sense of not having been designed, it may have no redeeming features at all. On the other hand, it may be of the greatest value. Hayek in his Cairo Lectures gave an account of the development of the ideal of the rule of law. This (valuable) ideal developed – according to what he says there – in a manner that in no way fits Hayek's specific ideas about evolutionary mechanisms. In his account, people discovered that the result of a particular concatenation of political interests, ideas and chance was valuable, and that it could then be understood, cherished, imitated and improved.

But what if there do exist institutions which have evolved in the sense of being the products of specific mechanisms?

They first must be recognised – we must pick them out from among things which are not of this character. We then need to understand what properties they have and to appraise whether these properties are desirable. Second, we must also appraise whether they are of value to everybody, or just for some specific group – and possibly against the general interest. Third, even if some such property has been useful in the past, it will not necessarily be useful in changed circumstances in the future. In addition, supposing that some product, such as a system of law, has evolved in a certain specific manner, and has desirable properties, we must take note of a point that Hayek himself makes:[95]

> The fact that law that has evolved in this way has certain desirable properties does not prove that it will always be good law or even that some of its rules may not be very bad. It therefore does not mean that we can altogether dispense with legislation.

What all this means is that Hayek cannot do without some ideas concerning the rational scrutiny and appraisal of institutions which have 'evolved' *in either sense*. He must, in short, be concerned with the 'duty' of critical scrutiny that Menger enjoined upon the historical jurists, and which Hayek seemed willing to take up in his earlier work. The move – in so far as it is suggested by Hayek's later writings – of offering a theory of social evolution *in place of* a theory about how inherited institutions are to be appraised is a will o' the wisp, and a source of confusion.

Hayek, therefore, must be interpreted more 'rationalistically' than some of his later writings might suggest, if we are to be able to make the best of his work. Such a 'rationalistic' interpretation may, of course, include an appreciation of the claim that, in the face of human ignorance, we may do best to try to solve our problems via social formations which allow for 'evolutionary' learning by trial and error. At the same time, Hayek is surely right to stress the way in which, at every stage of our endeavours, we will be taking for granted various biological predispositions, culturally inherited rules or patterns of behaviour, and personal habits, dispositions and preconceptions, of only a fraction of which we could possibly become aware at any one time.

If these points are accepted, we are left with a number of specific problems. In what terms should we appraise inherited or 'organic' institutions? What is the significance for Hayek's political thought of 'spontaneous orders' in the sense of large-scale institutions which allow for innovation, coordination and the use of socially divided knowledge? Can we make coherent the various demands on individuals within such institutions for innovation, critical appraisal *and* uncritical compliance? Finally, can anything useful be done with Hayek's specific ideas about the mechanisms of social evolution? Some of these issues we will take up in later chapters of this volume, as they involve us in issues that are opened up by, but not resolved within, Hayek's writings. Here, however, we will address one key problem: that of tradition and rationality.

TRADITION AND RATIONALITY

Under this heading, I will raise a number of related issues concerning Hayek's work.

A particularly important issue concerns the critical appraisal of undesigned institutions. This problem itself has two aspects. The first is the more concrete problem of how we should actually appraise such institutions. To this we already have an answer, for we have already argued that Hayek is suggesting a consequentialist (indeed, a broadly utilitarian) appraisal of the performance of certain institutions *as systems*, taking full account of human ignorance and of our need to learn, and that he also believes that systems selected upon such a basis will also serve to minimize coercion. Our argument above concerning the weakness of Hayek's 'evolutionary' ideas when they are treated as a *substitute* for the rational appraisal of inherited institutions suggests that we were correct in emphasizing the importance of the more 'rationalistic' themes of the 'early' Hayek, against his later self. The second problem concerns Hayek's understanding of the character of human rationality, which is relevant in so far as we are concerned with the rational appraisal of institutions. The difficulty here might seem to be posed by the scepticism towards 'rationalism' that is expressed by Hayek at various points in his work. Does what Hayek say on this topic call into question the role that our interpretation of his work gives to human reason?

There are several themes in Hayek's work that are relevant to this question. Consider his opposition to 'rationalism' as expressed in such pieces as *The Counter-Revolution of Science* and 'Individualism: True and False'. In these writings, Hayek is critical of those who wish – in a way that parallels Descartes' approach to human knowledge[96] – to make a clean sweep and to redesign our institutions from their foundations. As Hayek has himself later suggested,[97] his own language here was somewhat misleading. Rather than being opposed to rationalism as such – as his language might suggest – it was certain specific intellectual errors that he was combating; and his own view in these very essays, which favoured the *piecemeal* critical appraisal of inherited institutions, has itself been well described by Hayek as 'critical rationalism'.[98] I am thus suggesting that one takes seriously, and uses as a basis for the reconstruction[99] of Hayek's views, the links that Hayek himself suggests exist between his ideas and Popper's 'critical rationalism'. This identifies rationality with the piecemeal appraisal of our knowledge and our institutions.[100] It suggests that we do this while, at any one point, uncritically accepting various other theories or social practices. In the sphere of our knowledge it suggests that those ideas which we can appraise critically rest upon various unconscious expectations but that these can be brought to the surface in the light of criticism, albeit only in a piecemeal manner.[101]

Now all this clearly coheres pretty well with much in Hayek's work (and my account of Menger's views would also make him, in this respect, a precursor of critical rationalism).[102] But there is a problem. For the ideas of *The Sensory Order* and Hayek's other writings on perception, while in some ways compatible with this view, are, in other ways, at odds with it. On the side of compatibility, there is a common emphasis on our experience as structured by classificatory systems and predispositions, towards which a biological approach is taken. Moreover, there is a common emphasis on the idea that our knowledge is limited; that at any one time we can be conscious only of a small part of the mechanisms involved, and so on.[103]

There is, however, a difference. For Popper's view is, at bottom, close to the view expressed in Neurath's metaphor of our knowledge being a ship which we repair, piecemeal, while it is afloat (resting, in any one operation, upon other parts of our knowledge), and where no single element is in principle immune from our critical attention.[104] Hayek, on the other hand, develops his ideas in such a way as to suggest that there are certain intrinsic limitations to human knowledge. For he suggests that there is, at some level, an intellectual framework in which we are imprisoned in the sense that we are unable to bring forward as an object of conscious scrutiny, and to communicate, the classificatory principles upon which our conscious experience is based, since they are of a higher degree of complexity than is our mind.[105]

The ideas about the limitations of our knowledge appear in their strongest form in Hayek's 'Rules, Perception and Intelligibility', when he is reflecting on meaning, communication and understanding. Hayek there says:

> If everything we can express (state, communicate) is intelligible to others only because their mental structure is governed by the same rules as ours, it would seem that these rules themselves can never be communicated.[106]

He might then seem to qualify this point by writing:

> It is important not to confuse the contention that any such system must always act on some rules which it cannot communicate with the contention that there are particular rules which no such system could ever state. All the former contention means is that there will always be some rules governing a mind which that mind in its then prevailing state cannot communicate, and that, if it were ever to acquire the capacity of communicating these rules, this would presuppose that it had acquired further higher rules which make the communication of the former possible but which themselves will still be incommunicable.[107]

The opening sentence from this quotation might seem to be close to Popper's view. But there is a most important difference. For Hayek's reference to 'higher rules' indicates that he is concerned with a hierarchical structure, the top level of which, whatever it may be at any one time, is always incommunicable (and thus also, in a sense, something that cannot be an object of conscious awareness). But such a view, by contrast with Popper's, seems close to R. G. Collingwood's theory of absolute presuppositions in his *Essay on Metaphysics*,[108] and quite properly to be understood as a doctrine of the intrinsic limitations of our knowledge.

Now, if this thesis of Hayek's can be sustained, and assuming with Hayek that the classificatory principles in question are simply a particular product of experience (and could thus, presumably, have been other than they are), Hayek's theory would seem to be, in a certain sense, relativistic. For our (shared?) rationality, and thus our rational appraisal of other elements of our knowledge, would seem to depend upon certain presuppositions which may be arbitrary, or contain arbitrary elements, which we are not in a position to correct.[109] This contrasts with Popper's views.[110] And, as compared to them, Hayek's views seem to place limitations upon the character of human rationality which cannot be overcome by piecemeal improvement.

But is Hayek correct? While it would be too great a task to discuss these aspects of Hayek's ideas extensively here, there is an argument in Popper's favour. For we can develop our knowledge in this field in a piecemeal way, through the development of abstract theories about the way in which our own classificatory mechanisms work, and test them via computer simulations.[111] In this way we may obtain knowledge about the way in which *we* are classifying information, which is outside of ourselves (so that we don't get involved in problems of watching ourselves watching ourselves, etc.) and which is of a general and abstract character, such that we do not need to have experienced (or, at a certain level, to know about) all the particular operations involved in order to know something about the overall character of the classificatory system involved – and to discover something of its limitations.

Thus, I wish to suggest that while there would seem to be a genuine difference between Hayek's and Popper's views on the character of rationality, on this point Popper's should be preferred. If this is right, there is an *argument* for suggesting that Hayek's views should be more fully assimilated to Popper's critical rationalism – with which he has often linked it – even where what he has written is, in some respects, rather different in its character. And this, in turn, suggests that there is no problem presented for the Mengerian programme of the critical improvement of inherited institutions by this aspect of Hayek's work.

The third strand to Hayek's opposition to rationalism is the theme – running from his Inaugural Address at the LSE, through 'Individualism: True and False' to his 'Three Sources of Human Values' – that there are certain elements of useful inherited institutions which it is necessary for us simply to accept, and which we must not submit to 'rational' scrutiny, if these valuable institutions are to survive. This view is at odds with critical rationalism. For a key motif in Popper's work is that all claims to knowledge, and all social institutions, can – and, if they are problematic, should – be brought by citizens to the tribunal of conscious critical appraisal. The contrast between this and Hayek's views merits some detailed discussion.

Hayek, as we have seen, argues that a certain compliance is needed on the part of citizens if they are to be able to sustain useful social institutions. In 'Individualism: True and False' and elsewhere, Hayek argues that the continued existence of such institutions depends upon a willingness on the part of citizens to comply with certain rules and conventions, even though they cannot appreciate their rationale. In some of Hayek's formulations, this seems to mean simply that citizens should not break with institutions or conventions merely because they cannot see a positive reason for them and that they should be retained if citizens have nothing against them. But, as we saw earlier, citizens can be expected to have specific complaints against some of the very institutions which Hayek champions – for example, about the operation of an extended market order, about a legal system of the broad character that Hayek favours, and about a useful system of social roles.

As I have suggested earlier, Hayek cannot be interpreted as urging an uncritical compliance with all social rules and conventions. First, on Hayek's account the fact that we obtain benefits from the market order depends on innovation taking place within it. And this innovation will, itself, involve the breaking of many kinds of taboos, traditions and conventions – as is evinced by the resentment that is often directed against the innovator.[112] In consequence, Hayek's citizens need some way of knowing with what they should comply and in respect of what they may innovate. This very fact shows that a 'blanket' conservatism is not in order. In addition, as we saw in our discussion of Hayek's later account of law, he allows for the immanent criticism of institutions and for the revision of one standard on the basis of others. But this, while interesting, does not in itself provide for the external or functional criticism of institutions which we need; not least if Hayek's own ideas are to work.

Hayek does, it is true, offer some suggestions about how this problem might be resolved. For example, in his 'Freedom, Reason and Tradition',[113] he tells us that:

> There is an advantage to obedience to such rules not being coerced, not only because coercion as such is bad, but because it is, in fact, often desirable that rules should be observed only in most instances and that the individual should be able to transgress them when it seems to him worthwhile to incur the odium which this will cause.

And in *Law, Legislation and Liberty*:[114]

The contentious and courageous may on rare occasions decide to brave general opinion and to disregard a particular rule which he regards as wrong, if he proves his general respect for the prevailing moral rules by carefully observing the others.

But while on occasion this may be effective, it will not work as a general resolution of the problem. For those circumstances in which a person will find it most 'worthwhile to incur the odium' of others will presumably be those in which they can make a considerable gain as a result of breaking with some convention to which others are keeping. There seems no obvious way in which, within Hayek's structure, others may distinguish between a judgement that a rule is wrong and someone's simply breaking it because it is to their advantage to do so, and no reason why personal gain should relate to what is in the general interest. What we need is a path from one shared set of conventions to other – and better – ones which are shared; all that Hayek's suggestion seems to offer is a basis on which existing conventions may be eroded.

A defender of a conservative reading of Hayek might argue: these problems are resolved by the conventions of the larger culture in which one is living. Those cultures which are successful are those which allow for certain kinds of innovation (e.g. in market behaviour) but not others (e.g. breaking the rules of an established market order in the name of social justice). While this is perhaps a possible view[115] it is hardly one that coheres with the bulk of Hayek's ideas. After all, he has been concerned with the *evolution* of just those larger cultural institutions which the conservative reader must take as fixed – and this presupposes that they have changed and thus can change. In addition, one of Hayek's concerns – sustained right up to *The Fatal Conceit* – has been with the need to improve upon our inherited institutions.

What, then, are we to make of all this? One option would be to say that the individual must make choices on the basis of theories (perhaps present implicitly in his culture, but which may need to be made explicit in the event of things going wrong) about the kind of innovation that is in order. Such a view coheres with much in Hayek's own work, and with his enterprise of trying to spell out, and to think of ways to re-establish, liberal ideas which had tacitly guided people's choices in the past.[116] But it is at odds with that side of Hayek's work which stresses the limited role that can be played by the conscious appeal to theoretical knowledge, and the value of uncritical compliance, with which we commenced this section; and it is not clear how it will cope with that side of Hayek's work which stresses the imperfect character of even the best of our social institutions.

It would therefore seem that the 'critical rationalist' side of Hayek – that which involves the critical appraisal of institutions, and which is informed by specific theories about the working of institutions such as the market and the legal order – stands in need of supplementation. What would seem required is something that will allow for relatively uncritical compliance with the institutions of some culture, but for citizens to be able to voice their disapproval – or their attraction to the way in which things are being done elsewhere – by voting with their feet. One needs institutions that will allow for the instantiation of something like the evolutionary, group-selectionist, mechanisms which Hayek has discussed but which are not – *pace* the suggestions of Hayek's later writings – actually to be found in the ordinary circumstances of human history. These would require, rather, a distinctive and in certain respects rationalistic setting in which to operate. A suggestion as to how this requirement might be met is offered later.[117]

THE THEORY OF SPONTANEOUS ORDER[118]

As previously suggested, Hayek's idea of a spontaneous order may be interpreted in two different ways: as a property of certain kinds of institutional formation (such as the market order); and as a theory of the evolution or development of such institutions. I have already discussed – and criticized – Hayek's account of the evolution of spontaneous orders. There is, however, in Hayek's work, also a theory of spontaneous order in our first sense.[119] It is developed only in a programmatic form, but it is interesting for our purposes because it is accompanied by an account of a distinctively Hayekian form of social engineering! It is worthy of examination both for its own sake and because of some of the problems to which it gives rise.

In his 'The Confusion of Language in Political Thought', Hayek sets out a distinction between the idea of a spontaneous order, or *cosmos*, and an arrangement or organization – a *taxis*. This contrast highlights a theme that runs through many aspects of Hayek's work: in the course of his paper, he touches on the contrast between a market order and a planned economy, on his ideal of the rule of law and on his critique of legal positivism. He also says:

> A spontaneous order may rest in part on regularities which are not spontaneous [in origin] but imposed. For policy purposes there results thus the alternative whether it is preferable to secure the formation of an order by a strategy of indirect approach, or by directly assigning a place for each element and describing its function in detail.[120]

Now, while this contrast is one of degree (as Hayek himself notes in *The Sensory Order*),[121] the suggestion that there are two, rather different, approaches to policy issues is important and is illustrated by some of Hayek's own writings. Consider, for example, Hayek's suggestions about the 'denationalization of money'.[122] For many years, Hayek had been concerned about monetary stability and with the idea that it would be desirable if something could play a role comparable to that played, earlier, by the gold standard. In his *Constitution of Liberty* Hayek pointed to the actions of government as a cause of instability. He raised, rhetorically, the question why should we not rely on the spontaneous forces of the market to supply whatever is needed, and answered:

> This is not only politically impracticable today but would probably be undesirable if it were possible. Perhaps if governments had never interfered, a kind of monetary arrangement might have evolved which would not have required deliberate control.... This choice, however, is now closed to us.[123]

He went on, when discussing international issues, to canvass the idea of a 'commodity reserve standard' as perhaps the best alternative to a gold standard, but he was pessimistic even about that.[124]

In 1976, when he addressed this problem again,[125] and surveyed the impact of 'the onslaughts of popular forms of Keynesianism', he commented: 'I do not believe that we can now remedy this position by *constructing* some new international monetary order' – such as the gold standard. But he continued by suggesting that if one moved to a system of competing currencies, this would create a situation where those issuing currencies – including govern-ments – would be propelled by self-interest onto those paths of virtue that he had hitherto despaired of their ever treading again.

All this is a striking example of Hayek's ideas about spontaneous orders and social policy. For clearly we are dealing here with an attempt to *create* a 'spontaneous order' in order to resolve a particular policy problem. The fact that one can do this renders somewhat beside the point Hayek's occasional emphasis on the 'purposelessness' of spontaneous orders, as do his sugges-tions about how they might be improved. To be sure, spontaneous orders can be used for a variety of purposes, and they offer a framework for the pursuit of many different goals. But so can a created *taxis* – as is suggested, for example, by Michels' *Political Parties*. The idea that a social institution should be one in which various individuals should be able to follow their own aims and visions of the good is, itself, a goal in terms of which an institution may be assessed – just as, to use one of Hayek's examples, one may assess a language on the basis of its ability to serve as a general medium of communication.

The use of 'spontaneous orders' for the purpose of social engineering is also exemplified in the grand design behind Hayek's *Law, Legislation and Liberty*. There he proposes a new constitutional structure which he hopes – after the fashion of a spontaneous order – will have the kinds of consequences, in limiting the activities of government, that he would favour.[126] In addition, his specific policy suggestions in *The Constitution of Liberty* are informed by similar uses being made of the more familiar 'spontaneous order' of the market.

All of this, I suggest, indicates two things: first, that Hayek's ideas about 'spontaneous orders' stand independently of his ideas about the *origins* of spontaneous orders; second, that his own use of these ideas for policy-related purposes poses a problem. For in making such suggestions he is involved in an appeal to theoretical knowledge of a kind that will not necessarily be possessed by – or be accessible to – the individual citizen. But how, then, can such knowledge be utilized in a *liberal* society, in which the liberty of the individual – and, above all, of his judgement – is safeguarded?

4

COMMERCIAL SOCIETY, SOCIAL JUSTICE AND DISAGGREGATION

INTRODUCTION

One important theme of Hayek's later work has been the contrast that he has drawn between an extended social order based upon markets, and earlier forms of human organization. He has argued that the former, which he favours, is morally significant – not least because it is required if we are to be able to support the numbers of people who are at present alive. This theme becomes the focus in his work for a contrast between an extended, market-based social order, and a more face-to-face society. In the former, people pursue economic self-interest, in an appropriate legal and institutional setting, their conduct also guided by various inherited moral and behavioural rules. In the latter, to which Hayek thinks humankind is more instinctively attuned and for which many of its moral and religious traditions were well adapted, people respond, rather, to the direct needs of others with whom they are in more immediate relations.

All this, however, is more than a matter of speculative anthropology, as it forms the basis of some of Hayek's reflections about the problems facing a liberal social order and its defenders. Essentially, Hayek's argument is that such societies, while he thinks them the best for humankind, are vulnerable to criticism, just because they can be judged and found wanting on the basis of moral responses and traditions adapted to or inherited from an older social order. As we have seen from our earlier discussion, Hayek thinks that market-based societies face a particular problem here, just because they rest upon rules that may not have immediate intuitive appeal, and involve practices – and consequences – that have certain intrinsically unlovely features. A defence of such a social order – containing such features – would require that we take a theoretical overview of the character of such a society. But such a perspective is, clearly, not available to most of its members. As a result, Hayek thinks that market-based societies of the kind that he favours are particularly open to criticism from socialists, who are able to make their case in a powerful manner, just because, at a certain level, ordinary people can correctly judge that important features of the

118

societies that Hayek favours, and which socialists criticize, do not satisfy their moral intuitions.

These ideas seem to me interesting and challenging. The final chapter of this book will discuss how some of the problems to which they give rise might be resolved from a Hayekian perspective. However, there is more involved than just the problem of the complex and morally mixed character of such social institutions. Hayek has, in his contrast between an extended market order and a more face-to-face society, touched upon an issue which is of wider significance for his work. For it is the periodization of economic organization to which he alludes, and, more specifically, certain extensions in the range of people with whom we may form market-based relationships which, if developed, will help to resolve an even more significant problem that arises concerning Hayek's work. For as I have argued in the previous chapters, there seems to be something highly problematic about Hayek's liberalism. Not only is no real rationale offered for his shift from (mild) socialism to liberalism (the socialist ideas to which he, personally, was attracted seem closer to interventionism on the basis of socialist values than to the full-scale socialism which he did criticize effectively). But also his own ideas about liberty and coercion would seem extendible in directions which take us closer to Wieser, to New Liberalism and to the Welfare State than to anything that might seem identifiable with the classical liberalism with which one might more usually associate Hayek.

My argument in this chapter takes the following form. I wish to argue, first, that Hayek's ideas might be made more specific, and I would hope rendered less hostage to fortune,[1] if they were interpreted in the light of a specific aspect of Adam Smith's ideas about the transition to commercial society. I will be concerned not with Smith's general economic typology of historical stages, but, rather, with the more limited issue of that aspect of the transition to commercial society related to the development of a general market in grain.[2] This issue, which E. P. Thompson has discussed from a perspective that contrasts sharply with that of Smith,[3] is of some significance, as marking a transition which has important moral consequences that pertain directly to Hayek's concerns. This transition involved some people being treated in ways which they could quite properly consider to be immoral. But (or so I will suggest), not only did it have highly desirable overall consequences, but it also changed, radically, our moral circumstances. In particular, it changed the character of our obligations towards our fellows, in ways that seem to me to provide us with the missing argument in favour of *classical* liberalism.

The developments with which I will be concerned were not, however, an all-or-nothing matter. Indeed, there is a sense in which, in the words of *The Communist Manifesto*, I am tempted to assert that 'A similar movement is going on before our own eyes'.[4] For changes similar to those which, historically, posed problems for ideas about 'the moral economy' as a consequence of the opening up of an extensive market in grain, seem to me to be posed for inflated ideas about the moral significance of national citizenship by developments that are currently taking place towards a global market economy.[5] But here I get ahead of myself.

Why I am suggesting that the transition that Smith advocates – and which was actually taking place at the time at which he was writing – was so important, is that it had significant implications for property, as this was understood in the post-Grotian natural law tradition. To put the matter at its most stark, the transition to an extended market-based economy seems to me, morally, a good thing – essentially for the reasons for which Adam Smith himself favoured it: that it generates wealth in ways that are of benefit to all people, and that it led to autonomy for ordinary people of a kind that they had never enjoyed previously.[6] Further, as Hayek has argued, the fact that it has taken place has the consequence that whether or not the reader will find my moral evaluation of this transition one with which he can sympathize, there is no easy going back, in the sense that people are now alive in societies which have undergone this transition, whose very existence depends upon the continuation of such arrangements. However, the transition itself has important *moral* consequences. As these matters had been conceptualized in the immediately previous period, both at the level of high theory and – if Thompson and others who have written in this vein are correct[7] – in popular consciousness, wealth and property ownership were cast around with various moral encumbrances. But these encumbrances, I will suggest, themselves made sense only if one was dealing with a society in which those who were obliged, and those to whom they were obliged, stood in reasonably clear-cut, face-to-face relationships. If, as was widely held in the natural law tradition (see below), one had a right to subsistence from the surplus of others, it was crucial that one knew to whose surplus one could look for support, in the event of one's needing it. Similarly, the correlative restrictions upon property ownership would also seem to make sense only if it was clear-cut who might have a claim upon one's property in the event of famine; for it is only in such circumstances that people could take decisions with regard to their property, on the basis of information that would be available to them. Wider ideas about 'moral economy'-based rights and obligations, which Thompson and others have discussed, would seem to require that the people involved knew who could claim and from whom, and – if appeal was made to ideas about customary market prices for subsistence goods – upon whose customs and with what markets they were dealing.

My thesis, in short, is that these older relationships were shattered by the transition to an extended market economy (and also by the possibility of wider social mobility, such that ordinary people could expect to travel, in pursuit of work, and thus to live among people with whom they did not share immediate kinship, deep social customs, or even citizenship). Such a transition, I would argue, we should consider to be desirable. Not only, however, did it serve to break with the specific and localized moral obligations with which Thompson was concerned, but also, as I shall argue, the kind of society to which it has given rise has other important features, too.

These relate to two strands of argument which are worth mentioning immediately, as I appeal to them to provide me with an argument against the possible extensions of Hayek's views, such that duties are imposed upon us that go beyond what is involved in *classical* liberalism. The first is that, if it is claimed that people have rights, such claims must be assessed, *inter alia*, in terms of the moral reasonableness of the correlative duties that they impose upon others. This argument has been made – in my view with considerable effect – by Jeremy Waldron against classical liberal ideas concerning private property.[8] Waldron has argued that to assess the moral validity of claims about the right to private property – and thus that other people can legitimately be excluded from the enjoyment of some object – we must, among other things, consider the reasonableness of this exclusion from the perspective of those who are being excluded.[9] This is a challenge that any theory of property has to face, just because to grant the legitimacy to some claimed right is, at the same time, to grant the legitimacy of the correlative duties that its admission would impose. Waldron's argument in the context of property rights, however, would seem to me to be simply one application of an argument that is completely general in its character. Any right that is claimed must be assessed, *inter alia*, in terms of the moral reasonableness of the correlative duties that it may impose upon others. Further, any claim that the bringing about of some consequence is morally obligatory, or even morally desirable, must again be assessed, *inter alia*, in terms of the moral reasonableness of the duties that the acceptance of this claim would impose upon those whose actions (positive or negative) would bring it about. But, I will suggest, life within an extended moral order typically makes the duties that are correlative to the *extensions* of Hayek's argument morally *unreasonable*, just in so far as they are to be exercised in respect of people with whom we do not have the kinds of relations that would make them appropriate, and who enjoy autonomy from us of a character such that it is unreasonable that we should bear moral responsibility for their circumstances or for the consequences of their actions.

Second, the abstract argument that I have pursued above is given particular point by what might be called the concrete features of societies which have undergone the kinds of change with which Hayek is concerned, and in which there is the kind of disaggregation of decision-taking to which I referred in the first chapter of this book.

There are two parts to this argument. The first holds in respect of any society, and might be called the Burkean problem of institutional design. By referring here to Burke, I do not wish to endorse his views in any general way (indeed, it has always seemed to me that an exaggerated respect for Burke, a man who did not understand the difference between argument and long-winded rhetoric, is perhaps *the* mark of poor judgement in a political theorist). Rather, what I have in mind here is this. Burke, in the course of his criticism of

121

the early stages of the French Revolution, and of the radicals of his own day, stressed the way in which we, the material out of which political institutions are made, and upon whose actions the realization of any moral or political ideal will depend, are shaped by the institutions and settings under which we have grown up. To use more recent terminology, we are socialized, and this must be the starting-point for any reflection upon what it is now open to us to achieve. In saying this, I do not mean that change is impossible. It may be possible for us to respond to argument or emotional appeals concerning what should be valued, or otherwise to change our habits, beliefs, routines and the institutions that sustain them. But, and this is the crucial point, what can be done is affected by where we start from; and there may be many things which would be desirable if they could be achieved, but which cannot be achieved given the position from which we are starting (and especially, without coercion and if we have freedom of judgement and action). In part, my point here is sociological. I am not saying that one can't teach an old dog new tricks. But I am suggesting that he may be limited in respect of the new tricks that he may be taught. Things are similar with regard to institutions: there may be some things that cannot be accomplished, given the point from which we start. There may be other things that can be accomplished only in ways that may impose costs such that we would not, on balance, favour the change once we realize what it would involve. Or, as I will discuss further, shortly, we may find that they cannot be accomplished within a society of the kind that Hayek has discussed – although they might, say, be achievable within a particular and more disciplined institution within it.[10]

The sociological ideas to which I have just been referring become of particular interest when they are related to my earlier moral argument. For moral appraisal – especially of that to which we are asked to give not just assent at the level of abstract agreement as to its desirability, but concerning which we will actually have to change our behaviour – will be undertaken by ourselves as socialized characters, from the positions, and within the institutions, in which we are currently situated or to which we could understand ourselves as moving. In so far as we are concerned with issues upon which we have freedom of choice,[11] what is crucial is what, in that situation, will seem to us a reasonable action.[12] It is out of such actions that any change – to our values, habits and institutions – must be forged. All this, in my view, becomes especially important in the light of the second part of my argument, to which I will now turn.

My concern, here, is with the disaggregated character of decision-making that characterizes societies of the kind with which Hayek has been concerned. I do not need to say more, here, about economic decision-taking within such societies, a theme which has been explored, extensively, in earlier chapters. What is, perhaps, worth stressing are some consequences of such disaggregation. If economic decision-taking is disaggregated in the way that I have indicated, many large-scale decisions cannot be taken on the basis of collective decision-making, just because that is not, as it were, where the actions occur that give rise to the effects in question. For if economic decision-taking is disaggregated, then so too will be the decisions that give rise to many macro-level consequences in which we may be interested. And – here is the rub – they may well be taken by people who do not know and who (for informational reasons, related to Hayek's argument about economic calculation) *cannot* be fully informed about what these consequences will be.[13] Further, even though they may initially believe that some overall outcome is desirable, and even if they could have access to the information they would need in order to know how to act so as to bring it about, they may find that they have no reason themselves to act so as to bring it about.[14]

What is involved may be illustrated by a problem which we will discuss more extensively a little later in this chapter in connection with social justice. In a society of the character that Hayek has described, economic redistribution will – or so it would seem – have to be effected in large part by way of some combination of a rule-based taxation system, and a rule-based benefit system. But those who implement such rules – and those upon whom they are implemented – will encounter such rules in a disaggregated context, in which, as it were, they are dissociated from the overall goals or purposes that they are intended to achieve.[15] They instead become practices, the implementation of which by officials will involve what is reasonable as a routine, or actions that it is reasonable to take in the specific situations in which people find themselves. (Of course, we may consider how some goal that we desire to achieve could be achieved on the basis of different values and procedures. But given problems of information and motivation, some attractive goals may not be realizable at all, while others would depend upon the adoption of ways of conducting ourselves which would make nonsense of what – and where – we currently are.) Further, the rules and practices of officials become, for citizens, things around which they conduct their lives and plan their activities, sometimes with sophisticated professional help.

This last point possibly requires some clarification. I am not, here, concerned with, say, people's honesty in paying their taxes.[16] Rather, my point is that many such regulations are not encountered by us in the form of action rules, concerning which we are faced with a decision whether or not to comply, so much as obstacles around which we must navigate when planning our various activities. But, as I will argue later, this may well have the consequence that centralized decision-taking, including that in which we may participate wholeheartedly as sovereign (in Rousseau's sense), cannot achieve the ends that it desires, as each of its initiatives serves only to elicit new counter-initiatives from us as citizens, when we encounter it in our ordinary day-to-day lives. Of course, centralized decision-taking will be able to achieve *something*. But it will be a matter for discussion as to whether what it is able to achieve, and at the cost that it would involve to do so, is something that there is any moral case for achieving.[17] Alternatively, in some circumstances it may be possible to achieve an outcome more directly by supplying action rules that people will actually use as the basis of their conduct. Consider, here, coordination rules, or conventions as might be imposed on the conduct of some practice such as accounting. Consider, also, what might be achieved within a voluntary organization or a business organization, or in the armed forces during peace-time, within which specific rules of conduct may be imposed because member-ship of the organization in question is itself voluntary; or, alternatively, what gets done to people involuntarily within armies, during wartime. In such cases, a specific code of behaviour, or of rules, practices or incentives, may be imposed with an eye to achieving a specific and valued outcome.[18] But to make this point itself serves to highlight the way in which much of our lives is not of this character. A programme, say, of indoctrination in ideas about racial equality, and the dismissal of those who will not comply with its message, is something that is at least a possibility within the armed forces of an otherwise free country. But it is clearly utterly unacceptable as a model for social life in general, however desirable the intended outcomes might be.[19]

Finally, here, we must consider another feature of governmental decision-making in societies of the kind with which Hayek has been concerned. It relates to how we are assuming that governments will themselves behave. This is a point that, in my view, Hayek himself has not considered sufficiently – as is evidenced by the fact that from time to time in his writings, functions are allocated to government without his giving an account of how it is that such goals will be decided upon by those involved in governmental decision-taking and of the practices needed to bring them about.

There is an economics-derived literature in rational choice theory, and more particularly in public choice, that addresses these issues. This raises important points, but is over-restrictive in its view of the motivation of the agents with whom it is concerned. From the perspective for which I am arguing here, it is right in assuming that we need to think of the human behaviour that is involved in governmental decisions as in many ways disaggregated; wrong in that it takes too simple a view of human motivation, in situations in which there do not seem to me to be good *prima facie* arguments for working with such restrictive models.[20] By way of contrast with this, my particular concern here will be with issues that have been raised in the discussion, within political science, of the policy making process and the problems of implementation.[21] This material in a sense takes the concerns of pluralists and neo-pluralists inside governmental decision-making and its implementation, and offers an im-portant corrective to those who would see government as if it simply involved Rousseau's sovereign, making laws for itself. Rather, the specific content of legislation and what is implemented are seen as the products of the actions of various groups and interests both inside and outside government, and of what may be negotiated between them. There is no reason why we should assume that these people are narrowly self-interested; but what actually takes place will typically be an emergent product from their disaggregated activities, rather than something the specific content of which represents the product of any kind of normative consensus. Indeed, this occurs even when there may be a normative consensus that something is desirable (albeit one that has not been considered in the light of the disaggregative analysis that I am here canvassing).

In so far as such a picture holds good – and Albert Weale has made the important critical point that much of this literature represents as typical of government in general what may be distinctive features of governmental processes in the United States[22] – it imposes another important constraint upon what can be achieved by way of the realization of our normative goals through processes of collective decision-taking. Clearly, there could be much less fragmentation of decision-taking, much clearer lines of responsibility and a much stronger public sphere than is the case in the United States.[23] But whatever we can achieve here would seem to be subject to limitations imposed, on the one side, by policy-making communities and the various power relationships within them – many of which would seem inevitable features of the ways in which we would wish to do other things – and on the other, by the element of negotiation that would seem an essential feature of the process of implementation.

All this, in turn, indicates that there are important limits to what can be achieved within societies of the kind within which I – and I suspect the bulk of my readers – are living, and with which Hayek has been concerned. These limits relate, importantly, to the very issues addressed in discussions within normative political theory, and towards which many political movements are directed. My argument is not that there should not be such normative discussion, but that it is vital that those who undertake it should be aware of the ways in which what they are discussing are the products of various institutional practices and of what I have termed disaggregated decision-taking. Indeed, while I am in disagreement with many of his substantive views, Robert Goodin has made this point particularly strongly in a recent essay:[24]

> One of the central lessons of contemporary social science for contemporary political philosophy is that we cannot propound any values we like confident that an institutional shell can be found for pursuing all of them simultaneously.

Two additional points must be made before I launch into the details of my argument concerning Smith.

(1) I am here advocating an approach that in certain respects differs from Hayek's own, and which I am proposing as a correction to his. For while the themes which I have just been discussing are clearly inspired by Hayek's work – especially his critique of the ideal of social justice – my argument is, in certain respects, at odds with his own. Three things are involved here. First, I am making explicit and raising as a problem something that is glossed over in Hayek's own work. It is that his own normative concerns are often focused upon what are, in effect, macro or emergent properties of a society. His vision of a

democratic society is, in large part, one which has certain broad characteristics which, as it were, he is commending to us as desirable in themselves, and because they bestow benefits on members of those societies in general.[25] But it is by no means the case that each of these things is of immediate and readily intelligible benefit to each individual member of these societies. This, however, poses a problem that Hayek has not addressed: that his own ideas may not themselves pass the test of disaggregation. Now in some ways it is easy enough to see why this may not have struck Hayek as a particularly pressing problem. For he, after all, was by training an economist. And economists would seem typically to develop arguments about the consequences of human behaviour against a background of institutions, habits and assumptions that are taken for granted, and are not themselves typically made the objects of theoretical scrutiny. Further, there are traditions within economics – from Smith to the present day – which are suggestive of links between disaggregated individual action and desirable macro-level consequences, in the light of which such connections may seem generally less problematic than is, in fact, the case. What is required, I would suggest, is an approach which is rigidly endogenous. It can, indeed, take some things as given: people's actual preferences, traditions and institutions at the point at which analysis starts. But it is thereafter entitled only to this, and to the ways in which such things are transformed, with the passing of time, according to the theoretical approach itself. Links between individual action and specific social outcomes would have to be demonstrated. There would be no restriction on how this might be done, so appeals to 'invisible hand' mechanisms, 'evolutionary' themes, 'filter mechanisms' and other structural constraints are all in order. But what is invoked in such explanations must be made explicit. And for every step after the initial one, it must be shown that what is being appealed to for explanatory purposes – both by way of motivations, and things exercising constraints – will still be there, given our initial assumptions and what we then claim takes place. (And clearly, in so far as claims are being made about the existence of these things in the real world, appropriate tests must be made to reassure us that these claims remain plausible.)

Second, in developing such arguments there would seem to me to be strong reasons against using the economist's usual *homo economicus* model of human action. I certainly favour the idea that it is useful to look at human action as subjectively rational, and thus at people as acting in ways that make sense to them in the situations in which they are acting. But Hayek's own stress upon the distinctive rules, customs and so on that people may follow, should surely guard us against treating everyone as if they were undifferentiated rational economic men.[26] Also, Hayek's stress on human ignorance should lead us to think in terms of people acting in ways that seem to them to make sense, in the particular institutional settings in which they find themselves, and on the basis of the information that would be available to them in such settings, rather than in terms of the actions of agents who are fully informed. Unless there are specific theoretical reasons for working with models which provide a rationale for making this oversimplification, we should not assume that people act on the basis of knowledge that would not, in fact, be available to them.

This, however, is not the half of it. For within particular institutions, there is typically a distinctive ethos and way of doing things, into which people are socialized. By this, I do *not* mean that we should necessarily think of people as following socially shared rules. Rather, there are certain things to be done, and in our various institutional settings we develop ways of coping with this which, while they may be different in their internal structure, share, as it were, the mark of a common template. I would suggest that, unless there are specific arguments to the contrary, it is in such terms – and thus, in terms of an approach which is more hermeneutical than economic – that we should approach our task of understanding human action, and its consequences.

There is, however, a final argument to be made here. It is that we should be realistic about people's moral concerns. People, surely, are not narrowly morally self-interested. But it is difficult to imagine anyone actually being a utilitarian, either, in the sense that it is difficult to see a concern for the greatest happiness of the greatest number being an intelligible object of their moral concern. We may, of course, wish people well rather than not, and genuinely be moved by the occurrence of dire poverty, or some unusual misfortune, even where it affects people remote from ourselves. But our moral lives are made up of particular concerns, relationships and obligations, many of which are specific to particular institutional settings. This is not an argument for moral myopia. But it is an argument to the effect that our wider moral concerns must be built up from actions the intentional objects of which are limited in scope. For this reason, while we may be inspired – or may wish to inspire others – with Hayek's large-scale moral vision, we must think of what we are asking people to do in their day-to-day lives, and whether what we are asking is for them to do things which will, there, seem to them morally reasonable from the specific vantage-points in which they are acting. (Clearly, certain large-scale changes such, indeed, as those of the forms of economic and political organization under which we are acting may have a key role in structuring the very situations in which we are acting, and their pros and cons may be debated on a rather different basis, as is indicated by the overall argument presented in this volume. In addition, as I will suggest in the final chapter of this book, we may, further, think of ways in which forms of life can be deliberately created – and then chosen by individuals – from the vantage-point of which such actions may make more sense than, perhaps, they do at present.)

This argument, however, cuts both ways. It may pose some problems for Hayek. But it poses much greater problems for those who wish to argue that we owe much more to others, than does Hayek. For, to mention an argument that I will develop later, one of the major attractions of a negative view of liberty is that what it asks of everyone else is typically morally reasonable, in a way in which the obligations that go with a universalistic interpretation of positive liberty are not.

(2) A powerful case has been made by Thompson that action on the basis of the ideas which Smith favoured – and indeed, in some cases inspired by his very words – led to disaster. Sen[27] has discussed the problems of famine, in a manner that might seem to tell heavily against the case that I am making. In addition, it might be argued that a society based on an extended market order, and characterized by disaggregated decision-taking of both the economic and political kinds that I have been discussing, faces some distinctive problems when activities within it generate large-scale, undesirable consequences which are emergent products relative to the actions which take place within them; for example, certain of the environmental problems that are matters of current concern.[28] For even if we were to assume that no distinctive problems of public goods were involved, we would face problems concerning information and the structure of human motivation of the kind that I have just discussed, which would seem particularly difficult to handle.[29]

I wish here simply to indicate that problems such as these seem to me important and difficult; but that they are points to which I cannot sensibly try to respond on the present occasion. All that I will say here is that these problems seem to me genuine, and not open to knock-down solutions. One important point that relates to them, however, is that their existence – and, say, Sen's specific argument about the problems of famine – would seem to draw attention to the importance of a public forum. Whether or not we conclude that, in the end, what is required is action by the state or even a change in the form of our economic and political organization, the existence of these problems – real or possible – suggests that it is vital that there should be somewhere where we should be able to reflect upon them together. Hayek's stress on the disaggregated character of decision-taking, and the emphasis within 'economic' approaches upon individuals acting on the basis of preferences, should not blind us to the importance of issues which require deliberation and argument with our fellows – and to the fact that we stand in need of institutions within which this activity is to take place.

BEFORE CLASSICAL LIBERALISM

As I have indicated above, a defender of classical liberalism faces certain historically generated problems with regard to the ideas with which he wishes to operate. This is not the place for a full survey of these issues. That would take us far beyond what is appropriate in the present study. In particular, I will not address foundational questions here.[30] But at the very least, a defender of the view that universal welfare rights should *not* be recognized, faces the following problems.

First, liberal ideas about property rights would seem, naturally, to be an extension of ideas that arise within the post-Grotian natural law tradition. But here the liberal faces a problem, in that Locke – who in terms of substance if not in respect of his account of their basis would seem to be almost paradigmatic of the kind of views that the classical liberal wants to uphold – qualified individual property ownership with an acknowledgement of a *right* to charity on the part of the indigent.[31] As Locke himself puts it: 'Charity gives every Man a Title to so much out of another's Plenty, as will keep him from extreme want, where he has no means to subsist otherwise'.

Second, there are the concerns that E. P. Thompson has highlighted in connection with his discussion of 'moral economy', and in particular of disputes that arose with respect to trade in grain, when the local populace objected to a variety of practices (including the export of grain out of their area; the selling of grain through intermediaries, rather than directly at the market-place; and the keeping of grain off the market, or selling it at high prices, in times of dearth). Thompson has looked at popular sentiment, rather than high theory.[32] Part of what he considers might be seen as a popular correlate of the natural law right to charity, which we noted above. In part, however – and in particular, in so far as one was concerned with the idea that grain had to be brought to market, and sold there at a 'fair' or customary price – one is dealing with wider moral restrictions upon individual property rights.

These were genuine limitations upon property rights, such that, if they were accepted, people were not free to do just what they wished with 'their' property. Or, rather, we are in a situation in which what a modern (classical) liberal would wish to see as an unrestricted property right in fact turns out to be subject to qualifications, in certain circumstances. The right is conditional; and indeed, as Hont and Ignatieff – and Thompson – have discussed from their different perspectives, these qualifications upon property rights were, in situations of urgency, typically understood as constituting not just imperfect duties, but were made the objects of legislation or of action by courts. (For example, there were restrictions on the export of grain, and various emergency measures as codified in the *Book of Orders*.)[33]

The important issue for our purposes, however, relates to the character of these limitations; namely, that they are *local*. Propinquity seems to play an essential role.[34] For we can ask: if someone is starving, or if there is dearth, *whose* property ownership is qualified, and *who* is it that incurs obligations? The answer – in terms of the general debate about the export of corn, and Thompson's examples – would seem to be: those people in what was recognized as being the immediate neighbourhood. It was *here* where it was believed that people had claims. Over and above what might have grown up as the result of particular customs, this has a more general intelligibility to it. First, while such duties may have been conceptualized as general, when understood in the context of a location they take on the character of special duties, to the discharge of which there seems, as a matter of moral psychology, a certain intelligibility. In addition, it is over people in this same area that are exercised various forms of informal social control, such that there is a kind of interrelation between the person in question's exercise of their freedom, and the way in which others react to them.[35] Second, such duties also relate importantly to issues of knowledge and information. If you are a landowner in a certain district, then it will be possible for you to understand how your actions are likely to be impinged upon by changes that take place in that neighbourhood. If there is the failure of a certain crop, or if the local market for certain kinds of crafts or primary products is adversely affected, these are things of which you will have knowledge and so, as a result, you can take into account how these developments will impinge upon your responsibilities towards others. Further, in so far as one is dealing with what is, primarily, a local economy, those with whom you will be dealing will be in the same boat: it will come as no surprise to them, either, that you can't bring as much of your corn to the market as might initially have been hoped for.

It is such things that, with the transition to a more extended market-based society, become problematic, and in two respects.

First, within such a setting, trade takes on a more impersonal character. If subsistence goods are shifted, physically, over considerable distances, owner-ship can no longer be morally hedged around with the sorts of claims that were usual before. If agreements are made with those in remote places, the customs of a *local* market-place and its customary prices and practices can no longer serve as an intelligible constraint. Further, if the grain is shipped elsewhere, it is no longer physically there to be commandeered by the local magistrates in the event of a local shortage, and the very fact that grain becomes a standard commodity means that the earlier, locally based, restrictions can no longer be attached to it.

Second, contractual arrangements can no longer be understood to be subject to qualifications in the light of locally available information, without risk of serious disruption to the extended, market-based social order. The dealings of merchants and manufacturers come to involve the putting together of materials produced in different places and under different conditions by people of whom and of whose circumstances they cannot even hope to have detailed knowledge. Yet this, as Hayek has stressed, is perhaps *the* characteristic feature of an extended market order, transactions within which are coordinated by prices. In such settings, contractual arrangements must be understood as relatively unencumbered by locally generated restrictions that do not form an explicit part of the contract. It will no longer be possible for people to take into consideration the changes in circumstances which in a local economy would be common knowledge to all participants. Accordingly, the development of an extended market-based society would seem to be incompatible with natural law constraints upon property ownership, and with the ideas of Thompson's 'moral economy'.

But there is an additional argument to be made here, too. For one feature of commercial society in its full-fledged sense is clearly, also, that within it people may be more mobile, and in ways that are in tension with the notion of community to which the notion of moral economy – and, I would suggest, ideas about universal (but in fact locally realized) subsistence rights – implicitly appealed. It is one thing to have obligations to those who are on a regular basis in the environs of one's activities, and with whom one's day-to-day actions and life is bound up, quite another to suggest that such obligations should extend to whoever happens, as it were, to turn up. In a setting in which stable relations are the norm, there will doubtless be formal or informal rites of acceptance. It may even be the case that, if it is supposed that people will be becoming settled members of a community, the local norm is that they should be fully accepted at once. There may also be what amount to reciprocal arrangements for the treatment of strangers from different communities. And, if they are not too numerous, people may extend a helping hand to strangers, out of generosity. But in so far as we all become more transient, or transients become more common, it can hardly be the case that need, imported into some location, can reasonably be taken as establishing moral economy-style obligations on the part of others, when the only local connection is, as it were, that we turn up near them, with our begging bowl.

It may, however, be useful at this stage for me to comment briefly on what I take it that this argument has and has not established so far. My suggestion has been that there is an incompatibility between an extended market order, and moral economy type ideas about location-generated obligations. I have suggested, further, that subsistence rights are usefully interpreted in similar terms, i.e. as implicitly carrying with them ideas about propinquity (or some other kind of specific connection) in the generation of obligation, and thus in effect that they should be regarded as an odd form of special obligation, albeit one that occurs as part and parcel of people's customary relations, rather than being the product of any kind of contractual arrangement.

What I have not done, is to argue that there is a moral case that such a transition be made, or to consider what, if such a transition should be made, should happen to the moral claims that, prior to the transition, some people would have had upon others. To the first of these tasks, I now turn.

FROM THE TRADE IN GRAIN TO A GREAT SOCIETY

I have already mentioned that Adam Smith, among others, was involved in a debate about trade in grain, which is highly relevant to the question of this transition.[36] For if, say, grain is made a commodity; if people become professional middlemen in grain, and if, especially, it is exported – whether to another country, or outside its place of origin and the control of local rioters or the local magistrate – this marks a break with ideas and practices of a 'moral economy' and with the qualification on full property ownership that such practices involved.

What is the case for such trade? We may here discount the simple advantage to the owner of the grain. For while that is real enough, it is no argument that others should be deprived of their rights, simply because the owners would gain from their so doing. Rather, it would seem to me that there are two interrelated arguments here. The first is broadly utilitarian in its character. The full commodification of the production of grain would contribute towards efficiency in its production and distribution, and by this means, towards the well-being of people generally. In so far as some lost out; for example, in not being able to purchase grain at customary, 'moral economy' rates, this would be more than compensated for by gains to well-being on the part of other people; not least others who might well have starved without such a transition. (For their moral economy entitlements would have been of little use to them if there is nothing upon which they can make such claims in their local area or, more generally, if there is simply not enough to go round.) There is, as I will shortly argue, a case for the compensation of those people who, personally, lose out in the transition. While, within the conditions created after the transition, subsistence in itself would not seem to be a problem in the way in which it was, historically, prior to the transition.

This leads us to a second argument – which Hont and Ignatieff have represented as Smith's own view – which is that one might accept that there was an imperfect right to subsistence, in the event of people actually reaching the point of starvation (or even according government the power to act, should it be necessary). However, the long-term result of a transition to a fully market-based economy would be that one would not, in fact, have to act on the basis of this under any ordinary circumstances.

These broad arguments would seem to me telling; at least in respect of Western countries, and, more generally, those that have successfully made the kind of transition that Smith had in mind. It is simply not the case that the inhabitants of such countries, in normal circumstances, now have to worry about whether they will starve to death or, indeed, suffer the risk of absolute destitution that was the lot of much of humankind up to the development of such societies. Those who live in such societies also enjoy a multiplicity of other benefits, too; notably the opportunity for access to cultural and intellectual resources of a kind undreamed of in even the recent past,[37] as well as freedom from many unchosen dependencies. However, three issues must now be addressed.

The first concerns the moral desirability of the move to an extended market-based society. Here, my own belief is that if it can be accomplished, there is no question that it is morally desirable that it should take place; essentially for the reasons indicated above.

Second, there is the problem of those who lose in the transition. Three separate issues seem to me to be involved here. Consider, initially, people who lost out in such a transition in respect of subsistence rights, and other moral hedges round property. There would seem strong grounds for the idea that the right to (bare) subsistence be continued, although there would seem every reason to expect that it would seldom have to be acted upon, once the transition had been accomplished. Accordingly, it is not clear why the admission of such a right for those who were actually involved in such a transition should impose any significant burden on others, and thus why it could not be dealt with either by some form of insurance, by government or by charitable organizations, whichever should prove the more convenient.

Next, what of the wider entitlements that are included within Thompson's ideas about 'moral economy'? Here, one would need to distinguish between those who could be expected to benefit personally from the gains that take place in connection with the transition, and those who could not. The latter might include the elderly, who had made plans for their old age on the basis of the former arrangements (e.g. of the availability of corn at customary prices). They, on the face of it, would seem to have a strong moral case for the continuation of an entitlement of something equivalent. It is also clear from whom they should expect to receive it, in the first instance: those who gain directly from the abolition of older customary rights. For it is clear who gains most immediately from the transition, in the sense of losing what, from their perspective, were previously existing moral encumbrances upon their title to their grain. There would, however, seem no special reason for the compensation of other people who have the freedom and capacity to make their own way in the new circumstances that have come about. If, for some reason, the people in question were directly prevented by the changes from doing what they had done before (e.g. as might be the case in some sorts of non-consensual enclosure of common land), or if, culturally, they were left unequipped for life in a market-based society, there would seem a strong case for compensation, by way of an entitlement to training in respect of the human capital that would enable them to gain from the changes that had been forced upon them; something that could well be seen as a charge upon *all* those who benefit from the change. It is not so clear, however, that there is any special ground for compensation that extends beyond the generations who are immediately affected by the change.

Of course, the transition to such a form of social organization may have other distributional consequences. Particular skills and attributes may come to acquire a value that they never had before. The gangly seven-foot giant changes from a curiosity to a potential millionaire, as a consequence of the development of professional basketball, while the strength and practical capacity that might have enabled someone to make a good living as a village blacksmith may become of little use at all. Similarly, acquired human capital – say, the skills of an able handloom weaver – may suddenly become useless, while the skills of a mathematician or a logician which might previously have appeared the paradigm of useless knowledge may, with developments within computing, suddenly acquire a considerable commercial value.

Within such a society, with whom one has commercial relations is largely voluntaristic. (Clearly, most of us have to earn a living; but from whom we seek employment, and who grants it to us, is a matter that involves a fair measure of voluntary decision.) But this in itself suggests that we have no entitlement to a specific reward in respect of our services; and that, special relationships aside, no one else has a claim upon them. The very fact that our commercial relations may involve us in cooperation with people remote from us means that there is no reason why those in relative propinquity to us, but with whom we do not have special relationships, should acquire any distinctive claim upon us or our products. While the fact that such relationships are voluntary means that there can be no question of their bringing with them uncontracted moral appendages. (Indeed, it is important for those who are relatively vulnerable that they do not. For if, say, the mere fact of having had contractual relations with someone in this situation brought with it uncontracted moral obligations should they fall into unfortunate circumstances, prudence would lead people only to deal with those who did not impose such risks. As a result, the relatively disadvantaged would lose out on those very contractual relationships by means of which they might otherwise hope to improve their situation.) At the same time, moral obligations *may* grow, out of relationships that develop between such parties, over time.[38] (In addition, some such relationships may be of a quasi-cooperative character such that both parties willingly incur limited uncontracted obligations to one another, to their mutual advantage.)[39] Individual, or in some cases family-based, returns to people's labour and capital are, in effect, a prerequisite for the functioning of such societies. But no one has an entitlement to any specific level of return, or to the uncontracted benefits of anyone else's activity.

At the same time, people within such societies may be vulnerable, in ways in which they may not have been before. While, now, a local crop failure is no big deal (other than to the farmer), an entire way of life, and a level of income to which one had become accustomed, may become subject to radical change in ways which one cannot anticipate and which do not have any ready intelligibility, because of innovations or changes of taste on the part of people with whom one has no personal contact. This, however, is a practical problem, which those living in such societies need themselves to address through the creation of appropriate institutions, and in relation to which I offer some (very) modest suggestions, in the final chapter of this volume.

But what, it might be said, of those who lose out from the transition to a market-based form of social organization, because they are ill-equipped to function within it at all? In my view, two questions must be posed here. First, were they genuinely better off under earlier arrangements? One must, here, be realistic. But if there were people who could make a modest living out of low-grade agricultural work but not out of, say, shelf-filling in a supermarket, there might indeed be a case for assisting them so that they were no worse off, by means of a small levy on all commercial activity. If their position was not worse, there would seem no case for an entitlement to compensation. But if their situation is nevertheless markedly worse than that of other people around them, they might seem a worthy object of charitable activity; say, in the form of the provision of cultural facilities or sheltered housing. However, in view of the possibilities for mobility within such a society, and the fact that many forces within such a society may serve to weaken links of kinship or other forms of identity which many people feel to be valuable, there might be a case for linking their obligation to provide such assistance to those with whom the donors feel some tie in respect of shared identity, original location, or whatever. (This would, typically, not be a matter just of having the factor in question as part of one's identity, but of having chosen to make it something of importance to one's self.) That this should not be understood as a general moral charge upon those in the locality in question is vital, in view of the importance of the freedom for people to move from place to place. For if the arrival of relatively poor people into a community in itself set up a moral charge upon the people already resident there, one could, surely, expect them to resent it, and even to act, politically, so as to discourage such mobility.

I have already referred briefly to those who lose what, in effect, were special benefits that they enjoyed prior to the transition, e.g. of buying grain at locally customary prices; something that was not available to others. As I have already suggested, they should in my view be able to claim personal compensation if they are elderly or otherwise disadvantaged in ways that do not allow them the chance to gain from the new opportunities that are opened up. But they may well claim more than personal compensation: they may ask for compensation for their descendants, too. It would seem to me that any claim that they might make on this score is trumped by the broadly utilitarian consequences to be expected from the transition. There seems no moral reason why other people should recognize their dependants as having any special claim (not least, because it was to the products of other people's labour), and certainly not something that should impede the possibility for a full transition to an extended, market-based society. Within such a society, the responsibility for the well-being of those dependants falls – not unreasonably – upon those who generate them.

All this, however, leaves us with two further issues to consider relating to our obligations towards others in such societies; first, what can be achieved within them and, second, what, out of what can be achieved, have we an obligation to achieve? We will look at the first of these issues by way, initially, of a consideration of Hayek on the theme of social justice.

SOCIAL JUSTICE IN A GREAT SOCIETY?

Extended, market-based social orders have some distinctive characteristics, the full implications of which have not, in my view, been appreciated sufficiently by political philosophers. Hayek has stressed the idea of the division of knowledge and the coordinative function of prices within such societies. In societies characterized by such arrangements, many of the things that matter to the individuals within such societies, while the products, will not be the *direct* products, of the activities of themselves and of other citizens. Within a family, say, distributional issues *can* be relatively unproblematic: they may simply consist of the giving of items to one person by another, or the setting up of relatively simple action rules which will lead to effects which the people concerned wish to bring about. In an extended, market-based society, however, things are more complicated.

Consider, first, Hayek's account of the individual decision-maker in such an economy. He will have a variety of preferences, which he will manifest in various choices. However, he will also have preferences for things which, while the products of his actions – and those of others, in similar circumstances – he cannot easily relate to the actions that he will be taking. My concern here is not with problems of collective action in the usual sense, so much as with informational problems that face him and other citizens.[40] He and other citizens may wish to act such that the products of their actions have certain ecologically pleasing consequences; their problem may be that they have no idea what to do in order to bring them about.

Accordingly, even if various laws are passed with the aim of bringing about such consequences, people encountering these laws in the situations in which they actually act will react to them with the concerns and the knowledge that they have in those circumstances. As a result, it may well be the case that the initial aims of the legislation are not realized, and further, that one discovers that if there is individual freedom of action, there is no way in which they can be realized, at least in the form in which they were originally mooted.

Hayek's analysis – and the discussion above – is very much an economist's-eye view of the problems. In particular, it pictures its agents as rational economic men. But on the face of it, this is a useful account of us only in respect of a limited range of our activities. More typically, we act in particular organizational and institutional settings, within which, both what we have to do, and the kinds of ways in which we do it, are somewhat circumscribed. I do *not* want to claim that, in such settings, we are usefully described as rule-following, or acting on the basis of common meanings, not least because of the way in which there may be important differences between the ways in which institutions actually work, and the kinds of accounts that people customarily give of how they are supposed to work. But patterns of activity, and ranges of ways of going about it, are clearly given to us by the various different institutions in which we are involved. Our institutions, and how they operate, are not fixed. But clearly, at any one time there are limits to the extent to which changes are possible, given the place from which we start. And changes, themselves, are limited to what is possible – and, indeed, reasonable – for those who are already *in situ*.

The informational problems affecting isolated economic actors, however, also hold in respect of people acting in various organizational settings. Their behaviour also gives rise to various emergent products, concerning the character of which they – and other members of the societies in which they live, or upon which their actions impinge – will doubtless have their preferences. My argument is that the transition to a society like our own, of which such relationships are characteristic, imposes important constraints over what can be accomplished within it, and that this pertains to exactly the issues with which we are concerned in the present volume. The discussion of issues such as freedom, individual well-being, the rule of law, all pertains to objects which, in fact, would depend for their realization upon such disaggregated human action.

One way of looking at my suggestion would thus be that we can see all kinds of institutional practices, and the kind of conduct that people can undertake within them, as consisting of a variety of *Sittlichkeiten* which, together, produce as emergent products the kinds of things with which we are concerned. This, in turn, suggests a twofold strategy.[41] At the one level, it is appropriate for us to be engaged in the critical discussion of social ideals, after the fashion of normative political theory for, *pace* the image of agents offered by public choice theory, these are things about which we care and which we can discuss. At another, there needs to be discussion of what would be required for their realization. This is more complex than it might at first seem. For the realization of the ideals in question will typically involve not all the members of a society acting on the basis of a single action-rule, but a complex interaction of institutional practices, forms of accountability and actions undertaken by individuals with a variety of individual aims and concerns, where none of this typically relates *directly* to the achievement of the ideal in question. In so far as we focus upon the large-scale ideal, two issues arise: on the one side, what would be required to realize it, and, when we have understood this, whether the costs in question are acceptable. On the other – and this will be a particular concern of the final chapter of this volume – there is the problem of how we can create *Sittlichkeiten*,[42] which will produce the outcomes which we cherish, as an indirect consequence of the actions which we undertake within them.

We may, however, also focus upon our present conduct and institutional procedures, and their feasible transformations. And at this level, the ideas with which we are here concerned may have an important cutting edge, in so far as they may suggest that the espousal of a large-scale ideal is empty, in the sense that, when it is examined at *this* level, no one would have good reason for performing the actions which would be required to implement it.

My suggestion – for which I will argue later – is that this is, indeed, the case with regard to the wider conceptions of welfare entitlements which, as I have suggested, are in some ways compatible with Hayek's overall approach and which might also be suggested by considering the historical transition with which I have been here concerned. I would like to start, however, by offering an interpretation of Hayek's own critique of the idea of social justice, on the basis of which I will then suggest a response to some of Hayek's critics.

HAYEK'S CRITIQUE OF SOCIAL JUSTICE

Hayek's critique of social justice should, in my view, be understood as 'institutional' in character, in the sense of being grounded in the specific ideas about the institutional requirements of a liberal market order as a social system which we examined earlier. Hayek is to be understood as arguing that the realization of the ideal of social justice is not compossible with a liberal market order. Now by contrast with this, Hayek might well be understood as making a conceptual or linguistic point: as arguing that the idea of social justice is meaningless. Indeed, he has written that '[Social justice] does not belong to the category of error but to that of nonsense, like the term "a moral stone" '.[43] But to take such statements as constituting the heart of Hayek's view is misleading. Such formulations should, rather, be understood as a shorthand for ideas which are better explained elsewhere. For Hayek's point is not linguistic, but based on his ideas about human well-being and his theories about the institutions required for its effective promotion. This may be illustrated if we start from another passage in the same work[44] from which our earlier quotation was taken:

> The basic contention of this chapter [is] that in a society of free men whose members are allowed to use their own knowledge for their own purposes the term 'social justice' is wholly devoid of meaning or content.

What Hayek is getting at in this passage is easy enough to understand, given our earlier discussion of his views. Hayek believes that, to a considerable degree, we are living in an extended market order. Such a form of social organization allows for the use of socially divided knowledge and also accords to the individual freedom in the choice of occupation and as to what ends he or she should pursue. Hayek writes, for example, of '[individuals acting] on the basis of their own knowledge and in the service of their own ends, which is the essence of freedom'.[45]

Such a society, for Hayek, is to be valued on various grounds. It is esteemed by Hayek because it produces benefits which might be called utilitarian in character: it allows for the better coordination and satisfaction of individuals' preferences. It also accords an increased possibility of such satisfaction to an individual chosen at random in such a society, and Hayek therefore suggests that such a society might be chosen as a good society by people who did not know what place in such a society they would occupy. Related to this last point, there is the idea that such a form of social order is to be valued because it exemplifies the moral ideal that the law should give equal treatment to each citizen. Hayek thus thinks that it satisfies the kinds of demand concerning the character of law laid down by Rousseau and by Kant; demands which Hayek sometimes links to Stoicism and to the Christian tradition.

In such a society, people are in general rewarded on the basis of the social utility of their actions, at least in so far as this is captured by effective demand and its transformations within markets. Hayek argues that this is a *necessary* feature of a society in which the knowledge possessed by individual citizens is to be utilized, and in which such citizens are to be free to choose their occupations. But such rewards will correspond neither to our ideas of the reward of virtue, nor even of the reward of merit. Here, Hayek takes issue with certain widespread justifications of the distributive pattern of a market order. He suggests that had such a distributional pattern been brought about as the result of anyone's intentional activity, it would be condemned as unjust. However, Hayek claims, such a distributional pattern is in fact the unintended consequence of the actions of many different individuals, and it is inappropriate to speak of justice or injustice in such cases: it is closer in its character to a natural occurrence, such as an earthquake or a fine summer's day.

However, Raymond Plant has argued that

> even if we accept the bulk of what Hayek says about the fundamental nature of market transactions between individuals, it does not follow that his conclusions are valid. The egalitarian response to the so-called naturalistic outcomes of the market is not to concentrate on how they were *caused* but on how we *respond* to them. The weather may be a naturalistic phenomenon but we make collective efforts to avoid its ravages. Handicap may not be the result of deliberate action but injustice and justice come into the picture when we consider the *response of society* to these misfortunes.[46]

Plant's argument here is to the point. But it is not as damaging to Hayek as it might seem, as there are two fairly simple, and complementary, 'Hayekian' responses. (I set them out in what immediately follows, although I should mention that I will later be developing a third, but more speculative, Hayekian argument, which – if it is correct – in some respects calls into question not only Plant's challenge, but also these 'Hayekian' responses.)

The first response is that Hayek does not do justice to his own case against social justice. Further, he generates confusion by quite needlessly attempting to 'demoralize' the whole issue. Instead, a response could be made to Plant, along the following lines. The distributional consequences of a market-based society are, indeed, morally unlovely. But they are a necessary concomitant of a form of social organization which both generates wealth and which allows for the minimization of coercion; and these considerations are more important, morally, than are issues of social equality. If one makes such a (moral) choice for a market-based society, then one has chosen a form of social organization within which distribution will not fit any particular moral pattern. Further, one cannot make it fit any such pattern in ways that are compatible with the organizational basis of such a society. Accordingly, to call for the realization of social justice *within* such a society is to call for the social equivalent of a square circle. To demand social justice in the sense of a society ordered such that people receive what they merit, is to call for a small, face-to-face society, which in itself is less morally attractive than a market-based society (because it is both poor and does not allow for much individual freedom). To demand it in a situation where we have, in existence, a massive population of a kind that can only be supported by market-based forms of social organization, is wicked.

This first argument is in fact close to what Hont and Ignatieff suggest should be understood as Adam Smith's response to the 'civic humanists' of his day: a link that is particularly illuminating:

> Modern commercial society was unequal and unvirtuous but it was not unjust. It did not purchase civic virtue at the price of misery for its poorest members. However unequal men might be, in property and citizenship, they could be equal in access to the means to satisfy basic need. In this set of preferences, it is clear that Smith was choosing strict justice over civic virtue, passive liberty over active.[47]

It is important to note that Hayek's argument is couched in terms of markets (and their associated institutions) and is directed against the idea that social justice can be realized by such means. This makes it important to note, at once, Hayek's second argument.

The second argument is that Hayek himself explicitly favours a *non-market* welfare safety net. For example, he has written:

> There is no reason why in a free society government should not assure to all protection against severe deprivation in the form of an assured minimum income, or a floor below which nobody need to descend. To enter into such an insurance against extreme misfortune may well be in the interest of all; or it may be felt to be a clear moral duty of all to assist, within the organized community, those who cannot help themselves. So long as such a uniform minimum income is provided outside the market to all those who, for any reason, are unable to earn in the market an adequate maintenance, this need not lead to a restriction of freedom, or conflict with the Rule of Law.[48]

And earlier, in *The Constitution of Liberty*, he had written:

> All modern governments have made provision for the indigent, unfortunate, and disabled and have concerned themselves with questions of health and the dissemination of knowledge. There is no reason why the volume of these pure service activities should not increase with the general growth of wealth. There are common ends that can be satisfied only by collective action and which can be thus provided for without restricting individual liberty. It can hardly be denied that, as we grow richer, that minimum of sustenance which the community has always provided for those not able to look after themselves, and which can be provided outside the market, will gradually rise, or that government may, usefully and without doing any harm, assist or even lead in such endeavours.[49]

This complements the first Hayekian response to Plant, by suggesting that where the operations of a market-based society leave people in circumstances of extreme misfortune, then it is appropriate that they be assisted, but by extra-market means. Three points are worth noting about all this. First, that it does not involve a reversal of the first argument: it still rests upon the idea that the case for markets and their associated institutions is morally pressing, but also has some morally unfortunate consequences, which may be palliated but not removed if such a society is to deliver the (moral) goods. Second, Hayek is not suggesting that they can be palliated via market mechanisms, or arguing that market mechanisms should be changed. Rather, he argues that these problems should be palliated by non-market means: that the institutions of a market-based society are not themselves to be altered. (Hayek, notably in *The Constitution of Liberty*, seems to set high hopes on the idea that by placing emphasis upon what is permissible by way of the form rather than the content of government action, the role of government in all this can be rendered innocuous, something, however, which the problems of his formalism may give us reason to doubt.)[50] Third, Hayek might seem to be on strong ground in placing emphasis upon the relief of 'extreme misfortune'. This can be identified fairly easily. And – as indicated by the second quotation, above – as wealth grows, its relief might seem fairly unproblematic; it also accords with ideas about residual entitlements from older natural law or moral economy obligations, which we have discussed above. In addition, as Hayek grants this point, those who would argue against him from the side of more extensive welfare entitlements are left with a case that is slightly more difficult to argue. As even a recent and highly unsympathetic critic of conservatism and market liberalism has concluded, the case for the moral importance of equality as such is problematic.[51] While the problem about the moral inflation of citizenship rights so as to include more extensive welfare rights – to consider another popular attempt to address this issue – is surely that there are no good moral grounds for discriminating, in the way that that would involve, between the moral entitlements of citizens and non-citizens.[52]

What reasons does Hayek offer for believing that there are incompatibilities between the operation of a market-based social order and the achievement of social justice?

Within such a social order, distributional issues are (for the most part) not a matter of deliberate intentional activity. Rather, they are – on Hayek's argument – the result of rewards that people happen to receive, as a result of what their goods or services are able to command in the particular situation in which they are offered, and where these rewards are the products of disaggregated decision-taking on the part of economic agents throughout the entire economy. Further, while what distributional patterns eventuate are not the direct intentional products of human activity, this does not mean that distributional consequences are underdetermined by human action, such that some distributional pattern can be imposed upon economic activity, without otherwise affecting it. From Hayek's perspective, the material upon which any such ordering would have to take place is already structured by free, purposeful and *functional* human activity, conducted under the rule of law. In addition, given the character and complexity of the processes which lead to such distributional consequences, it is not clear that, even if all the actors in some economy wished to bring about some particular distributional pattern as a result of their activities in the market-place, it would be possible for them to discover what each of them would have to do, in order to accomplish this result as the product of their market-based activity.[53]

Hayek has argued that in a large, market-based economy, we simply do not have – and cannot have – access to the kind of information that would be needed to reward people on the basis of merit.

Now one reasonable reaction to all this, on the part of a proponent of social justice, might be to argue that their ideals should be recast, and pursued through the actions of the state within the general guidelines of a market economy. Thus, while they might agree that Hayek's arguments are telling – on the grounds both of freedom and of economic well-being – against those who would pursue some goal of social justice by replacing a market-based economy by a centrally directed economy, or by trying, somehow, to manipulate market signals, they would argue that other alternatives are open to them. If market mechanisms are to remain, and if coercion (in anything like the sense with which Hayek was concerned) is to be limited, some outcomes will no longer be available to them. For example, the pursuit of strict economic equality would be recognized not to be an option (just because it would swiftly disappear, as a result of market-based transactions). But it would, surely, be open to government to pursue a policy which limits economic disadvantage, by giving a (reasonably high) level of cash benefits to those who are disadvantaged. In addition, they might argue that while economic transactions within markets generate inequality, current distributions of property are typically inherited from pre-market societies, and that continuing and substantial advantages accrue to people who have received these advantages, typically because their ancestors engaged in all kinds of predatory activities of which classical liberals would surely not approve.

A Hayekian response to this is possible, but it would seem to me not all that powerful. Consider the meeting of the basic needs of the disadvantaged through the activities of government. Hayek – in his views on a welfare safety net – is himself already in the same ball-game. By proposing that it should take place, he is granting that such activity is possible, and – although it is based on coercive taxation – morally legitimate. The only real argument between Hayek and his critics would seem to be as to the level at which it should take place. In this connection, three broad kinds of considerations could be raised.

First, there is the question of what is possible. There are clear limits to what can be accomplished by any single, reasonably liberal, government: beyond a certain level of taxation, capital, income and potentially highly taxed citizens will decamp elsewhere. This is, clearly, a factor of growing importance with the development of a more fully international economy. In so far as goods are, increasingly, produced with different components manufactured in different countries, the freedom of action of government would seem to be placed under ever-increasing restrictions.

Second, there is the question of the cost of such measures and how this should be evaluated. There are clearly arguments – from considerations about eating seed corn (more prosaically, the risk of shifting capital resources into consumption), the effects of high taxation on incentives upon efficiency, and the effects of, say, an extensive and officious taxation regime – which would suggest that there may be efficiency and liberty costs to the institution of such a regime. The problem, however, is to determine what they are, and – second – how they should be evaluated. However, it is not clear how easily such issues could be addressed from Hayek's own perspective. Given that his argument is not made on the basis of an appeal to rights, it is difficult to tell what he is suggesting should be the basis of – or the limits to – other people's entitlements. As to consequentialist argument, in so far as one is dealing with redistribution, one is concerned with issues concerning which Paretian considerations are useless. Hayek, however, faces special difficulties, because of his doubts about the interpersonal comparison of utility. It is also not clear that his substantive ideas allow us to say much about the – crucial – trade-offs that would be involved. And his methodological writings suggest that the kinds of quantitative evaluation that would here be crucial cannot, in fact, be undertaken. As I will argue at some length in the next chapter, to make an argument for Hayek's views here, would seem to me to require some revision to his ideas about welfare.

A third argument – which has more to it – relates to issues of distribution; to this I will turn in the next section. Before doing so, I will address, briefly, the other argument to which I alluded above, about the distributional effects of pre-market predation, i.e. the problem of the monarchy (if one has one), of aristocracy and of others who are still benefiting from the consequences of their ancestors' successful predation. The appropriate response, here, within a developed market economy, is presumably a Humean one: that such entitlements are, by now, so tangled up with others that were come by honestly, that there is no easy way in which they could be disentangled. Further, the benefits of stability in a system of property rights in such a society would arguably outweigh any gains that individual citizens might hope to enjoy from such an exercise. But again, such an argument would seem not to have much bite unless it could be offered in quantitative form.

REDISTRIBUTION WITHIN A MARKET ECONOMY

I have referred, above, to the issue of distribution, and to that I will now turn. In fact, two different issues arise here. The first concerns what in fact can be redistributed within a market economy; the second, how the burdens of any such measures will be distributed, and their equity. In both cases, we are involved in moving from the aggregative approach that we have taken so far, to the disaggregated processes and moral judgements that would underlie the realization of this aggregated goal.

The first point again raises issues which I discussed earlier in this chapter; namely, that it is insufficient to discuss normative concerns without considering also how the ideas which one is discussing could be put into effect. To pose this question immediately raises the point that it is one thing to take the view that it would be desirable if the disadvantaged were, say, to acquire additional resources; it is another to claim that this can actually be achieved within a market-based economy in which people enjoy a fair measure of negative freedom. Yet the fact that we are dealing with a market economy in which individuals enjoy a fair degree of freedom from coercion would seem to have important consequences as to what can be achieved, distributionally. Much could be said on this issue, but I will restrict myself here to three general points.

First, as I have suggested earlier, we must think about these issues not in terms of pious collective resolutions, but of what can actually be accomplished. Here, Hayek's picture of disaggregated social action may I believe usefully be supplemented by ideas drawn from the study of public policy. We need to note the extent to which the actual agenda of public policy is set not, as it were, by what citizens judge to be most morally pressing, but by a complex process of negotiation and trade-offs between individuals and groups with agendas and interests of their own. Indeed, the experience of reading work on the policy-making process might well lead one to consider that there was something to be said for Enlightened Despots, after all![54] Once decisions are made, one then faces problems of implementation. From this – fascinating – field, two issues are of particular note. The first emerged from Pressman and Wildavski's classic study *Implementation*, and relates to the way in which the achievement of some outcome will, typically, depend on the agreement and cooperation of many people for whom its achievement is not – to say the least – their most pressing priority. As a result, what can be achieved will, typically, be the product of deals and negotiations rather than simply the putting into practice of some measure that, say, has been agreed upon by Parliament or Congress. As in Pressman and Wildavski's account, this effect is heightened in so far as what is required is cooperation among different agencies. The same thing is also true, to a lesser extent, within individual agencies and organizations, too: in order to accomplish their various tasks in an effective manner, people must be given a degree of autonomy. This, however, means that their interrelations then become a matter of negotiation, rather than of the simple giving of orders.

This brings us to our second theme: to what Melvin Lipsky has discussed as 'street-level bureaucracy'. Lipsky urged that those interested in the analysis of public policy should pay special attention to the activities of 'street-level' bureaucrats; those who, as it were, provide the interface between a bureaucratic organization and those independent agents with whom it is dealing. As Lipsky wrote:

> The decisions of street-level bureaucrats, the routines they establish, and the devices they invent to cope with uncertainties and work-pressures, effectively *become* the social policies they carry out.[55]

Lipsky's point seems to me to be of the greatest importance when we consider our ability to implement normative ideals upon which we have agreed, collectively. It is one thing to lay down rules which relate to such goals. It is quite another for these to be things on the basis of which people within the bureaucratic structure can actually operate, in the accomplishment of their tasks. What it is open to us actually to achieve will be the products of Lipsky's 'routines and devices', and their possible transformations.

Of course, there are certain exceptions to all this. On the one side, there are those situations in which some outcome can be laid down in some simple form, akin, say, to that of profitability in a commercial enterprise. But there is a danger that when this happens, e.g. in terms of fines levied by traffic police or underpaid tax recovered by tax officials, what actually goes on as they successfully meet these targets may be morally unlovely. On the other side, there are those organizations which run along militaristic lines. It is striking that the US armed forces, for example, seem to have been able to change social attitudes within their ranks with regard to race, in ways that have attracted the envy of those concerned for the welfare of other groups.[56] Much the same picture emerges from Herbert Kaufman's classic study of *The Forest Ranger*,[57] which offers a picture of control being imposed over what would otherwise seem a situation ripe for disintegration and corruption, by means of a militaristic-like form of organization and conditions of service. Such examples, however, surely indicate the limits to this kind of model as a general pattern of social organization. Not only would we not tolerate militaristic organization in much of our social life, but also such forms of organization surely have massive disadvantages, too: while the military may be highly effective in the accomplishment of certain tasks, they are hardly a byword for either flexibility or efficiency.

In the light of all this, when considering what can be accomplished we must typically think of people engaged in specific routines and interactions with others, acting on the basis of habits and rules of thumb that enable them to accomplish the tasks with which they are concerned. Further, we must consider them as behaving in ways that seem reasonable to them in those settings, both with respect to particular actions that they might take, and also in respect of changes that might be made to those arrangements. What can be achieved must then be seen in terms of what can be built up from such activities and what, realistically, could be their modifications.

What is especially important in such a context is to bear in mind that measures that may be introduced by government or by those running an organization with the aim of accomplishing some overall goal – such as redistribution – will be experienced by citizens or members of a large organization simply as regulations that impinge upon their activities. They may well not see what such regulations are intended to accomplish, or experience them as morally telling; not least as the overall moral goal they are designed to achieve is remote from the actions upon which they are actually taking, and the concerns – moral or otherwise – that are central to their activity as they are acting. Rather, they will typically be experienced as constraints under which they will have to operate or – for my purposes, more important – as obstructions around which they will have to steer, in accomplishing what needs to be done (consider, here, compliance with such matters as health and safety regulations). Of course, it is possible to deal with some of these problems by means of monitoring. But this is costly, and there are well-known problems about this, especially relating to the ways in which those engaged in such monitoring are dependent upon information and cooperation from those whose activities they monitor.

Such an approach is suggestive as a way of approaching the material discussed in Robert Goodin and Julian Le Grand's collection, *Not Only the Poor*.[58] This volume considers, on a comparative basis, ways in which the middle classes have benefited from the operation of the Welfare State. Its broad conclusion is that the middle classes will typically give (essential) political support to those programmes from which they also benefit, and that from such programmes they will typically do rather well, not least because they are likely to have more in common with professional providers, and greater skills at handling bureaucratic procedures, such that they can pursue their concerns relatively effectively. It is striking, however, that in their concluding remarks,[59] Goodin and Le Grand suggest that

> from the redistributivist point of view, [the benefits gained by the middle classes] would be a price that would indeed be worth paying just so long as the tax-transfer system on balance shifts resources from the non-poor to the poor.

But this leads me to my next point. Goodin and Le Grand end their quoted statement by expressing a pious hope about the possible operations of the tax system; something that, again, would stand in need of the kind of 'disaggregative' analysis which I have recommended above. A plausible hypothesis here[60] would seem to be that there are significant limitations as to the kinds of transfers that can be made, within an extended market-based economy. What I have in mind is that the wealthy will have access to specialized advice that is likely to help them round almost any legislation (given that this must pertain to the circumstances of an international market economy). In addition, there will be differential opportunities for people to escape taxation on consumption. Thus, a senior figure in an organization, public or private, will be involved in numerous decisions concerning expenditure which will affect his or her well-being, or more generally his or her preferences concerning issues not related essentially to the business or administrative decision at hand, and it will be very difficult to distinguish between consumption and legitimate business expenditure. It must, similarly, be very difficult to distinguish between consumption and legitimate business expenses in the case of the non-labour-only self-employed. Even the employed in relatively lowly white-collar positions will, typically, have personal access to telephones, computers, fax machines, photocopiers and, increasingly, electronic mail; while those in some blue-collar positions may have access, out of working hours, to valuable equipment, all of which may be significant, even if a charge is imposed for personal use. By way of contrast, the lowest-level governmental or private employee may enjoy almost no benefits other than their actual income, and may thus bear the brunt of taxation in ways that differ significantly from other members of the community.

If there is anything in these points, it certainly does not mean that government cannot decide that some section of the community should enjoy benefits of some particular kind. It does, however, suggest that who in fact benefits, and who on balance pays for it, may be something that, within a market economy in which there is also a fair degree of individual freedom, it is difficult to control. What we are dealing with must be understood not at the level of what is set out by a legislature or by those at the top of an organization who make up rules that others are supposed to follow, but by an examination of what is actually produced, of the practices of the street-level operatives who actually produce it, and by a realistic appraisal of what else they might do in the face of regulation or incentives.

Further, these considerations raise problems about the equity of the transfers that are involved. Three broad issues arise here, upon which I can clearly touch only very briefly, as they would easily merit books in their own right. First, what do we owe to other people, and how do such obligations relate to the nation state? Second, given that who actually benefits from welfare provisions – and who pays for them – are to be understood not just in terms of legislative fiat, but as the complex results of social processes, how does this affect the individual's obligations? Third, should not our approach – as indicated above – be, also at the individual level, not to focus upon pious expressions of moral generosity, but on what is appropriate to people's day-to-day lives in the social situations in which they are living? Let me take these points in turn.

The idea of the nation state as a focus for positive moral entitlements (even to the degree to which this is accepted by Hayek) is really rather strange. On the face of it, there seems no special reason why shared nationality should bring with it any form of mutual obligation of this kind. The fact, say, that I am English seems to me to bring with it no more moral obligation towards, say, someone with whom I have had no personal contact or shared affiliation in South Yorkshire, than it does with, say, someone in Austria, and much less than I have towards people living in places – anywhere on the face of the earth – with which I *have* some measure of personal contact. One can look at the nation state as a vehicle through which various coordination rules, public goods and various forms of mutual insurance have been provided. It is also the case that any of these are likely to involve a measure of redistribution. Some will benefit more than others even from the provision of coordination rules of a particular degree of specificity, to say nothing of gestures towards their uniform enforcement. But given the advantages of uniformity within a geographical area, and economies of scale, such redistribution might seem unproblematic, and to be no more significant than, say, such redistribution as takes place through the sale of some commodity, such as a glass of beer, in a standard size. In respect of provision by means of the state, however, I would suggest that this is not the case, just in so far as the decision-making processes there are such as to lead to forced redistribution, within a geographical area, which may be neither innocuous nor have a distinctive moral basis.

This, I would suggest, is enhanced by my second point: that what state-run entitlement programmes amount to is – as we usually decide upon them – something like buying a pig in a poke. We do not, as the decision is put before us (to the extent to which this can be said to occur at all), know what it is to which we are committed, other than that investigations like those of Goodin and Le Grand may confirm our suspicions that at least some of what is extracted from us may well be ending up in the hands of people to whom we may believe that we have no moral obligation whatever. This is not, emphatically, to suggest that we should be understood as self-interested, and as not having obligations towards others. Rather, it is a suggestion that the combination of the actual effects of the taxation system and the welfare state is a mighty odd realization of what those obligations are.

But how, then, should those obligations be understood? I would suggest that these should be looked at in terms of our actual situations, routines and practices (and their possible transformations) and the outcomes emergent from them. Whether or not some obligation is reasonable, is a matter of whether it is reasonable that a person should act in such a way as to discharge this obligation, given the situation in which they are acting. This is not to suggest that moral concerns do not have a degree of autonomy from our day-to-day activities. Rather, they have to be sustained through our interactions with others in such settings, and the degree to which they can be acted on will itself be strongly affected by our setting, and the routines that they impose upon us.

Of course, we clearly have moral concerns that go beyond those things with which we are involved in our day-to-day activities. But how such concerns are to be realized is more problematic than it might at first appear. For what is required is an account of how the outcome is to be constituted from actions which it is reasonable for us to discharge: something that must take into account both the character of our obligation, and also the (often complex) social construction of the result. In such settings, it may well turn out that there is nothing that can be done in respect of what may seem very worthy causes (in the

148

sense that what it seems compelling to do cannot, in fact, be done, while what can be brought about are results that, once we realize what they are, we feel no obligation to bring about). But it is exactly these connections that are broken in a structure like the welfare state, which uncouples entitlements from their correlative obligations.

Let me offer a brief characterization of the view to which all of this leads (these are ideas which, for reasons of space, I can here only state, rather than provide argument; a task to which I will return on another occasion). On the account that I am offering here, we have various obligations, of both an uncontracted and a contractual or quasi-contractual character, and both in respect of things which are our responsibility because we played an important role in bringing them about, and in respect of things which we did not bring about. The latter sort of obligation is generated by our coming across things which generate *prima facie* obligations: it is a matter simply of our recognizing certain things as being morally compelling.[61] These include, most obviously, the Good Samaritan's experience of coming across someone who needs his assistance. However, with regard to such cases, it is important that we distinguish between three things.

First, there are those cases in which we have an obligation to help, either by way of an individual or cooperative action, or in respect of trying to effect those changes to our institutional practices which will bring about the results in question. Such cases seem to me those in which there is either an element of personal connection or of propinquity, i.e. that we are involved here in what are, essentially, special duties;[62] or those in which we have had a personal role in bringing about the state of affairs in question; or those in which, while none of the former connections hold, what is asked of us is relatively trivial in relation to the issue at hand.

Second, there are cases which are like the first part of the former – in which there is an element of personal connection or propinquity – but in respect of which any claim that the person may have had upon us can be defeated. For example: one has no obligation towards relatives who have behaved in ways that are unacceptable; or to fulfil social roles the distribution of advantages to disadvantages within which is inequitable. Contributory negligence does, in my view, diminish the extent to which it is reasonable that we can be considered to be obliged towards people who get themselves into silly situations. *Pace* Goodin, the existence of vulnerability as a social fact does not carry any telling moral weight, unless the idea that we should have responsibility is itself morally reasonable, i.e. that we are not dealing with something that the party who becomes dependent should themselves have taken care of (although I would not wish to exclude someone's choosing to take responsibility even in such a case). Consider, say, a situation in which someone was enslaved, and where it turns out that the person who did the enslaving in the end becomes vulnerable to his victim. In such circumstances, I would argue that the slave has no obligation to continue his ministrations when he could

149

escape, and indeed that while it might appear as if he was behaving morally if he did continue them, none the less, the better course of action would be to dispatch the enslaver swiftly, and to then go about living fruitfully what was left of his life. Matters, however, typically do not have this nice simplicity to them; and what is more usual is that some people come (relatively) innocently to depend on things which are the products of the exploitation of others.

Here, however, there would seem to me to be every reason to take freedom as our default position. If this were the case, people would need to scrutinize the arrangements upon which they were expecting to depend, and to make alternative arrangements if what they were proposing would depend upon the servitude – moral or otherwise – of others. Transitional cases – those depending on arrangements made prior to such a change in social attitudes becoming widely accepted – or various forms of accidentally generated dependence for which there was no insurance provision, would seem a proper burden for the charitable activity of those with whom the people in question had some broad special relationship, rather than a burden that should fall upon the specific individuals to whom the people in question happened to be closely related. Such ideas would, of course, have important implications for domestic division of labour; but this is not a theme that I can pursue here.

There are also issues posed by the overall character of the political, economic and social orders under which we live. These are important in themselves and – as I have suggested in this chapter – for what it is open to us to achieve within them. Over such things we may be able to exercise some choice, and about them, deliberations within a public forum may be of some importance. But the choices facing us may be significantly limited; not least by our own past history, by what kinds of traditions and institutions we have, and by what kind of people we are, in the sense of what all this has made of us. Radical change, however, is clearly possible. And – as I would suggest was, for example, the case with regard to the abolition of slavery in the United States – it may sometimes be the only way in which changes can take place which people might judge to be desirable, but find it difficult to initiate given the situations in which they are acting on a day by day basis. It is, indeed, with the pros and cons of such moves, and with the analysis of the implications of possible such choices, and of how we are limited within any one such system of institutions, that works such as this are concerned.

Within a liberal regime of the kind for which I am here arguing, it may, however, be possible to set up more specific regimes, geared to the production of particular forms of social order – a topic which I will discuss in the final chapter.

It is, however, to the ideas that I have developed in this chapter that I think that we may usefully have recourse, in answering the problem posed for Hayek by those who would pursue socialist values in a market-wise manner, such as Wieser and David Miller. For the response that is suggested is, first, that it is not clear that the kinds of outcomes that they favour can be achieved in a market-based society in which people enjoy a fair measure of (negative) freedom. While, second, there seems no good reason to suppose that, if they could be achieved, there are telling reasons why people should consider themselves morally obliged to others in the manner that these views presuppose. For, on the one side, there seems no reason why we should have any special obligation in respect to other citizens (and not to those who are not citizens). While if their proposals were genuinely universal in their scope, they would also seem to involve the idea that we have obligations to others to whom it is not clear that we have any obligation at all, other than to respect their persons and justly acquired property.

However, what is sauce for the goose is also sauce for the gander. We must, therefore, ask whether Hayek's views stand up to the kind of critical scrutiny which we have considered. In so far as Hayek's views involve a negative conception of liberty and, thus, respect for persons, they would seem to me to have a strong advantage, just in the sense that such views are easy enough to act upon, on a disaggregated basis. At the same time, it would seem to me that Hayek has not given us an adequate account as to why it is important that negative freedoms be respected. I will discuss this issue further in chapter six; but as my discussion there may suggest, this poses a more difficult problem than liberals, today, seem customarily to think.

Other aspects of Hayek's work are more problematic still. In so far as he is offering us a more specific account of a market-based economy and its associated institutions, Hayek's account is problematic just in the sense that he does not provide a satisfactory account of how it can rest upon disaggregated action. There are special problems here, posed by the way in which the institutions that Hayek favours possess undesirable yet ineliminable features, as we have discussed earlier in this volume. I offer a response to this problem in chapter seven.

A third problem relates to Hayek's ideas about a non-market safety net. Here, the development of an international market economy poses a particular problem for Hayek. For making of Hayek's concern a universal entitlement would seem inappropriate; not least because of the lack of connection between those who would be obliged, and those to whom they would have an obligation. In my view, the appropriate reaction is to treat our obligations as special obligations, albeit ones which depend upon a continuing bond, and reasonable behaviour on the part of those who wish to call upon such relationships for assistance. Of course, over and above this, we may hope that if, say, we suffer from the consequences of some natural disaster, or from bad institutions, or more generally that if we are in a situation of adversity that others might do something to alleviate, they would respond to us in a generous manner. But this would not seem to me something to which we would have a right.

5

POST-HAYEKIAN
POLITICAL ECONOMY

INTRODUCTION

In this chapter, I address a group of interrelated problems that arise in Hayek's work. My aim is critical and programmatic: I wish to identify what, in my view, would have to be done in order for Hayek's broad approach to be vindicated; to criticize ideas to be found in the work of Hayek – and elsewhere – which seem to me to stand in the way of doing what is needed, and then to offer some *highly* programmatic suggestions of my own. I can hardly myself aspire to solve the problems which I raise, least of all in the compass of the present volume. But I believe that it will make a positive contribution simply to identify the problems facing a Hayekian perspective, and to argue that the way those who favour such an approach typically approach them has been ill-conceived.

First, as I argued earlier, Hayek faces a problem concerning the basis upon which he is advancing claims for markets, when he starts to develop his interesting ideas about the significance of human ignorance and of the social division of knowledge. For the points to which he is drawing significance would not seem compatible with the kind of general equilibrium theorizing which formed the backdrop to his earlier work, and which would seem to be implicit in his arguments for the efficiency of markets. In so far as the dispute in which he was engaged was about the proposal that markets should be completely replaced by central planning, or about programmes for interventionism of a character that would lead government progressively towards full-scale central planning, this is, perhaps, no big deal. For *whatever* the imperfections of markets, they would seem better than this. But even here, there is a gap in Hayek's argument, concerning how one is to characterize the target towards which markets are able to approximate, and from which central planning falls short. Once, however, the concerns of a Wieser or a Plant are brought onto the scene – once one starts to consider, not proposals for the abolition of markets, but for the accomplishment of ethical goals *within* a market-based economic system – Hayek's approach faces three more serious problems.

First, Hayek offers various characterizations of what he thinks the kind of system that he favours will produce. However, both these and his various formulations of specific normative concerns do not appear to be equivalent. More troubling, it is never made fully clear how some of his more fundamental concerns relate to one another at all. In particular, just what are the relations between his concern for liberty (especially as related to his ideas about the rule of law), his concern for the realization of the plans of individuals taken at random in a society, and the concern for welfare and the relief of suffering from which he started?

Second, what does Hayek tell us about the ability of the kind of social arrangements that he favours to deliver the results that he favours? This issue becomes particularly pressing, once we consider the options – suggested by Wieser and Plant – of the state acting within, and in ways that do not disrupt utterly the workings of, a market economy, to address various value-related concerns. We are here involved in the appraisal of the pros and cons of various different institutional arrangements, and the merits of trade-offs between them.

Now, Hayek has things to say about these matters. As we have noted, Hayek himself allocates various functions to the state, including – in a country that is sufficiently affluent – the provision of a welfare safety net. But these activities have to be funded, and we have to consider the mechanisms through which they (and only they?) are to be provided. Hayek has developed arguments – after the fashion of public choice theory – which raise some problems concerning the operation of interest-group democracies. But as I noted earlier, Hayek does not, in any systematic way, link such theories to his own ideas about the maintenance of a market order which also has the forms of state provision which he himself favours – but only these.

Accordingly, we stand in need of a theory in terms of which we can address these issues. First, we need to be able to discuss what we can expect from the performance of different kinds of institutions: of how the adoption of them, and the kinds of actions which people can be expected to take within them, relate to the various things that we value. We also need to be able to treat of trade-offs between the possibilities of the achievement of different goals in different institutional settings. And we need, further, to treat institutions realistically, in the sense of taking a hard-headed view of how they will work, and of how people are likely to behave within them, rather than simply *assuming* that they can be depended upon to realize our various normative goals.

One special problem here is that while these are issues to which one needs to develop a response from Hayek's perspective, there are strands in Hayek's methodological writings which would seem to indicate that he thinks that we cannot address such issues. *If* Hayek is right, this would seem to me to lead to an awkward impasse – he would be a consequentialist who tells us that we cannot have knowledge of those consequences of our actions that we need to resolve certain crucial disputes. But I am not sure that things are quite as he would suggest, and it may also be possible here that forms of learning by trial and error might be brought in to supplement weaknesses in our theoretical knowledge.

A third problem concerns the shift from Hayek's initial concern with misery and its relief to a terminology of preferences, individuals' plans and so on. Here, Hayek is making a move which places his approach close to the spirit of many neoclassical economists. For there is a widely shared approach to welfare which combines a professed scepticism about values with an approach which treats each individual's preferences as something the satisfaction of which is good in itself. (It may be seen as a general and informal version of ideas which occur in Paretian-based approaches to welfare economics.) From this comes a view that the only proper form of appraisal that can be made of states of affairs by an economist is by saying that a state of affairs is better if at least one individual is better off (in terms of their own preferences), and no one else is worse off.

Why economists should have become attached to such an approach is an interesting historical issue. But there is no good reason why economists should restrict themselves to appraising arrangements upon such a basis, or even why we should be *all that* interested in such appraisals at all. I will argue, instead, that there is nothing wrong with economists being concerned with welfare in the more concrete sense in which Hayek was, as a young man, concerned with the well-being of the citizens of Vienna, and with how different substantive values are realized by various institutions. Indeed, the line of argument that I developed earlier clearly calls for work of exactly this kind. Yet economists – the very people who historically were involved in just this kind of appraisal – have instead turned to ever more sophisticated work which seems to throw less and less light upon these real-world issues: the issues that matter.

Now there is a variety of arguments – part, in effect of the folk-lore of economics – which economists will produce if questioned about such things, of which the patron saint is Lionel Robbins. They include the idea that one cannot make interpersonal comparisons of utility. To this there is a back-up: that one cannot do this upon a *scientific* basis – whatever that might mean. And there is also the idea that, in offering Pareto-style appraisals, economists are not involving themselves in normative issues at all. My argument, by contrast, will be that the proper task of the economist is the discussion of how our institutional choices relate to our various values. I will suggest that while values are matters for argument, there is no mystery about the kinds of values we are interested in and to which the work of economists should thus relate. Further, the view that we cannot talk about people's well-being – as opposed to just their preferences – is simply a mistake. And the idea that preferences are something that should be respected is a view for which we may require argument in the face of problems that can be raised about it.

All these issues are particularly pressing for Hayek. For he is dealing with the dynamics of markets, and with situations in which individuals must revise their plans in the face of the discovery that their initial moves are not in coordination. To deal with such issues, one has to have recourse to ideas about

POST-HAYEKIAN POLITICAL ECONOMY

what should be revised, in what circumstances and on what basis; ideas which clearly go beyond the compass of the economist's usual concerns with Pareto improvement.

Now it may indeed be true that one cannot do work of the kind with which economists have become increasingly concerned during the twentieth century in quite these terms. The appropriate response, in my view, is so much the worse for technical work in economics. Pure economics is hardly a subject that is worth pursuing for its own sake, in the way in which, say, this might be said of pure mathematics. And it is that much more the case, when such work is done by people who might otherwise be concerned with assisting us with pressing problems of institutional choice and design.

One further point should here be added. I am not suggesting that the economist, *qua* economist, has to be involved in philosophical disputes about values. He can, quite appropriately, take as his task the analysis of how different institutional arrangements pertain to values which, for the purposes of his analysis, are given. Yet, at the same time, one of the central thrusts of Hayek's own work is that arguments that have been developed by economists are of great significance for arguments about values. It would also seem to me difficult to imagine how, say, arguments about rights could be developed without reference to the consequences of admitting rights claims. Accordingly, the role of my argument in the present chapter is to open up space within which work in economics – and more generally political economy – has to be developed to take further issues opened up by Hayek's work and the responses of his critics. And such work would, in my view, have as an important component the taking further of many of Hayek's own programmatic suggestions. This still, however, leaves open arguments about values themselves, and in particular some unresolved issues concerning the relationship between welfare (in a non-subjectivist sense) and the other values with which Hayek is concerned, as well as how these, notably his later concern for freedom in the 'negative' sense, could be made compelling to Hayek's own, earlier self. Those issues we discuss in the next chapter.

SUBJECTIVISM AND WELFARE

What does Hayek claim for the market order, and on what basis? The story of Hayek's own contributions to the socialist calculation debate, and of his other papers of around the same period, such as 'The Facts of the Social Sciences' and 'Economics and Knowledge', together with his later paper, 'Competition as a Discovery Procedure', is fascinating. In these papers, Hayek gradually differentiates his views from those of other neoclassical economists. He also moves towards the articulation of a distinctive view of the way in which the economy, and especially prices, are to be understood. Rather than a general equilibrium perspective, within which his own earlier work had been situated, Hayek moves towards the development of a dynamic, disequilibrium-orientated perspective as the setting within which prices, competition and entrepreneurship are to be understood.[1]

I do not wish to question the interest and the significance of these developments. But they seem to me to pose some problems for the argument of Hayek's Inaugural Address, and, more generally, for how we are to interpret his arguments for liberalism. For Hayek offers us what John Gray has identified as an indirect utilitarian argument for liberalism.[2] But if one offers such an argument, it is clearly only as good as one's case that liberalism will deliver the goods. But just what does this argument look like, as Hayek's views develop?

There are, in fact, two separate issues here. The first is metatheoretical in its character. Hayek broke with his teacher Wieser with respect to the intersubjective comparison of utility. Hayek does not offer us much argument for so doing.[3] Yet it is hardly surprising that he took the view that he did, given the emphasis placed upon this point by both Mises in Vienna and Robbins in London. But can one conduct Hayek's argument while eschewing all intersubjective comparisons of utility? And is there any reason for so doing? Second, Hayek placed considerable emphasis upon subjectivism, not only in the methodology of social science, but within economics itself. Thus, he has written:

> it is probably no exaggeration to say that every important advance in economic theory during the last hundred years was a further step in the consistent application of subjectivism.[4]

This poses the question: can one sustain the argument of Hayek's Inaugural Address, and more generally his indirect utilitarian argument for liberalism, on the basis of a subjectivist approach within economics? In particular, what happens to it if subjectivism is applied to welfare theory? We will investigate this issue, after which we will return to the issue of intersubjective comparisons of utility.

Subjectivism has considerable merits in many areas of economics, and much of importance to contribute to the discussion of welfare. However, subjectivism does not, of itself, provide an adequate basis upon which Hayek could make his important points about the welfare characteristics of a market-based economic system. In his Inaugural Address, Hayek was concerned with human misery, and its relief. But what does welfare economics look like from a subjectivist perspective?

The purest attempt at a subjectivist theory of welfare is probably Murray Rothbard's theory of 'demonstrated preference'.[5] His reinterpretation of the theory of utility and of welfare economics takes seriously the idea that there can be no interpersonal comparisons of utilities. He also takes seriously the subjectivist idea that we do not have access to other people's preferences except in so far as they reveal them to us. The 'very fact that an exchange takes place', writes Rothbard,[6] demonstrates that both parties benefit (or more strictly, expect to benefit) from the exchange . . . . The free market is the name for the array of all the voluntary exchanges that take place in the world. Since every exchange demonstrates a unanimity of benefit for both parties concerned, we must conclude that the free market benefits all its participants.

The idea that both parties benefit in free exchange is of the greatest importance. But there seems to me to be three problems concerning Rothbard's view – and concerning related views which have been upheld by other economists in the modern Austrian tradition – if we consider them as the basis upon which we should interpret Hayek's argument.

First, Rothbard's argument will shift our attention to the basis on which exchanges are to be judged voluntary, and on which we are to judge whether or not negative externalities can legitimately be imposed upon others, i.e. to a theory of rights. But in discussing the merits of different such theories we will need to have recourse to considerations about the consequences of admitting one rather than another claim. It simply is not the case that rights theory can spring full-fledged from the head of the philosopher like Athena from the head of Zeus (consider, say, the problem of *how* property rights are to be established, and of just what someone acquires in virtue of establishing a property right). Yet what we will wish to have recourse to will, on the face of it, involve issues which go beyond the scope of subjectivism, but to which the subjectivist cannot let us have access except in so far as they can be discussed in purely subjectivist terms.[7]

Second, Hayek has written of markets as examples of 'spontaneous orders'. But we need, in the context of Rothbard's approach to welfare, to look closely at what we mean by 'order'. Rothbard's approach seems to suggest that the *only* question that we can ask of some state of affairs is whether it came about as a result of voluntary exchanges between consenting agents. In that case, to call the result a 'spontaneous order' is to say no more than that it is the unintended consequence of such voluntary activity. But to call something an 'order' is suggestive of a contrast with 'chaos'. If we are saying something more about certain of the products of voluntary human activity than that they are the product of voluntary human activity, then we are using a criterion to appraise them *over and above* that suggested by Rothbard.

Third, one additional point might be made by the Hayek of his Inaugural Address. It is that the very starting-point of Rothbard's approach seems to rule out, as beyond the scope of economics, the very thing that was Hayek's concern: human misery and what might be done towards its alleviation. For, from Rothbard's starting-point, it would seem as if one could not say that someone (other than – possibly – oneself) was in a condition of misery. This, to be sure, is in its way a dramatic solution to the problem of human misery. But it is hardly the one which Hayek needs for the purposes of his Inaugural Address.

An alternative theory of welfare that is open to the subjectivist is along the lines of an informal version of the Pareto criterion. It differs from Rothbard's view, in that it allows for judgements to be made about the well-being of actors other than are manifested in their actions. But it does not presume to go beyond the preferences of economic agents, to consider the relation between these and deeper issues concerning their well-being.

I am open to being convinced that there is theoretical interest in the study of Pareto optimality and the conditions under which it might be realized.[8] But it is strange why economists should have considered that it enabled them to discuss significant welfare issues without being involved in what is ethically contentious. Or rather, it is all too easy to understand how they do this, in the sense that this approach seems to allow them to have their cake and eat it. What are the typical views of the economist, on ethical matters? On the basis of several years' casual observation, I would suggest that they consist of a combination of subjectivism or scepticism with regard to value issues, a disavowal of the idea that it is possible for us to know more about people's well-being than is exhibited in their preferences, and the view – a kind of ghost of classical liberal ideas about rights and utility – that preferences should be respected. I would conjecture that the attraction of the Pareto approach is that it allows economists to give full reign to these predispositions (into which, I suspect, they are socialized by their education as economists), while at the same time disavowing that they are going beyond the scientific.

To be sure, in so far as they are simply working with these particular values, rather than espousing them, they are doing economics rather than moral philosophy. The problem arises, rather, with the question: why *these* values, and with the assumption that it is only those who wish to work upon some other basis who are involved in the 'development of an ethical postulate'.[9] It is clearly open to Pareto-influenced economists themselves to decide whether they are undertaking non-prescriptive economics, or economics on the basis of what they consider to be minimalist and uncontentious moral assumptions. But whichever it is, the moral assumptions involved in the Paretian approach play an important role, whether as substantive assumptions of their work, or as the values that, in the sense of Max Weber, give their (non-evaluative) work value relevance or direction.[10]

My argument here is that the issues in political economy to which Hayek's social philosophy gives rise cannot, for the most part, usefully be discussed by work which is directed by the Paretian approach. In particular – and for reasons that I have spelled out at some length earlier in this volume – the values involved in the Paretian approach are unsuitable for the direction of work that is crucial to the evaluation of the Hayekian programme, and indeed, in my judgement, in any significant issue that arises from contemporary discussions within politics. *This* criticism is, thus, a criticism of these values *qua* their role in the direction of the activities of economists. In so far as the values in question are held as a kind of minimalist social philosophy by economists, I would like also to criticize them directly. For such an approach takes for granted a vast range of contentious issues, and allows its proponents to take positions on them while pretending that they are not really involved in contentious issues in political philosophy at all (which, after all, is something that would sit ill with their non-cognitivism).

Let me mention a few of the issues I have in mind. First, who is to count? Second, why do the preferences of each person who counts matter? Third, how are resources initially allocated? Fourth, how did we get a specific system of property rights, which not only allocates resources to each person, but which also sets out what is and what is not an externality that one person can impose upon another... and on and on and on. In addition, the approach does not say anything about virtually any real-world occurrence in the economy. In actual competition, some are successful and others are not; we learn by trial and error; innovation typically involves costs as well as benefits. And even in cases where two people trade in relative isolation, their actions may generate pecuniary externalities.

But what of Pareto improvement *per se*? Is it always uncontentiously desirable? I suggest that it is not necessarily so.

First, it is not obvious that the satisfaction of people's desires is necessarily of moral significance. Imagine that a person were, one day, to visit a room in which a number of people were engaged in a variety of activities, in an apparently purposive manner. However, he could not tell what they were each doing (his understanding of them would be as the subjectivist economist wishes to treat the activities of all of us). It might appear, for example, as if they were performing actions that related to properties that those people seemed to suppose that objects possessed, but which those objects did not seem to him to possess. In addition, their plans and projects, in so far as he could discern them, seemed inchoate and fleeting. For while they exhibited a propensity to truck and to barter, and exchange things with one another, they would sometimes be observed to exchange much the same things back again, a little later.

Now, suppose that someone were to tell our visitor that it was of some moral significance – that it was better – that these individuals whom he was observing should be free to conduct these 'exchanges', but that the only rationale offered for this judgement is that, at the time at which those individuals made the 'exchanges' in question, these were in accordance with their preferences.

He might well take the view that, on the basis of the information that he had so far, it is a moot point as to whether the situation after these exchanges has taken place is to be judged better than was the situation before. For, so far, we have not been told anything about the relation between such exchanges and the stability of the people's desires, their rationality in anything but the most short-term of senses, and the relation between these transactions and the well-being of the individuals who are making them. And all this is not yet even to say anything about the relation between the satisfaction of these preferences and the people's pursuit of significant ends and goals, or the relation between what they are doing and the well-being of others.

A lot would, in my view, depend on what other information he could gather. If it turned out that our visitor was making his first visit to the stock exchange, then these activities and people's freedom to engage in them would assume great moral significance. If, on the other hand, he was watching people in a nursing home for the senile, it would be appropriate if nursing assistants were, from time to time, to restrain these people's pursuit of their preferences, and instead make sure that they were fed and washed and that they slept. But the level of description that our economists wish us to work with would seem neutral between these two very different states of affairs.

To put this point in more general terms, individuals may have preferences. But this fact in itself says nothing about how other people should react to them. It is, I would suggest, because we can link those preferences to something that is of value – such as the well-being of the individual with the preferences; the consequences for himself and others of his being free to act on the basis of them, or to their rights – that we accord them ethical significance. Without any of this (and no argument about such links is typically supplied to us by the economist) then it is not clear why we should care about these matters.

Second, there are cases in which our observer may correctly judge that the state of affairs after a Pareto improvement has taken place is morally worse than the state of affairs previously. For suppose that we were to take individuals' preferences as an indication of their well-being. Should we not, then, welcome every Pareto improvement as desirable? I would suggest not. For consider a society that includes three people, two of whom are already in very comfortable circumstances and one of whom is in misery. Consider, then, a reallocation of resources, such that the first two people become better off, and no other member of the society is made worse off. The younger Hayek – as we have seen from his Inaugural Address – could well respond: but, in this setting, what matters is the alleviation of the condition of the person who is in misery! The gains made by the other people may be to their satisfaction, but there is no reason why an impartial spectator should agree that the condition after the reallocation of resources is better than it was before.

Now it might be claimed that the conclusion that I have reached should not surprise us. For it is widely admitted that Paretian criteria are almost never satisfied in the real world; that, it might be said, is why economists, when discussing welfare issues, do not in fact use the pure Pareto criterion, but instead ask whether there would be a Pareto improvement if those who are made worse off in some transaction were compensated by those who gained.

This, however, raises many problems. First, it would only be ethically acceptable if the compensation were actually to take place. It is, say, no argument that Donald Trump should be given the meagre contents of my savings account (held, to satisfy the purist, in what from an economic point of view is probably an unnecessarily short-term form, given my use and likely use of it), that *if* it were given to him he could make more productive use of it than could I.

Second, without its proponents suggesting a *mechanism* through which compensation is to be assessed and then effected, the whole idea is pointless. But how is anyone else supposed to tell how much I value some possession? How is compensation to be effected? And what of the costs of whatever mechanism is supposed to handle all this, to say nothing of the problems of the motivation of those who have responsibility for all these matters?

Indeed, the sceptical outsider might at times be tempted to think that economists, on these issues, suffer from a strange form of manic-depressive illness. On their depressive side, they seem overcome with scepticism about our ability to know that others are suffering, on grounds that are about on a par with philosophers' concerns as to whether I am experiencing 'redness' in circumstances in which everyone else is experiencing 'greenness' when there is symmetry with respect to all intersubjective claims that either of us might make. On their manic side – when they are engaged in cost-benefit analysis – they seem willing to make all kinds of wild *a priori* assumptions about others' tastes and well-being, and the value that they place on (or ought to place on) features of their environment, and to make assumptions about the knowledge, motivation and virtue of planners that are reminiscent of those that the advocates of central planning attribute to the Platonic guardians of the Central Planning Board.

The suggestion that I am here making – so that the reader is not left in any doubt – is not that there is something desirable about inefficiency. It is, rather, that provided we take a less elevated idea of what a theory should be in these areas, it is perfectly possible for us to discuss the pros and cons of different institutional choices and courses of action within them. There is *not* a big problem about the kinds of things that people find valuable. But at the same time, there are also well-known disagreements and points at which there seems no sensible alternative other than to leave matters up to individual choice. The economist, however, does not himself have to make choices or offer arguments about such matters, if he does not wish to do so. But there is no reason why he cannot offer us assessments of the kinds of institutional and individual choices open to us in terms that pertain to the full scope of human concerns, rather than to the highly restricted assumptions involved in Paretian approaches.

HAYEK ON WELFARE

A critic might, however, claim that Hayek hardly stands in need of the ideas about welfare that I am pressing upon him, on the grounds that he has some perfectly good ideas of his own. These I must therefore discuss.

161

Hayek has sometimes argued for the advantages of markets in relation to the desirability of the coordination of people's expectations.[11] This is an interesting idea, in so far as it shows a concern with welfare issues relating to dynamic processes in which people discover that their expectations do not cohere, and must then revise those expectations if their behaviour is later to be in better coordination. Hayek's ideas are suggestive, and it would be interesting to see how they might be characterized in more detail. (There is, on the face of it, a considerable difference between discoordination of a kind that might be dealt with by the arbitrage activities of a Kirznerian entrepreneur[12] and, say, that which would require more radical changes to be made; for example, to production.)

However, if we consider the revision of expectations and actions in the face of a lack of coordination, what may matter from the point of view of welfare is how these revisions take place, and to what result, rather than just that the result involves (better) coordination. Suppose, say, that initial discoordination resulted from people not being willing to give me as much for my services as I felt that I deserved. Suppose that revision then takes place within a 'black box' and afterwards that they give me everything that I want. We must surely enquire what went on and how the result relates to human well-being if we are to judge the development from the point of view of welfare. If, say, in the 'black box' the other people were menaced by my assistants, it is clear that we may not regard the outcome as an improvement. But on just what basis is it that only some kinds of transformations are to be counted legitimate? After all, we are not here dealing with anything like Pareto improvement, but with a process of adjustment, in which one – or more – of the parties will be revising their plans and expectations, in ways that may well promise them less satisfaction than they were hoping for before.

One response here might be to have recourse to some theory of rights, implicit or explicit. But Hayek is somewhat guarded on this topic. In so far as there is anything of the sort in Hayek's work, it would seem to depend on his belief in the undesirability of coercion, on his *Rechtsstaat*-derived ideas about substantive equality before the law, or on a consequentialist argument that the treating of people in such a manner can be justified in terms of some notion of welfare. However, the latter ideas may pose problems (not least as people may have tastes for the coercion of others); while, as we will discuss in the next chapter, the rationale for the first group of ideas and their relation to Hayek's welfare-based arguments are less than clear-cut.

One other criterion for the judgement of social systems that is sometimes offered in Hayek's work is his version of a veil of ignorance argument: an appeal to the idea that we should appraise a society in terms of the well-being of a member of that society chosen at random within it.[13] It may be interesting to compare different societies on such a basis. But it is not clear why evaluations in such terms are supposed to carry any special weight. I might, for example, be more interested to hear how overweight, balding philosophers who like cats do in such societies than I am in the fate of people chosen at random. If, on the other hand, I am told that any such appraisal is to be conducted from behind a veil of ignorance, such that it should have nothing to do with my personal interests (whether of self-interest, altruism or simple curiosity), I need to be told why I am supposed to adopt such a standard of appraisal. The explication of this will, in effect, amount to the advocacy of a substantive moral theory (and one, what is more, that would seem to me to have some features that are totally unacceptable, for reasons hinted at in the previous chapter). Accordingly, while this idea is to be found in Hayek's work, it is not clear what argumentative force it is supposed to possess – other than to those who just happen to think this slightly strange characteristic of a society valuable.

Two other discussions by Hayek also demand consideration here. First, there is Hayek's exchange with Galbraith on the 'dependence effect'. Hayek there discusses Galbraith's argument that, as Hayek puts it:

> the great part of the wants which are still unsatisfied in modern society are not wants which would be experienced spontaneously by the individual if left to himself but are created by the process by which they are satisfied.[14]

Hayek himself argues that this is true of the 'amenities of civilization', and that we want these things because 'they produce feelings or emotions which we would not know if it were not for our cultural inheritance'.[15] But he then argues that consumers are not determined in their choices by the efforts of individual producers, but, rather, are influenced by producers who compete with one another, and also by the choices made by their fellows.

Hayek's argument is compatible with the idea that we should be concerned only with individuals' preferences. But its rhetorical force is not. For his references to civilization and – as are disclosed in the full text of his argument – to music and painting, and to his own literary taste for Jane Austen and Anthony Trollope, carry with them the idea that these are tastes that it is desirable for him to have acquired (a *purely* subjectivist argument would run, equally, if its author had listed only various works of pornography, devoid of literary merit). Similarly, Hayek's writings on the theme of competition as a discovery procedure seem to me to obtain their force from our reading into them the idea that what is being discovered is conducive to human well-being.

Of course, claims that, in appropriate conditions, markets produce well-being may be contested. Indeed, an important strand in the history of ideas since the mid-eighteenth century has been an extended discussion about the pros and cons of markets and of alternatives to them. Much of the work of Hayek and of other members of the Austrian school, forms a vital contribution to this debate.[16] But to take a purely subjectivist view of these matters – to accept that 'progress is movement for movement's sake'[17] – is to turn one's back upon this argument by suggesting that we cannot engage in it, rather than to contribute to it.

THE INTERSUBJECTIVE COMPARISON OF WELL-BEING

One reaction that is certainly possible for the economist is to take seriously my jibe at Rothbard and to ask: can we judge that some 'unfortunate' individual is, indeed, in misery? Would not to attribute any such condition to him be to break with the idea that there can be no intersubjective comparison of utilities? To this it could be responded: such intersubjective comparison is not necessary – we are merely responding to our belief that the individual is at a low point on *his own* scale of well-being. However, this in itself would seem of no particular ethical significance. Unless we were to interpret his being in that situation as unpleasant – in much the same sense as something is unpleasant for us – it is not clear why we should be concerned about it at all.[18] After all, one might well imagine that, in Paradise, there are some things that people prefer to others; but it is not clear that, should we come across one of the Blessed who is at what, for him, is a particularly low point in his scale of well-being (indeed, one that, for him, is actually unpleasant), we should do anything but wish that we ever were to experience something similar in our greatest moments of bliss. Accordingly, unless we know something of how the points on a person's range of experience relate to our own, the fact that he is, in his own terms, not doing particularly well has no particular significance for how we should react to him.

Someone might deny that we can have knowledge about other people's well-being. But this is to deny the obvious. Lest, however, this judgement seem simply a personal prejudice, let me call upon the testimony of a distinguished economist, whose views might be of interest in this field: Lionel Robbins. He wrote, 'in daily life we ... continually assume that [interpersonal comparisons of utility] can be made'.[19] Robbins, however, goes on to argue that such claims 'cannot be justified by appeal to any kind of positive science', and that there is a need for 'a substantial curtailment of the claims of what now assumes the status of scientific generalization in current discussions of applied economics'.[20]

Hayek himself, in *The Constitution of Liberty*, notes that 'individually most of us have definite views about whether a given need of a person is greater or smaller than that of another'. But he suggests that 'The fact that we have an opinion about this in no way implies that there is any objective basis for deciding who is right if people differ in their views about the relative importance of different people's needs; nor is there any evidence that they are likely to agree'.[21]

Now, while Robbins was arguably correct in his rejection of the specific work in welfare economics with which he was taking issue,[22] the basis on which he argues is less convincing than he – and many economists who have followed him – have supposed. He has certainly offered us no good reason to call into question our common-sense knowledge in this area. As Robbins himself noted, common sense is against him. We readily attribute well-being and its absence to other people. If we are told that there is a famine in some part of Africa, or that someone has been stung by a wasp, other people would quite properly wonder what was going on if we did not take this information as also informative about the victims' well-being. Our reaction would depend on our knowledge of them as members of the human species, tempered with knowledge about what they were used to and of local peculiarities (the person who was stung might be allergic to wasp stings). Further, we all know that individuals' reactions to circumstances may be different – that some people are more sensitive to stimuli than are others; that other people make a greater fuss about their well-being. And we may know, further, that it may sometimes take a bit of time and trouble to sort out which are which. But to depart from all this in the direction of a general scepticism about our knowledge of others' well-being clearly requires an argument. What is on offer?

Robbins himself suggested that we imagine that 'the representative of some other civilization were to assure us ... that members of his caste ... were capable of experiencing ten times as much satisfaction from given incomes as members of an inferior caste'.[23] He argues that while we might be affronted by such a claim, we cannot refute it. But this is too quick. For the people making the claim seem to believe in intersubjective comparisons of utility – as that is what their claim is about. We might ask them more about their claim, and about whether, in their view, it could be tested. For example, is the difference innate; if so, what if babies were exchanged at birth – they might have some local equivalent of the story of the Princess and the Pea. Alternatively, the claim might rest on some theory of the cultural formation of taste. Now, either claim might, of course, be true. There is no reason why the defender of interpersonal comparisons must claim that each person has an equal capacity for pleasure. Robbins, however, might well retort that all this gives us no reason to suppose that such claims will, in fact, be open to refutation.

But is this true? Economics is, after all, dealing (for the most part) with the activities of members of our own biological species. And even if our experiences are not plausibly to be identified with properties of our physiology,[24] they are, none the less, closely dependent upon them. If someone were, say, to lay claim to an extreme subjective sensitivity, it would surely be strange if this were unrelated to any physical characteristics whatever. Thus, when Robbins writes 'there is no means of testing the magnitude of A's satisfaction as compared to B's. If we tested the state of their blood streams, that would be a test of blood, not satisfaction',[25] he would seem correct only if satisfaction were a purely mental state, with no physiological dependencies or concomitants. But as, after all, that which is giving rise to satisfaction will act through various states of a person's physiology, it would seem to me quite amazing if this were to be the case.

But what of the idea that, while interpersonal comparisons can be made, this cannot be done 'scientifically'? Three issues are raised by such a claim.

The first is the idea that goes back to logical positivism or to the work of Karl Popper: that it is important to distinguish between science and non-science. However, the positivists' view – that the non-scientific is meaningless

– has itself been criticized. Popper's ideas, while important, are not pertinent in the present setting. My reason for saying this is that Popper's work on demarcation has, in effect, two foci. On the one hand, he was arguing that confirmation should only count if the theories in question were genuinely testable. This is a valuable suggestion about methodology, but it does not apply here. On the other, he suggested that it was highly desirable that a theory should be falsifiable, an idea that he later generalized to stress the importance simply of openness to criticism. But here, there is no special problem concerning the interpersonal comparison of utilities. To be sure, it might be the case that someone offered a theory in such a form that it could not be criticized, or was determined to hold some view intact in the face of criticisms, making changes anywhere else in their views but to this theory. However, while if a theory concerning the interpersonal comparison of utility were of this character it would be open to criticism on this very ground, there is no special reason why theories which involve the interpersonal comparison of utilities have to be of this character.

Second, such theories may be thought unscientific because they pertain to things which are not directly open to observation. But direct observability is too crude a tool to use in such a context. If it were adopted, we would lose much of science in the process. Rather, what is pertinent is that a claim be open to intersubjective appraisal. There is an interesting range of techniques which have been used for the intersubjective appraisal of introspective claims (compare, in this context, the extensive body of knowledge that we have on the phenomenology of visual illusion). And claims about the well-being of other people would also seem to have a dimension to them which is also more directly amenable to observation of this kind, too.

Third, what might be meant by the claim that such work is not scientific is that it cannot be developed to too great a degree of precision, that it must always have a rough-and-ready character. To this I would agree. But there is nothing wrong with that. Indeed, we should here surely take our lead from our subject-matter and our concerns about it, and develop theories of a degree of precision that are appropriate to it. It would, for example, seem to me an absurdity if someone were to claim that meteorology could not be a science, because it was not possible, within it, to produce detailed predictions (we should, here, bear in mind what Hayek has said about the importance of having criteria of explanation and evaluation appropriate to complex phenomena). It would also, in my view, be absurd if, in the face of this, meteorologists decided that rather than studying the weather, they would instead develop models of an idealized climate in which everything was fully predictable, and spend their time exclusively in the exploration of the formal properties of that.

To sum up on this point. I do not wish to deny that it may be difficult to make judgements about others' well-being. But the idea that we cannot make intersubjective comparisons of well-being at all seems to me incorrect, especially when – as in the area of Hayek's interest in his Inaugural Address

– we are concerned with their misery rather than their pleasure. Given the variety of human values and interests, and of our reactions to the various different situations in which we may find ourselves, it may well be that we cannot produce a 'scientific' welfare economics involving interpersonal comparisons of utility after the fashion of, say, modern welfare economics or social choice theory. But this is, I would have thought, not necessarily to be regretted, just in so far as these disciplines seem able to contribute so little towards any real-world problems of political economy. (Or, in so far as non-Paretian approaches are used in welfare economics to deal with practical issues, important questions about subjective well-being, distribution and the variety of human concerns are simply begged.) I wish to argue, however, that it is in principle possible to develop theories and to argue in a non-arbitrary way (i.e. such that our claims are open to intersubjective criticism, argument as to their formal cogency and empirical tests) about major issues of human welfare. Such discussion must take into account the various different dimensions of our concerns and the trade-offs between them. It is a discussion from which most economists have excluded themselves, in their professional capacity, for far too long.

Let us now turn back to Hayek. Hayek's argument for classical liberalism requires that we be able to say more about the connection between the operation of markets and other voluntary institutions under a minimal state, and human well-being, than Hayek himself seems to allow for. It is also perfectly possible to do so. For, as was suggested by my critical remarks on Robbins, we can make informed judgements about the well-being of my cat, or about that of a fellow human being, both of which are intersubjectively discussable, and which may even be tested on the basis of biologically grounded knowledge.

There is, however, a significant difference in respect of the human being. For it is possible for me – in a way in which it is not possible for my cat – to understand that I am overweight and that I should diet and thus, as a matter of choice, undertake behaviour which an external observer could correctly understand to be unpleasant, because I feel that I ought to do so; for example, because of my responsibilities towards others. I might, alternatively, decide to fast during Lent for religious reasons. In such a setting, I would imagine that someone might correctly be able to say to me, from an 'external' perspective: you are unpleasantly hungry. However, I might well respond that while that is the case, I have chosen to be hungry, and to explain to him the moral or religious significance of my choice.

In making this point, I wish to suggest that it is perfectly possible for us to say something about the well-being of other people from an 'external' perspective. Indeed, if we could not do this, we would (to plunge recklessly into the middle of what is actually a very complex argument) be unable to learn a shared language with which to talk with other people about all kinds of 'subjective' matters. And this, in turn, gives some weight to my claim that we can say rather more about human welfare than a pure subjectivism would allow.

More specifically, we can evaluate societies in terms that relate closely to considerations raised in Hayek's Inaugural, by asking about human misery, and, further, as to whether those who are in unpleasant situations are in those situations as a matter of choice. Of course, these are not the only things that matter. There is room for argument about what constitutes choice, and there are obviously important differences between a society in which people are left pretty much free to go to hell in their own way,[26] and others in which much more assistance is offered to those who initially make poor choices, or, more generally, in which children are to a greater or lesser degree at the mercy of their parents. Membership of one or other such society, however, might itself be made a matter of choice: this is an issue to which we will return later in this volume.

A critic might claim of this whole approach that it ignores an important fact, upon which the subjectivist tradition has placed so much emphasis: that there is such a diversity of human ideals and concerns. While, say, it may be possible for any member of our species to discover that I am hungry or thirsty or that my situation is otherwise unpleasant, and while they might discover that I am miserable, there would seem, *prima facie,* little chance for someone who did not know me well to realize that the fact that I am miserable might have something to do with an absence of a tabby cat, Häagen-Dazs butter pecan ice-cream, a pinball machine, or Tuborg Paaske-Bryg beer. How, once we have moved beyond biological necessities, can we say much about what society is a good society, given the diversity of human concerns? To this, I would make two responses.

The first is that there is a neat affinity between that in respect of which we have biologically based knowledge and the limits of our *prima facie* duties to others. If someone is hungry or thirsty or in pain, the relief of this, if it is within our power, seems pressing. It is not our concern, in the same way, if someone does not have access to a particularly interesting new film – even if that person would, in fact, rather purchase a cinema ticket than eat. Further, our duty to assist others on such a basic level is only a *prima facie* one, and may properly be outweighed by other considerations: that we could only assist them through their eating seed-corn; that to assist them in this way would simply lead to them to return to us for support – along with their new offspring – later on; that to assist them would lead to an unacceptable sacrifice of our other concerns, or impinge on the rights of others, and so on.

The second point is that the sheer diversity of human concerns and interests in itself suggests the importance of choice, both at an individual level and in respect of one or another form of social organization; and both for reasons of welfare and of self-realization. This is an issue to which we will return later in this volume. But in so far as such issues are important – rather than sheer issues of the relief of misery – the ability of a socio-economic

168

system to enable people to realize their choices becomes an important desideratum.

My point in raising this argument, however, is not to suggest that economists should give up economics in favour of arguing about human welfare. It is, rather, to suggest that non-arbitrary argument about this subject is possible. And indeed, a lot of it has been going on. My point is, rather, that there is every reason for economists to take the issues raised in such discussion – what we know, in general terms, about human well-being – as that in relation to which they should tell us about the pros and cons of different kinds of economic arrangements. The usual discussions of the economist do not avoid substantive judgement relating to human welfare. Rather, they are conducted under the assumption that one particular such view is correct.

Yet, other things being equal, while efficiency and Pareto improvement are doubtless worthy concerns, and while dramatic fallings short from what can be achieved on such scales are morally important, in most usual settings these are not matters that we will rate particularly highly in aggregate terms. And they are certainly not matters to which we are likely to give significant weight in our day-to-day lives. Hayek's case, for the kind of society that he favours, must be made in terms that go beyond subjectivism.

HAYEK, MARKETS AND WELFARE

In the previous section, I suggested that there is no reason why we cannot make assessments of the welfare-related characteristics of different forms of political and social organization. At the simplest level, this is fairly straightforward – although, of course, there might be trade-offs between, say, our ability to meet different people's most basic needs, or between these and other concerns. All this is less a matter for purely technical argument, than for a mixture of theoretical, historical and empirical discussion, where we will have to draw on ideas from – and skills developed in – various different disciplines.

Hayek's work is oddly divided upon such issues. At one level, he offers a battery of arguments that are of vital importance for any such discussion. Consider, here, his arguments about markets and the use of knowledge, and competition as a discovery procedure; about the problems of collective decision-making without consensus, and of the importance of freedom of entry within a market as a check on the abuse of power. At the same time, there is a lack of specificity to the claims that Hayek makes. This, I think, is no accident, for reasons that become clear if one looks at Hayek's intellectual development.

As we noted earlier, Hayek's early work was undertaken within a general equilibrium perspective. At the London School of Economics, John Hicks, as a new member of the lecturing staff with good mathematical skills, was asked by Lionel Robbins if he would try to put Hayek's work on the trade cycle into mathematical form. Hicks tells us[27] that he became convinced that the notion of equilibrium with which Hayek was working was not, in fact, the usual one, but, rather, was dynamic in its character. He also suggested to Hayek – who agreed – that there was an oddity about Hayek's presentation of his theory. For Hayek had gone straight from a non-monetary economy to the introduction of money, whereas, Hicks argued, it was necessary that expectations were introduced first. Hayek, it appears, referred him to a paper of his own, in which certain of these issues were explored.[28]

As we have already noted, Hayek's contributions to the socialist calculation debate, his work on economics and knowledge, and eventually his *Pure Theory of Capital*, articulate an approach to markets as dynamic processes, and equilibrium as an idealized situation in which individuals' plans are coordinated. Hayek makes use of these, critically, in the socialist calculation debate, and they form the setting in which he works out his ideas in his later work on capital theory. However, and this is the point that is crucial, once Hayek makes the moves on which I have reported, he also needs to rework the argument of his Inaugural Address: the argument in which he presented his rationale for parting company with his early socialism. For, as we noted in our earlier discussion, Hayek seems, for example in the course of the argument about economic calculation under socialism, to make use of ideas that are most obviously understood within the context of general equilibrium theory. If *that* is being replaced, it would seem as if Hayek's claims about markets also stand in need of reinterpretation. The whole issue also becomes that much more pressing in the light of our discussion earlier in this volume: in the light of the approach – of Wieser and Plant – that socialist goals should be pursued within the setting of a market economy, in ways that are informed by a knowledge of how that economy works. Let us look back at the economic calculation debate from this perspective.

In Mises' article on economic calculation under socialism, it *looks* as if he is throwing down the gauntlet in just the terms that Lange – and the other writers – picked it up. The central claim of the article might appear to be that planners can make technical but not economic decisions, because in order to make economic decisions they would need to have access to prices for capital goods. It is true enough that there are various phrases which might suggest that Mises has other concerns in mind; but these are certainly not explicated at all clearly. In particular, what one does *not* get stated clearly is the argument that he developed in the second chapter of his *Theory of Money and Credit*, that there was no way in which one could measure people's preferences other than through their actual decisions in a market, in which people could articulate their preferences through the use of money.

It would be possible – as, for example, Peter Boettke has done[29] – to interpret Mises as presupposing this point. And as I noted in my earlier discussion of the economic calculation argument, Don Lavoie has brought out distinctively 'Austrian' themes in Mises, in his reinterpretation of the debate.[30] What is not so clear is that they have given an account of what we can expect from the market process, under various conditions. Now Hayek, in his contributions to the debate, develops the argument in two ways. First, he introduced what might be called a dynamic aspect to the argument, in the sense that he stressed that in a market setting there is *competition*, and that what gets into the decision-making process is what wins out in such competition. Second, he developed, in various different forms, what becomes his argument for markets and the utilization of tacit knowledge. To these may be added his later arguments on the theme of competition as a discovery procedure. These are, indeed, most interesting arguments. But they are not developed by Hayek in a form that goes beyond an explanation sketch. By this I mean that Hayek does not give us any account of these matters in either systematic or quantitative terms. It could be objected that this is to suggest that his views should meet requirements that he would, himself, contest; after all, he has argued that, in areas where our subject-matter is complex, all that we can hope to do is to develop explanations of the principle, rather than detailed predictions. But here, I would suggest, there is a need to produce rather more than Hayek has himself done, and that there is no obstacle to our doing so.

First, in his own critical discussion of equilibrium, 'Economics and Knowledge', he argued that to understand equilibrating effects, one must go beyond the pure logic of choice, and look also at empirical matters concerning how knowledge is acquired and communicated.[31] But if this is the case, an indirect utilitarian argument for the market would seem to require reference to the fruits of the investigation of such matters.

Second, it should be noted that at the time at which Hayek was writing, arguments had been developed in England for economic planning on the basis of knowledge-related defects of the market.[32] Examples offered included the way in which companies might well duplicate capital expenditure because of their ignorance of the activities of others – as, for example, when two factories were constructed to meet a limited pool of demand for a certain kind of product; or when, say, the competitive provision of transportation might result in two under-used railway lines serving much the same areas (an example, it might be argued, of overall losses from competition); or the way in which capital expenditure may not be undertaken at all if a company cannot obtain assurance that there will *not* be competition from others, an illustration here being offered of what was claimed to be the under-provision of railway lines in parts of London.

Clearly, much here will depend on what is being advocated as an alternative or a supplement to markets. But once the general power of Mises' and Hayek's arguments is appreciated, and there is a commitment to handling economic organization by broadly market means, such arguments may recur as arguments for certain kinds of piecemeal intervention. If this entire argument is supposed to be broadly consequentialist in its character, and if at least parts of it are empirical, then it would look as if there is no option but to try to develop more specific arguments about the pros and cons of such activity. I would personally hope that, if developed, the arguments would come down on Hayek's side. But it is striking that one can match some of his arguments about knowledge and competition with arguments that there are problems concerning markets and competition in just these same fields.

To be sure, once public choice considerations are invoked and one also brings in the issue of how those supposed to be handling such matters by extra-market means are supposed to be informed about what they are doing, then Hayek's case looks stronger. (I would stress here that there is no special reason why such behaviour has to be modelled as if undertaken by rational economic man; the key issue, rather, is the disaggregated character of much of the decision-taking, and the interesting point of the macro consequences of people pursuing actions which make sense to them in the institutions, settings and relationships in which they are working.) It is in just such situations that Hayek's argument would seem to require detailed theoretical and empirical exploration. However, as I have suggested earlier in this book, Hayek's own ideas about what government should do must be treated from the same perspective.

Third, as we have already noted, in the course of his arguments against those who would, say, concentrate industry and put government-assembled monopolies in the hands of managers, Hayek claims that such moves would be wasteful of resources. But at this point – when he has himself invoked dynamic factors – one also needs to know something about how resources would be used in markets as he depicts them.

It is, perhaps, worth noting two other points in just this setting. First, let us bring expectations into the picture. These may be correct or incorrect. Also, people will sometimes be acting upon, and prices will thus be transmitting, false theories. It is by no means obvious that, when we take such factors into account, individuals, when guided by prices in their immediate location, will be taking actions that will be equilibrating (or coordinating, or however else one wants to put the desirable characteristic that markets are supposed to have) in their consequences. On the face of it, how markets will perform will differ in different circumstances – which will include how good, as a matter of fact, people are in their theories, how aware people are to genuine entrepreneurial opportunities and so on – all of which are topics on which we might well ask for illumination from economists who follow in Hayek's footsteps.

Second, the picture of the economy offered by the liberal economist is one in which markets respond to the preferences of consumers.[33] But in such a setting, some preferences are more equal than others. If consumers have preferences concerning the conditions under which goods are produced – social or material – it is by no means clear that they will be able to exercise these preferences through markets. For producers will be taking decisions on the basis of what might be described as their economic ecology – which may involve factors that, to the consumer, seem in no obvious way to be linked to choices that he is making concerning the product in question. The consumer, on the other hand, will be making choices between objects in situations in which he will not know

172

what it is that he is choosing – in the sense of not knowing that the consequences will be, for decisions about production, of his making one choice rather than another.

In each of these cases, however, to raise some problems about the operation of markets is clearly not itself to argue that there are better ways in which we can organize things. And what we may end up discovering, through such investigations, are just further ways in which even the best institutions that we can choose fall short of what we might hope for.

Finally on this general topic, Hayek's discussion of economic issues in 'Competition as a Discovery Procedure' and in *Law, Legislation and Liberty* (volume three), is especially suggestive, just because he is able, within it, to pull together the different strands within his later work, and to convey a picture of what his approach to political economy looks like. As I have mentioned in my earlier discussion, his explicit break with perfect competition and development of an account of the relation between freedom of entry into markets and power is most suggestive. He even says a little about what we can expect from the performance of markets:[34]

> Competition, if not prevented, tends to bring about a state of affairs in which: *first*, everything will be produced which somebody knows how to produce and which can sell profitably at a price at which buyers will prefer it to the available alternatives; *second*, everything that is being produced is produced by persons who can do so at least as cheaply as somebody else who in fact is not producing it; and *third*, that everything will be sold at lower prices, or at least as low as, those at which it could be sold by anybody who in fact does not do so.

And while Hayek refers to such results as 'modest', he also stresses that he does not know of any other method that would bring about better results. Hayek's discussion in that material as a whole is programmatic. But it seems to offer an interesting programme for research in political economy and to suggest ideas which, if they could be developed, might make a real contribution towards showing how the argument of his Inaugural could be developed in more specific terms.

There is, however, a strand of argument upon which Hayek has placed particular emphasis in some of his most recent work which does not seem to me as valuable: his emphasis upon the size of the population that a society can support as a basis upon which comparisons can be made between different kinds of economic and social system.[35] While, as Adam Smith argued, we benefit from being members of a society in which the market is large and the division of labour is advanced; and while, if there is a large population, their existence and well-being is a constraint on the activities of the rest of us, I find Hayek's case for emphasizing population unconvincing. Rather, John Stuart Mill's discussion of 'The Stationary State' in his *Principles* is very much to the point:

It is not good for man to be kept perforce at all times in the presence of his species. A world from which solitude is extirpated, is a very poor ideal.... Nor is there much satisfaction in contemplating the world with nothing left to the spontaneous activity of nature.[36]

Hayek's revision of Bentham (from The Greatest Happiness of the Greatest Number to The Greatest Number)[37] does seem to me to be of interest in one respect. It is that in the face of the diversity of human ends or goals upon which the subjectivist insists, one must probably have recourse to a non-subjectivist but human-related measure in order to discuss the comparative ability of societies to satisfy human well-being. And while the actual goal of sustaining a large number of people in an existence in which their biological needs can be satisfied is an unattractive ideal, the potential to do this might be a revealing measure of a society's potential ability to generate human well-being.

To conclude, pure subjectivism is insufficient as a basis upon which Mises and Hayek can make the claims that they want to make – and should make – about what we can expect from markets. Rather, the properties of markets with which they were concerned seem to me to be of importance largely because of the idea that, through them, human well-being is enhanced, and in ways that are compatible with notions of individual freedom that many people will, independently, find attractive. But to argue in this way involves the elaboration of criteria external to markets, in the light of which markets and other forms of social organization can be compared. In addition, faced by the challenge of socialists who wish to pursue their ideals as ethical goals to be achieved within a market-based economy, it becomes urgent to develop theories about the working of the institutions of a mixed economy. And in so far as, here, public choice analysis and related approaches are used as a stick with which to beat the socialist, the classical liberal has also to apply these same theories to his own proposals for governmental action.

In so far as there are limits to our theoretical knowledge about such matters, it is important that we look at other ways in which we may learn. And here, Popperian ideas of learning by trial and error may usefully be combined with Hayek's ideas about experimentation in a market setting. As I will suggest subsequently, there may be strong arguments for a form of social arrangement within which different ideas about social organization may be tried out on a voluntary basis.

I should stress, in view of my earlier emphasis upon the biological, that I do not mean to limit what we can say about human well-being to the biologically based. But the biologically based is not a bad starting-point. We can, indeed, talk about gains in well-being in terms of people's not being frustrated in their biologically based desires; or, if they wish not to eat, drink, live in decent conditions and so on, of this being a matter of their choice, rather than something that is forced upon them by their circumstances. To admit such ideas is not in itself to advance a case for economic interventionism. For it was against a context of such general ideas about human well-being that the young Hayek, and before him Adam Smith, set out their case for the market. It is to this argument, in my view, that we should return.

Further, however, a key line of argument about markets should be about the relation between what people can produce within them (and the unintended consequences of ordering our affairs by means of markets) and human well-being. If *all* we have produced by markets is the creation and subsequent satisfaction of an unending but fleeting succession of subjective whims, then it is by no means clear why we should care much about them. Of course, other things being equal, we may say that it is better that desires be satisfied than not; we may also have some strong theory about human rights which gives an import to the satisfaction of non-aggressive human desires, whatever they may be. However, defenders of markets – from Mandeville to Hayek – have fully admitted that markets have their disadvantages, too. In assessing their pros and cons, those of us who have read and have been impressed with the work of Mises and of Hayek will do ourselves – and markets – less than justice if we try to argue their merits in purely subjectivist terms.[38]

My argument is thus that we should return to a conception of human well-being that goes beyond the purely subjective. It is only with such a theory that we can do justice to Mises' and Hayek's own arguments for markets. By saying this, I do not wish to downplay the importance of the insights of subjectivism. But I do wish to argue that we can go further, in talking about human well-being, than pure subjectivism would allow. Some of the most important insights of the classical liberal tradition, to which Mises and Hayek have done so much to contribute, relate to the importance of private property and of markets, and the liberating of the human imagination and the learning that they make possible. For this case to be made properly and for those who are impressed with it to engage with those who have objections, it is essential that a more powerful theory of welfare be developed: one which can give weight to the biological; to our choices in which we put our particular human concerns above the biological; and also to our concern for individual freedom. And as part of this theory, the insights of subjectivism should be recognized: it is important that individuals may prefer to choose not to eat or to copulate, and may even, in some circumstances, prefer to die.[39]

6

WHY OUR FREEDOM MATTERS TO OTHERS

INTRODUCTION

I have suggested that Hayek, originally concerned to improve a world which gives rise to profound dissatisfaction, was led, through his encounter with Mises, to espouse a form of classical liberalism. This, he argued, would provide a better path than would socialism to the realization of his ideals. Now, one important theme in Hayek's liberalism is the ideal of equality before the law, that, in constitutional or procedural terms, individuals should be treated as ends in themselves. Such an ideal makes its appearance in *Freedom and the Economic System* and in *The Road to Serfdom*. But it is in Hayek's *Constitution of Liberty* that it appears in a full-fledged form. Indeed, John Gray, when discussing Hayek's work, while he noted the 'fundamental utilitarian commitment in [Hayek's] theory of morality'[1] also said that Hayek has always been an ethical Kantian and that:

> What is distinctive in Hayek's Kantian ethics is his insight that the demands of justice need not be competitive with the claims of general welfare: rather, a framework of justice is an indispensable condition of the successful achievement of general welfare.[2]

While I would have reservations about Gray's 'always' – at least if it is intended as a statement about Hayek's published work – his description does seem to fit Hayek's *Constitution of Liberty*. It is also striking that, when Hayek discusses 'the end-independent character of rules of just conduct' in 'The Confusion of Language in Political Thought', he cites both Hume and Kant.[3] However, Gray's statement seems to me better understood as describing a claim rather than an 'insight'. For that there is such a connection between Kantian and Humean concerns is itself a thesis that must withstand critical scrutiny. And what – one might wonder – would someone make of this claim who accepted the younger Hayek's arguments for liberalism on broadly utilitarian grounds, but who did not feel any particular sympathy for the idea that each individual should be treated as an end in himself if this should prove a barrier to significant measures to relieve human misery? They might well wonder: has Hayek actually provided an *argument* as to why individuals should be treated in this way?

Since I wrote an initial version of this chapter,[4] Chandran Kukathas has published an excellent book dedicated to an analysis of whether Hayek manages to reconcile Kantian and Humean concerns.[5] Kukathas concludes that he does not, a judgement with which I concur. The present chapter could be read as a response to Kukathas's book, although it was not written as such, just in so far as, after raising some problems about attempts to derive Hayek's ideas about liberty from his concerns about welfare, it ends up by offering some suggestions as to a way in which such a reconciliation might be accomplished. Just for this reason, however, I need to explain briefly how my work does – and does not – relate to Kukathas's concerns.

First, I do not think that the Kantian strand in Hayek's work can be taken too seriously. Hayek does stand in need of a rationale for the strand in his later thought that places emphasis upon individuals as having substantive equality before the law, and for his – slightly different – ideas about the desirability of the minimization of coercion. (Hayek's approach to the individual, in my view, is thus best seen as what Nozick called a 'utilitarianism of rights', rather than a rights theory in anything like Nozick's sense.) However, while Hayek was clearly appreciative of *Rechtsstaat* approaches to the rule of law which owed a good bit to Kantian ideas, I do not see, in Hayek's work, any sign of a systematic Kantianism.[6] Accordingly, I take the task that faces Hayek to be to provide a rationale for the 'Kantian' features of his legal and moral concerns, rather than to offer a theory that, in any deep sense, reconciles Kant and Hume.[7] In much the same way, it seems to me perfectly in order to see Hayek as committed by his own position to the enterprise of providing an argument as to why individuals have rights, at least in the sense in which they are accorded these in his legal and moral theory. The particular character of the intellectual task that is before him would seem to me determined by his own intellectual history. For the problem that faces the older Hayek is, surely, to provide an argument that would be found telling by the younger Hayek – the young man who was concerned with human misery and the creation of a more just society – as to why *he* should be concerned with the minimization of coercion and with a negative conception of human liberty.

Second, I will not treat this issue by way of a close examination of Hayek's own textual arguments. In part this is because Hayek does not seem to me to confront this issue head on. In part, it is because Hayek's own work, while suggestive, contains many incompatible strands that he never seeks to reconcile in a systematic manner. (It is one of the particularly useful aspects of Kukathas's book that he brings out this issue so clearly, through his careful analysis of the different strands in Hayek's thought.) It would have been nice had Hayek sorted out these matters himself. But in my view the thrust of Hayek's work comes from political economy rather than analytical political philosophy, and it would perhaps have been too much to hope for that someone could combine

Hayek's range of interests and his fruitfulness in so many fields, with close analytical skills.

However, the problem of how these different aspects of Hayek's work are to be reconciled – if, indeed, they can – does seem pressing. And Hayek's own history shows the form that the argument would have to take: to make the case for his later concern for liberty pressing to his younger self. My reason for putting the problem in this form is not that I am unwilling to allow Hayek to change his mind,[8] but because for Hayek's later views to be compelling, one of the most pressing sources of criticism which they will have to meet will be those with the concerns of the younger Hayek.

The task of offering an argument for liberty – in the sense of why our freedom, i.e. the freedom of each individual, should matter to others – is pressing, yet strangely neglected. It is pressing for two reasons.

First, there are reasons that relate to the history of liberalism. As I have argued elsewhere,[9] the universalistic aspect of liberalism – that each person is to count, equally – would seem to be a heritage, within liberalism, from the Christian tradition, but not one for which it is easy to provide telling secular arguments, while theological arguments are of little use in a setting in which religious belief cannot be taken for granted. The key problem would seem to me to be not in respect of moral equality – we are all happy enough to claim that no one is intrinsically better than ourselves – but as to how universalism and equality of our treatment of others is to be generated from the particularisms of our moral lives, within which, quite properly, we seem to have *moral* reasons for treating different people differently. While for the Christian there may be an overriding moral obligation that comes from our all being God's children, for the non-believer, there seem, *prima facie*, to be very different moral relationships between, say, us and those who are our children, or the children of those who are our kin or with whom we share some particular tie, and those who are strangers.[10]

Second, as I have suggested in chapter three and as I will discuss more fully below, the liberal stands in need of an argument that makes his concern for *negative* liberty morally telling, which, at the same time, does not spill over into an argument for positive rights of a kind that are incompatible with his social theory.

In my view, to offer telling arguments here – and by this I mean not the construction of philosophical foundations, so much as considerations that other people, coming from wherever they do, will find telling – is perhaps the major theoretical problem facing liberals today. I am not sure if it is a problem that can be solved, and I suspect that a telling argument might require that one marshal a whole bundle of different considerations as to why the freedom of other individuals should matter to us. These might include valuing each individual as a unique cultural object, and also as representing a distinctive point of view on the world, through arguments in which one discloses how the ways in which individuals claim moral consideration for themselves also commit them to giving consideration to others who share the same morally relevant characteristics, to arguments which try to suggest that there are prudential reasons for treating one another as if we had rights, on a contractual or a utilitarian basis. In so far as such arguments worked, one would have, further, to show that they complement, rather than are at odds with, one another, and also that they add up to an argument for classical – as opposed to welfare – liberalism. One would need, also, to show how they could be extended to provide a rationale for a classical liberal view of property rights.

The reader will be relieved to discover that this is not a task that I propose to undertake in one chapter of a book on Hayek. Rather, my concern, here, will be to explore a line of argument suggested in Hayek's work, and which I will reinforce by the links that I have argued in chapter three can be made between Hayek's work and Popper's epistemology. They lead to a view which I believe to be distinctive, although it is also suggested by a strand in Popper's own discussion of ethical themes,[11] and which I believe to make a genuine (if limited) contribution towards the wider problem facing liberals, of making plausible why the freedom of each of us should matter to other people.

The path that I take is not to show that there is an argument in Hayek's text which will resolve the problems that I have discussed but to offer an argument which it would be possible for him to accept, because it extends an argument in his own work. I do this by way, initially, of developing an indirect utilitarian case for liberty, drawing on Hayek's own arguments. I find it in some ways telling, but in the end, inadequate. I then offer an argument of my own, which draws upon the critical rationalism that I have earlier argued it makes sense to use as the basis for an interpretation of Hayek's work. It is not possible, in the present chapter, to present this argument more than briefly. But I endeavour to show how problems that I raise for the indirect utilitarian argument for liberty can be met from such a perspective. I further suggest a link between this argument and a minimalist, property-based liberalism. This latter is an idea that I have already commended, at various points in the book, as a more natural conclusion to draw from Hayek's arguments than are the conclusions that Hayek himself offers, which give a greater role to the state. In the final chapter, I develop further this idea, and also use it to offer solutions to what, otherwise, would seem to me some unresolved problems in Hayek's work.

The aim of the present chapter, accordingly, is to suggest how the concern for the minimization of coercion of the later Hayek could be given a rationale to Hayek's younger self. The direction in which my argument takes me is towards a more minimalist view of the state than Hayek himself favours. It is a view, however, that I think that he ought to have favoured.

One point should be added. My concern here will be to explore some of the connections between concerns about well-being and liberty. Yet it could be argued that while the younger Hayek was concerned with well-being, he was not concerned with well-being in general, so much as with the well-being of those who are worst off. In so far as this is the case, one would need also to have

179

recourse to my earlier discussion of social justice. Here, our concern will be with the argument about the relation between welfare and liberty.

SOME HAYEKIAN ARGUMENTS FOR LIBERTY

It would seem that, by the time he wrote *The Constitution of Liberty*, Hayek did not wish to disagree with those who believed in 'the value of liberty as an indisputable ethical presupposition'.[12] But he was well aware that 'to convince those who do not already share our moral suppositions, we must not simply take them for granted'.[13] He went on to say that 'We must show that liberty is not merely one particular value but that it is the source and condition of most moral values' and further, that 'We can therefore not fully appreciate the value of freedom until we know how a society of free men as a whole differs from one in which unfreedom prevails'. But this – other than indicating that Hayek's argument will be consequentialist – gives no indication of the terms in which he will be arguing. Indeed, it seems to me that Hayek never really gets round to offering a sustained argument for this aspect of his views. I think it telling that, when Hayek later refers to the universal character of law in his preferred society, in *Law Legislation and Liberty*, he refers simply to his wish 'to continue on the path which since the ancient Stoics and Christianity has been characteristic of Western civilisation'.[14] This, however, would not cut much ice with the younger Hayek, who showed no obvious sympathy for arguments drawn from Christianity or Stoicism. What would the later Hayek have to do to show his earlier self that he should be a liberal in the later Hayek's sense? And is it really the case that arguments couched in terms of well-being lead to liberalism at all?

On the face of it, the later Hayek would have to show that circumstances can be expected to arise within a liberal social order which would be favoured by his younger self, and that alternative forms of social order would be likely to have defects such as to make them less attractive to him. But over and above this, he would face another problem close to that which, on some interpretations,[15] also faced J. S. Mill. For Hayek would seem to have to argue a case for taking each individual as an end in themselves, and for respecting the contents of their choices (or at least for minimizing the coercion of them), from broadly utilitarian premises. (Or, at the very least, to argue that there is no conflict between these things and the concerns of the younger Hayek, and that they have features that make them independently attractive. However, as I will be suggesting that the initial derivation does not go through because the ideas are incompatible, this option is not available either.) In addition, as Raymond Plant has argued, there is a constraint over Hayek in his responses to such problems. He must provide responses that lead to individuals being accorded rights of the sort that he favours (i.e. appropriate to the economic and legal arrangements of classical liberalism and a non-market welfare safety net). But the basis on which he argues for these rights must – presumably – also support the according to individuals of positive rights of a stronger kind; ones which are incompatible with his liberalism.

Let us briefly consider some of the problems that confront the older Hayek as a liberal who wishes to argue his case in broadly utilitarian terms. (The reader interested in such issues might note that very similar problems would seem to arise in the work of those liberals who wish to argue for similar views on a non-moral contractarian basis, such as Buchanan, Gauthier and Narveson; I will not, however, pause here to indicate how the argument of this section would require to be modified so as to apply to their positions.)[16]

EQUALITY BEFORE THE LAW

First, what is the younger Hayek to make of the idea that the law should apply equally to all citizens?

The older Hayek can of course point to the advantages to all citizens from membership of a large society in which there is practised the social division of labour; where individuals, under the rule of law, are free to choose their own occupations, act on the basis of their own knowledge and where their activities are coordinated through market mechanisms. Suppose (for the sake of argument) that the older Hayek is correct that such a society, with a welfare safety net, will, all things considered, do better in terms of the well-being of its citizens than a centrally planned society or a society in which social justice is pursued politically.[17] This would not, however, in itself explain why the laws should give equal legal rights to *all* citizens.

Clearly, there are utilitarian arguments for this, related to the kind of social order that Hayek is envisaging. For example, in such forms of social organization citizens are typically dealing (in economic transactions regulated by the legal system) with individuals with whom they do not have face-to-face relationships. There is thus a clear advantage to them if they can deal with such people as legal agents in as abstract and general a form as possible. And so, *ceteris paribus*, they will not want to face the information costs that variability in the law with respect to different individuals may bring with it.

There may also be some (although smaller) costs that follow from the problem of identifying individuals who have different rights even in situations where we are in face-to-face contact with them. More importantly, in face-to-face situations most of us[18] would feel that all kinds of human and cultural disadvantages result if people have radically different rights, as opposed to all relationships being with citizens who share a basic legal equality. However, it is by no means clear that the quantitative gains that one might make from engaging in interactions with other individuals as formal equals, together with qualitative gains of the kind indicated above, will constitute sufficient utilitarian grounds for the law being genuinely universal in its character (and thus for every individual's having the same legal rights).

After all, identification and informational problems may be susceptible to various forms of technical solution. It is striking that the credit card, with machine readable information, already provides ways in which discrimination may easily be made between individuals of different status.[19] Human beings have (unhappily) shown themselves all too adept at the construction and successful living out (by *all* parties) of cultures in which there is not formal equality (think only of the history of the relationships between men and women). It is also by no means clear that the results of a comparison of exploitation and of freedom will go the older Hayek's way. There may be huge gains to the exploiters if a minority is exploited – say, most radically, by their being 'farmed' as an organ bank for transplant operations for the majority. In this grim situation, their use for transplants apart, the minority may engage in the ordinary transactions of a liberal society with their exploiters. It might also be the case that the exploited minority are not all that unhappy. If someone is so used, their heirs may be given a sum of money (as I write, children are being sold into prostitution by their families, in some parts of Asia). If the risk of their being 'used' in this way is low, they may not be able to feel any more about it (until it occurs) than we do about, say, the risk of being struck by lightning. They might be chosen by lot. And it is also quite possible that – as a rationalization of such a relationship – they might come to accept some belief, custom or ideology that enables them to feel *good* about being exploited (again, think only of the history of the interactions between men and women).

Now it is by no means clear that, on utilitarian grounds, all this will be outweighed by the gain in well-being on the part of the minority due to their not being so exploited, together with such gains as there might be to the majority from the fact that they are now only interacting with citizens with *one* status before the law.[20] It might, however, be objected – along the lines explored by Gauthier in his *Morals by Agreement*[21] – that considerations of self-interest and sentiment, especially over the longer-term, may lead us towards non-exploitative cooperation. But while such considerations may tell against the enslavement of people, they may not tell against genocide and the seizure of the resources of those who are thus exterminated or decimated, provided that it can be done with little effort or feedback effects upon how those who do such deeds subsequently treat one another.[22]

All this might seem to be highly artificial and to have no relevance whatever to real-world situations. But consider, for example, the European settlement of America and Australia, or the situation of the Indians in the Brazilian rain forests today. Such cases exhibit the kind of disregard for the lives of others for reasons of greed that would be required for the kind of case with which I am concerned. And it would not have required circumstances to be much different before a European settler who was also a utilitarian could argue in the following terms: I am faced with an aboriginal population who own the land and what is growing upon it. At the same time, they are hunter-gatherers, or are engaged in subsistence farming, and are making what – from our perspective – is very inefficient use of the land. What is more, they do not seem to be interested, other than marginally, in giving up their current patterns of living and adopting other patterns such that we can obtain land from them; land which we can put to productive use and which would be of benefit not just to ourselves but to the relief of suffering among humanity as a whole.

Now in such circumstances, it would seem to me that the situation of the original inhabitants would be very precarious, especially if, say, the settlers possessed the ability to kill them without the infliction of much pain. (Historically, diseases brought by Europeans wiped out a large population of American Indians. My worry is that it would seem that in circumstances like those which I have sketched, a would-be liberal utilitarian's own moral theory might lead him to perform much the same actions deliberately, provided that they could be accomplished without the infliction of much suffering.)

The older Hayek, who wants to extract the ethics of Rousseau or Kant from a doctrine of utility, would thus seem not to be in a strong position. But what of the argument – which appears both in *The Road to Serfdom* and in *The Constitution of Liberty* – that 'liberty is not merely one particular value but . . . it is the source and condition of most moral values'?[23] If this is meant as an argument to the effect that well-being is promoted by liberty, it will also be open to criticism on the grounds indicated above (i.e. that it would look as if there are cases in which general well-being is promoted by some individuals *not* being accorded full legal rights).

RESPECT FOR THE PREFERENCES OF EACH INDIVIDUAL

Some account also needs to be offered as to why all individuals' preferences should be respected in the way that the older Hayek wishes. Again, there are some arguments which can be offered to the person who wishes to argue in terms of welfare. For example, he can argue that, other things being equal, the individual is a better judge of his or her own self-interest than are others (not least, for reasons of access to relevant information). But there are many cases in which it might be argued that other things are not equal – in which we may have reason to distrust an individual's expressed preferences as not representing his best interests, or as in some way inauthentic,[24] and where a degree of paternalism might seem in order. In addition, it might seem possible – following an argument of Martin Hollis's – to develop a utilitarian argument as to why individuals' preferences should be manipulated rather than respected by the utilitarian. This we will discuss below.

Let us first look at these issues in more detail. Hayek believes that we should respect the preferences and choices of each individual. Why should we do this? Presumably, because they are thought to provide the best path to knowledge of what will satisfy and what will dissatisfy that individual (to say nothing of their relevance to higher-flown ideas about individuality), and because the according of such respect will also enhance the contribution that the individual will make to the well-being of others. A case can be made here for paternalism. But it is one to which it is not too difficult for Hayek to reply, if he makes use of arguments about the availability of knowledge along the lines of Mill's *On Liberty*, and he demands that we take a *realistic* as opposed to an 'enlightened despot' view of the likely performance of those manning the political institutions that are allocated a paternalistic role. I will thus assume that Hayek could make out a reasonable case for confining paternalism to children and to governmental measures of a sort that do not call into question his ideas about the legitimate sphere and mode of governmental action.

More serious perhaps are problems about the manipulation of individuals' tastes: of whether individuals' preferences are a good guide to their well-being, given the influences to which these preferences may be subject in a market-based society. These influences might be argued to fall within a continuum, ranging from brainwashing, through socialization, to the influence of advertising in a pluralistic setting.

At first sight, it might be thought that Hayek has a strong case, just because he would seem to have something pertinent to say about either end of the spectrum. Brainwashing would seem to be ruled out, for Hayek, by the fact that it would involve coercion; while on advertising Hayek has written briefly, but spiritedly (for example, in his response to Galbraith)[25]. Here, he argued that the influence exerted by advertising poses no serious problem provided that the power to influence people is not in the hands of just one person or organization.

Hayek himself was clearly concerned only with down-to-earth issues that Galbraith had highlighted, rather than with the deeper problem of the multiplication of needs in commercial society and their relation to the kind of 'virtue' that is required on the part of citizens if their compliance with its norms and institutions is to be sustained. However, there is more depth than one might suspect to Hayek's response. For he also raised an important problem for those – like Galbraith – who complained about the manipulation of preferences. Hayek pointed out that tastes such as those for opera are clearly not natural to us, but that they are something that Galbraith would presumably not wish to condemn. He might have added that such tastes may well have to be acquired initially through processes involving cultural snobbery, the wish to impress, etc. (that is, if there is a threshold that has to be crossed before people begin to enjoy the things in question, and if one does not wish to coerce people into such tastes). All this would seem to make it incumbent upon Galbraith – or some 'deeper' critic of liberalism on such grounds – to offer a theory relating the desirable conditions for the formation of preferences to considerations of individual well-being. If my argument here is correct, the critic of liberalism would seem to be faced by a massive problem which he would need to solve prior to his being able to make his criticism. However, this weapon may prove double-edged, in that if the problems that I will discuss below concerning the authenticity of preferences amount to anything, some such theory might also be needed by the liberal.

I would indeed suggest that cases exist of inauthentic preference or of false consciousness which are generated and sustained by forms of social interaction which need not involve coercion. This may happen in interpersonal relationships (see, for a possible case, which, while initiated in a way that involved coercion, seems to have been later sustained without it, Linda Lovelace's account of her relationship with Chuck Traynor, as recounted in her *Ordeal*).[26] Similarly, it is plausible that some patterns of group interaction (such as those found in certain religious sects) may sustain beliefs in such a way that they may deserve to be called an ideology and, in consequence, that they may generate preferences which can be described as inauthentic. Those who participate in such social relationships may be insulated from anything that can call their beliefs into question. Such groups may thus practise forms of behaviour that – perhaps unintentionally – render their beliefs 'immune' to criticism, while those involved may not be aware of the fact that this is taking place.[27] What is more, such cases of individuals and groups highlight – in an extreme form – things that occur more widely in the day-to-day lives of us all.

If we consider such social factors as affecting the way in which beliefs are maintained,[28] it is not difficult to see the beliefs of many people in many kinds of situation as less than authentic, and their preferences as therefore not necessarily constituting a reliable indication of their interests. To the extent to which this is the case, it is not clear why those preferences demand the respect that is accorded to them by liberals. Clearly, should we argue thus, we would then stand in need of a theory to assist us in discriminating between what is, or is not, an authentic preference, or what are and are not conditions under which people's views are open to criticism. However, as is the case with more ordinary arguments concerning paternalism, it could be that while we can recognize a problem about preferences as they currently stand, the likely consequence of any alternative set of institutional arrangements might seem worse.

A further problem concerning the respecting of individuals' preferences is raised in a fascinating paper by Martin Hollis.[29] Hollis argues (with reference to *Brave New World*) that from a utilitarian perspective, the simplest way of getting people to be satisfied would presumably be to change their physiology, such that they would then be more easily satisfied in existing or even more modest circumstances. Some substance (which, I would suggest, might be called 'Stoite'), which would render people deliriously happy in the most modest of circumstances, is something that any utilitarian might find difficult to resist, for him or herself, or on behalf of others.

The most obvious response to such problems would be to have recourse to Mill's arguments for the higher pleasures. Mill's argument – as reconstructed, for example, by John Gray[30] – was essentially that the Socratic pleasures of a life involving risk and responsibility outweigh the piggish pleasures of a lower-grade existence. But this reply is here of no avail. For the kind of satisfaction accorded by Stoite might be engineered so as easily to outweigh the pleasures of a life of autonomy and responsibility – to which, if the argument is to stay utilitarian in character, appeal must be made. The arguments for liberty as an engine for the production of utility would also seem to be trumped. As the taking of Stoite promises optimal satisfactions, research on alternative ways of achieving satisfaction becomes pointless. And Hollis's own way out of his problem – a normative theory of human nature – seems to me to be of no use either, unless it is explained how this is other than an arbitrary stipulation.

Let me sum up the situation as it stands at present. Our discussion has raised some problems for Hayek's synthesis of broadly utilitarian and Kantian concerns. And we may well question whether rights of the kind with which Hayek is concerned in his writings on law, and on the minimization of coercion, always pull in the same direction as his concern for human well-being and the relief of suffering. However, a reader sympathetic to Hayek might suggest that Hayek's case does not look too bad. To be sure, there are problems posed by settlers and natives; but there, cannot our feelings of sympathy for the exploited stand on their own? And while Hollis's argument is interesting, it might be dismissed as science fiction. Does not Hayek's argument stand more or less intact?

This is not a conclusion with which I am happy. To meet it, I wish to offer a line of argument of my own. It is, however, one which I feel happy offering to Hayek, just in so far as it draws on the critical rationalism that I have already argued should be used to interpret other aspects of his work.

FROM CRITICAL RATIONALISM TO RIGHTS

I would like here to explore one way in which the arguments which we have explored above might be met. One of our concerns was to see if something akin to a Kantian ethic of respect for persons could be generated from a con-sequentialist position which, at its toughest, was a form of utilitarianism. This has customarily been done via the adding to utilitarianism of some ideal or moral – often Kantian – element, whether directly, or through an analysis of the supposed properties of moral language.[31]

Let us eschew any direct appeal to moral theory, and (initially) restrict our argument to the confines of a hard-nosed utilitarianism. Is there anything that, from such a perspective, might assist us? I believe that there is. For if we are utilitarians, we are concerned with the relief of suffering and with the promotion of happiness. And these depend on matters of fact. As a result, *qua* utilitarians, we have an interest in pertinent matters of fact, and thus – I suggest – in other people through the contribution they can make to the discovery of the truth or falsity of claims about such matters of fact.

If one feeds into the argument at this point the ideas of critical rationalism which, as I have argued earlier, make good sense of much else that is to be found in Hayek's work, one has an argument for treating people as ends in themselves generated *within* utilitarianism. For, to put this point at its most stark, while the utilitarian might be able to outweigh respect for the preferences of one individual by those of others, things are very different when one is concerned

186

with the individual as a source of cognitive judgements. For here, one single counter-example – one single judgement – is enough to show that some statement is false. And there is a *prima facie* argument for treating individuals as ends in themselves *qua* sources of such judgements (a point suggested by Popper's discussion of the idea of the 'rational unity of mankind').[32] The contribution – or indeed the possible contribution – of each individual becomes something of interest in itself and, as a consequence, so does the individual who is its bearer. Individuals, that is to say, should be accorded what might be called 'dialogue rights' by the utilitarian.

To be sure, particular judgements made by individuals may in some sense be overruled (e.g. if others cannot find the effects which they claim exist). But this overruling is not simply done as a matter of head-counting.[33] And one striking feature of critical rationalism is that it indicates that we may always have something to learn, even about those things which seem most clear-cut; and even from – as Popper points out, citing Burke[34] – those people who, on the face of it, might seem to have least to offer.[35]

My suggestion is thus that via our appeal to critical rationalism we can move *within* utilitarianism to the according of 'rights' to individuals who can – or might be able to – make such contributions, however humble, in their role as bearers of cognitive judgements.[36] Furthermore, the character of these rights is given to us by epistemology, in the sense of a theory of the growth of knowledge (there is here, clearly, a parallel with Habermas's theory of communicative competence).[37] Popper's ideas about 'conventionalist stratagems' may also serve as the basis of a theory which can explain which kinds of social formation illegitimately protect people's views from openness to criticism.

The theory of knowledge also furnishes us with an argument as to why individuals should be accorded autonomy, in the sense that their judgement should not be dominated by those of other people. For their judgements are supposed to provide independent tests of claims made by other people.[38] Individuals will thus be accorded a measure of respect as if they were ends in themselves, at least in this area of their activities. However, our approach also suggests that these rights might be subject to certain qualifications. The rationale for the according to individuals of rights, and the character of those rights, is derived from considerations in the theory of knowledge. It is on the basis of epistemological considerations that individuals are to be accorded freedom from involuntary domination. But what of domination that does not involve coercion – and the right that individuals may claim to join, voluntarily, a religious sect, or a monastery, membership of which may have the unintended consequence of cutting the individual off from participating in the wider learning process?

It would, indeed, seem to me that *prima facie* they would not have such a right (or, to put this another way, their dialogue rights would be inalienable).[39] However, on practical grounds one might argue that there is less of a risk – to the growth of knowledge – from giving people such rights than from the

187

setting up of some social institution with the power to pass judgement as to what institutions an individual is – or is not – to be allowed to join.

FOUR OBJECTIONS

It may be useful here to respond to four possible objections to these ideas.

1 The introduction of Stoite might seem to pose an insuperable difficulty: why should individuals be accorded 'dialogue rights' on utilitarian grounds, given that Stoite acts as ace of trumps when we are playing the game of utilitarianism? It might be thought that the obvious response from my position would be: don't take Stoite, as you (and others) need your wits about you to think how you might best be satisfied, to solve problems and, generally, to engage in dialogue about issues relating to utility, etc. But against this, it can be argued that if people take Stoite, such activity is not needed, as everyone will be fully satisfied anyway. The objection is, I think, valid if the argument is put in such a form. However, all that needs to be done is to raise the epistemological argument to a higher level. For rather than debating about happiness, we can debate about Stoite itself. All kinds of claims have been made about Stoite and its properties. But are these claims true? These, like any other such claims, stand in need of scrutiny and thus scrutinizers – and thus individuals with dialogue rights of the sort that we have described. (What is more they also should not be taking Stoite while engaged in such activities if it affects their judgement.)

2 This naturally leads on to the next issue: haven't we simply created a paradise for abstemious intellectuals, in which all resources would have to be diverted from enjoyment into investigation – which is an odd view for a utilitarian to take? An answer of sorts can be given from within our approach. For in order to evaluate certain claims we will have to be concerned not just with abstract argument, but also with trying out various ideas in a practical way. Such appraisal will require command over resources, the development and use of practical skills and even experiments in living.[40]

3 A critic might also object that all that we have given rights to is a person's intellectual capacities; and, pointing to the fact that in the classical world intellectuals were sometimes slaves, he might ask whether the 'dialogue rights' we have developed so far might not be more restrictive in their scope than they may have seemed. Could not intellectual emancipation be quite compatible with social domination? An answer to this is, I think, provided by the ideas developed in the previous paragraph. For if we are also concerned with experiments in living and tacit knowledge, rather than just with abstract theoretical knowledge, it would seem that we would have the basis for an argument for rights that go beyond the merely intellectual, to encompass fuller social liberties of the sort needed for experiments in living.

4 It might further be argued that I have been engaged in some sleight of hand. For I started with the problem of the respect for the *preferences* of individuals; but I have discussed only their *judgements*. It does seem to me that a cognitive approach can be taken to much of what is often treated as mere preferences, but I cannot discuss this issue here.[41] What I can say, in mitigation of the line that I have taken, is that it is certainly possible for us to take many of our preferences as having a cognitive element, i.e. as involving a judgement that some object has the property of, for example, giving us pleasure of a particular sort. Now, the cognitive aspects of these preferences will be accorded weight and protection by virtue of our epistemological argument. But the non-cognitive aspects of our preferences, and non-cognitive uses of rights which people are accorded for cognitive purposes, may also receive protection as a side-effect. That they receive such protection is a contingent claim, and it rests on the hypothesis that there is no practical means of protecting one without the other which will not, in its turn, generate other, more undesirable, unintended consequences. This claim may itself prove incorrect. It is also possible that, even if this claim is correct, it may be felt that there is something wrong with our argument: is it acceptable that such steps in our argument have such a contingent character? To this, the appropriate response is: but Hayek's own entire argument depends on such contingencies. For, clearly, an omniscient God could be a central planner; and many of Hayek's own arguments depend on (presumably contingent) facts about the ways in which human beings are limited in their knowledge.

It might be argued, however, that in so far as any of the above is successful, it walks into a version of the trap set for the market-liberal by Raymond Plant.[42] For if people are to be accorded rights of the kind favoured by (classical) liberalism, because of the epistemological role that they might play, should they not also be accorded 'welfare rights' too? For could these not also be presented as having an 'epistemological' rationale: if a citizen is to be able to contribute, he would seem to need such resources as would enable him to play a full role as an active civic participant.

It would seem to me that, as Hayek's argument – and our argument here – is at bottom utilitarian in character, the issue of whether such rights are admitted, and to what extent, must be empirical. Aside from the existence and quantity of such entitlements, should they be called 'rights'? Nothing much depends on words – provided we remember that such 'rights' are derivative in their character from utilitarian considerations. Hayek does espouse the idea of a welfare safety net. And if that *is* desirable on utilitarian grounds (compare our discussion in chapter four) there would seem to me no reason why an individual's entitlement to it should not be called a right – although it would, in some ways, be rather different in character from other rights.

THE RIGHTS OF THE TALKING CHICKEN

There is, however, one major difficulty about the approach that we have taken so far. It is that the point of valuing the individual's cognitive contribution is through the contribution that this can make to the goal of utility. And it is, here, competing with *other* contributions that that individual might make – most radically, as an object to be consumed by others.

Now I suggested, above, that from a utilitarian perspective it might be possible to sanction gruesome arrangements in which, say, a minority were treated as something like living organ banks for the majority. In such a situation, does our 'epistemological twist' cut any ice? It may not, in that the cognitive contribution which the people in question might reasonably be expected to make might well be outweighed by the contribution that they could make as objects to be consumed. The situation is not unlike that, say, of a talking chicken who tries to preserve its life through pointing out the cognitive contributions that it might have to offer. But its interlocutors might be hungry, and getting hungrier. And they might *correctly* judge that the chicken could contribute more to utility if it is eaten than through its contributions to our factual knowledge. Even when their interest is concentrated exclusively on eating chicken, it might stall them by engaging them in discussions about chicken recipes. But not only would this seem demeaning (and thus far from the kind of respect for persons in which the liberal is interested), but, as they got hungrier and hungrier, there would come a point at which what was to be gained from one recipe rather than another was simply of no further interest to them. The end – utility – in terms of the achievement of which rights were being accorded would, in such a case, itself serve to trump those rights. Is this the end of the road – not just for the chicken, but also for our line of argument? For if so, while it has got us some way, it has fallen short of what we were setting out to achieve.

There is, I think, a further move that might be made here. For all the above – including the sad fate of the chicken – was conducted within utilitarianism: a substantive ethical theory, the correctness of which was taken for granted (or, more precisely, our concern was to see if rights of a character familiar from classical liberalism could be generated from within utilitarianism). This, in itself, would indicate that there is a further move that the chicken might make: it might engage with its would-be butcher not over the utility of killing it as opposed to listening to what it might have to say, but over the correctness of utilitarianism.

At this new level of argument, a further case can be made out for rights for the sake of individuals' cognitive contributions. The situation here is somewhat more complicated, given the fact that there are clearly disanalogies, in terms of both goals and the methods appropriate for their achievement, between ethics and empirical knowledge. But it would seem to me that there are sufficient similarities for an argument like that in the previous sections to go through.[43] For there is no reason why we should not view moral claims as open to argument, much – on Popper's account – as are factual claims and claims about the correctness of say (criticizable) philosophical theories.

That such an approach is possible as an interpretation of critical rationalism is suggested in an appendix Popper added to *The Open Society* in 1961. In this, he suggested that the idea of the validity of an ethical norm can play a role in moral argument similar to that of the regulative idea of truth in science.[44] Popper himself did not discuss these ideas further; and while Watkins elaborated upon them a little in his 'Negative Utilitarianism', he has been criticized for developing this parallel between scientific and moral argument by Bartley.[45] In my personal view (which I will not elaborate here),[46] not only may such a parallel be drawn, but it can be developed into an epistemologically centred version of a non-naturalistic moral realism, which in turn has some interesting parallels with Adam Smith's *Theory of Moral Sentiments*. For our present purposes, however, all that we need is the idea that claims about moral judgement and about the validity of moral theories may be the objects of intersubjective discussion.

This idea would strengthen the argument, developed within our utilitarian setting, for the according of 'dialogue rights' to the individual. For it would allow the individual to call into question utilitarian values if they should seem to him morally contentious – as indeed they might well be prompted to do, should they prove a threat to his own existence. For once one applies critical rationalism to ethics, he and other citizens are accorded dialogue rights of an enhanced character: ones that cannot be trumped by utilitarian appreciations of themselves as objects to be consumed.

But what of the acceptability of these ideas concerning dialogue about ethical issues? If we are faced with people who are cognitivists and fallibilists in ethics, and are willing to accept that the patterns of argument in ethics are close to those in matters of fact, then our argument goes through very simply. But such strong assumptions are probably not needed. For many non-cognitivists accept the legitimacy of just such argumentation concerning the formal character of ethical discourse; and they accept, further, that such discourse may pertain to matters of substance in the field of ethics (they might thus be called meta-ethical cognitivists).[47] The biggest problem might seem to be with the ethical nihilist. If he can be engaged in argument, then there is a toehold for the establishment of 'dialogue rights' of the sort with which we have been concerned. But why should such a person be interested in talking? As Nozick justly said, Thrasymachus's response to Socrates should not have been to argue with him, but to hit him over the head.[48] The liberal who is after 'dialogue rights' even here seems to have an advantage, in that, as a matter of empirical fact, people seem to be moralizing animals, and typically to wish not just to do things, but to feel that they are right in doing them. Into such feelings our dialogue apparatus – and hence something that will serve as the basis for the according to others of dialogue rights – might be plugged.

I will not here discuss further issues concerning the philosophical status of these ideas.[49] More to the point is the question whether the argument works. Have we saved the talking chicken?

Two problems with the argument should be noted. First, the 'rights' accorded to the chicken are conditional in character: they depend upon its interlocutor's interest in the ethical validity of its actions and of its moral theories. This concern may, I believe, give our chicken *some* protection; but it is not, on the face of it, clear that it will give it much. For our concern for ethics is, surely, competing with our other concerns, too. And may they not outweigh our concern for ethics?

Second, there is the question of what our interlocutor has to offer.[50] For it might be questioned how we are to interpret the universalism that is implicit in the ideas to which I have appealed. In some sense, on the view being canvassed, when we make a claim, factual or moral, we make it for everyone, and this means that it stands open to their appraisal. But just what are we to make of this in the context of our argument? For – *pace* Popper's quotation from Burke – it may well be the case that we can judge that the value to us of someone's critical input may be very slight.

Imagine, for example, that we were asked about the concern that we should have, on the basis of such an argument, for the autonomy of a peasant farmer in some physically remote part of the world – say, Peru. Now it might well be the case that he is likely to make some useful contribution to our factual or moral concerns; after all, he may well have a perspective on our affairs which we had never even considered. What is not so clear, however, is what the second such person might have to contribute, over and above what has been contributed by the first. Everything that the first person had to contribute was, it might seem, a result of his occupying the role that he did; it is not clear that a second such person would have anything to add, even on issues concerning which he had an intimate knowledge. Accordingly, if we have, here, a theory of rights generated from epistemological considerations, it would seem to be very limited in its scope.

This is a genuine problem: we may seem, on reflection, not to have helped our talking chicken very much at all. However, this is misleading, and for reasons to which we have already had occasion to allude in our discussion of welfare issues in a previous chapter. For what the second Peruvian peasant has to contribute is largely to the moral and factual knowledge of those around him: it is his critical input, along with that of others, which goes to shape the culture and personality of his fellows. The relevant moral knowledge is in part highly context-dependent (and factual knowledge, too, may depend significantly on locally generated tacit knowledge). Yet it is from a culture into which he has made an input that we may well have something to learn. Accordingly, that we may be able to learn from the first Peruvian peasant – which is surely not a matter of contention – itself depends in part on the contributions to his local culture of the second. While the critical input of those immediately around us to our moral persona may be of the greatest importance.

Let me sum up. We have developed an argument which accords moral weight to each individual, and to their freedom, by way of the role that they play directly or indirectly in the evaluation of moral claims. For such a view, it can be said that their significance to us is derived from the role that they play in the conditions for the evaluation of any substantive moral claim; such that, formally at least, they seem to have a kind of priority. Against it, it might be said that the contribution or potential contribution of any one person may be minuscule, and easily outweighed by our other, more immediate, concerns. Further, if we invoke the 'contribution to local culture' argument in respect of our second Peruvian peasant, we owe our potential critic a further argument, to the effect that such a culture is best sustained upon the basis of people's enjoying autonomy and formal equality (as opposed, say, by some people undertaking all the drudgery, while an elite can specialize in cultural activities). As a result, we have here an argument, but not one that I am convinced has any great strength. Further, its universalism may be more than a little formal: do we, in fact, have much to learn, in respect of most things, from more than a tiny proportion of the world's population? I am happy, on the present occasion, to leave that issue open. Instead, I would like to explore a little further what might be extracted from it, should it prove sustainable.

FROM DIALOGUE RIGHTS TO PROPERTY RIGHTS

In the previous sections we discussed the problem, arising in Hayek's work, of generating respect for each individual as an end in themselves from more or less utilitarian premises. We suggested that this might be solved (or, more realistically, that a contribution to it might be made) through an appeal to critical rationalism, first in respect of factual matters, and second in respect of moral judgements. We generated the rights which we were seeking as 'dialogue rights' accorded to individuals *qua* participants in factual and, finally, normative dialogue.

Suppose that our earlier argument was in order. A problem might be raised concerning the pertinence of the conclusions to which we were led. For it might seem as if our approach depended, crucially, on actual, face-to-face dialogue. It might then be suggested that, in political terms, it must generate a variant of the *polis*-sized democratic ideal that has so bedevilled modern political thought. It would, indeed, be ironic if such a view were to be the conclusion of an argument developed in the spirit of Adam Smith and of Hayek. For it was Smith who argued – in contrast to the views of Rousseau and the civic humanists of his day – that the good society was a big society. And Hayek has described the kind of society that he favours as the 'Great Society'.

However, in Popper's *Open Society* an account is offered of the principles that should underlie a large-scale democratic society. This society is, explicitly, not of a face-to-face character. And it is implicitly arrived at by Popper generalizing his view of an idealized community of scientists in dialogue. Does this not show that my argument, above, is incorrect?

I think not. First, Popper's view of scientists as engaged in such dialogue is itself perhaps a little misleading. For even on Popper's own account, scientists will be working within specific and competing metaphysical research programmes. Between these, dialogue is possible, fruitful and extremely important. But for such dialogue to take place is by no means a simple matter or a matter of routine, and it is often inconclusive in its character.[51] Second, scientists are able to engage in dialogue to good effect, even when they are not in face-to-face contact (e.g. through letters or journals). But they can do this just because the scope of the issues that they are discussing is restricted. There are also widely accepted conventions about how such dialogue should proceed.

However, in politics, an inconclusive dialogue is not enough when collective decisions are being taken. For without consensus these decisions will override the very dialogue rights for which we have argued – unless there is explicit agreement to act on, say, a majoritarian basis, on pragmatic grounds. In addition, political issues are multi-dimensional in character (we are back with Hayek's problem of different ideas of the good). But it is difficult to have a fruitful dialogue between more than about four people, unless its scope is severely limited (as anyone with experience in taking group tutorials in a British or Australian university would surely testify).

What all this implies, I would suggest, is that actual dialogue has its limitations as a model for politics. It certainly has an important role to play: at the level of most general principles, or in the determining of the level at which a welfare safety net should operate.[52] It may also have its uses as a forum in which people may be called to give an account of what they are doing, and to respond to criticism. But here we would not expect that consensus will result, and no collective action will necessarily follow.

Does this bring us to the limits of the relevance of the 'dialogue rights' which we spent so much time developing in the present chapter? My answer is: no. For while dialogue itself does have such limitations, the gains which we there made may be preserved in another form. For dialogue may be simulated by means of an 'invisible hand' mechanism.[53] And individuals may be accorded rights, on epistemological grounds, in order to participate in such a mechanism. What this amounts to is the suggestion that there is a natural path from our ideas about dialogue to the ideas about a minimal state, with individual property rights, which we had previously argued was a more appropriate conclusion to draw from Hayek's arguments than was his more interventionist account of the state. If individuals are accorded property rights; if they and their property are protected by a 'nightwatchman state'; and if they are free to engage in what others might regard as experiments in living, and to move between such experiments, all this can serve as a surrogate for that more general dialogue which is not directly attainable.

The character of such property rights, the kind of protection that they are accorded, and what sorts of activity are so protected, are themselves determined by considerations from both epistemology and social theory. Social theory comes in here, because we are concerned with those arrangements which will best allow us to learn, in conditions of scarcity and of uncertainty. And it is in the face of these that Hayek's arguments, together with the public choice argument that we should not treat the state as a benevolent despot,[54] seem to me to tell in favour of a minimal state rather than an approach that would grant individuals more extensive welfare rights for the sake of their contributions to such a surrogate dialogue. In a similar way, we can argue against diverting resources to any considerable extent to bring someone who is very severely handicapped into participation in our dialogue – just because of the high opportunity cost of so doing. However, it is clear that there may be disagreement about such issues. As a result, we may have to agree to differ. Those citizens who believe that the level of support that should be accorded to the disadvantaged in order that they can play a participatory role in our surrogate dialogue is greater than is allowed for by the consensual judgement of other citizens, should be free to use their own resources for this purpose.

This approach provides a rationale for the protection of individual judgements – and, in consequence, of individuals themselves. To this, it adds an argument for the protection of property and of experiments in living as these would be a way in which judgements are externalized (there is a certain parallel here with Hegel's view of property). The nightwatchman state must itself be as neutral as possible between substantive ideas that are being tried out. But it would maintain rules of the game so as to prevent coercion or the entrapment of individuals within experimental communities, and to deal with overspill effects or externalities (the exercise of judgement concerning causality in this latter connection may well involve a policy of non-neutrality concerning the substantive ideas of some particular group).

A model for such ideas is, in fact, to hand in the (unduly neglected) 'utopia' section of Nozick's *Anarchy, State, and Utopia*. Nozick noted a discontinuity between the utopia section of his book and its earlier parts, in that the utopia section did not depend upon his earlier assumptions about rights. In addition Nozick pointed out[55] that there were parallels between the ideas of that section and Popper's philosophy of science. He has later noted a parallel between the 'utopia' section of his first book and the pluralistic (yet truth-directed) approach of the Introduction to his *Philosophical Explanations*. Thus, the link between the epistemologically grounded ideas of this chapter, and this suggestion for their social instantiation, is not without its precursors.

Two points, however, should be made explicitly, because of my reference here to Nozick.

The first is that, by contrast with the earlier parts of Nozick's *Anarchy, State, and Utopia*, in the final section of his book, rights – as in Hayek's work – are being accorded as a means to an end: the pursuit of the good (as in our dialogue about ethics), utility (where there is consensus about this) and truth. This, however, means that while judgements, individuals as the source of them, and property as instantiations of them are accorded protection, the basis on which this is done is instrumental, and arrangements here will be shaped by argument as to what represents the best use of our resources. This will mean that, as we noted above, we are not committed to saying that resources must be used come what may to give someone a voice in our dialogue if the opportunity cost of so doing would be high.

The second is that, because of the epistemological basis of our argument, the character of property rights may not prove quite the same as is familiar from classical liberalism. For, while substantive judgements will as far as possible be protected (so that there will be a presumption of freedom of contract between adults), property rights may be limited, as a consequence of Popper's epistemological ban on 'conventionalist strategies'. That is to say, there may be an epistemologically generated restriction on the right to use property for the construction of certain kinds of social formation which protect people's judgements from critical scrutiny.

In particular, this has the consequence of giving us a picture of classical liberalism rather different from that which we obtain from the economist. For while all that the economist stresses – and our forms of experimentation – are there, they operate in the context of a public forum. This serves both as the place within which the rules of the system are legitimated to its inhabitants, and also within which different specific forms of life must give an account of themselves.

In our liberal metautopia, experimentation and learning take place via the activities of individuals. Individuals back their own judgement with their own resources in the membership of some society, organization, club or, more radically, experimental community. Learning takes place via those individuals deciding they had made a mistake and pulling out; or staying and making whatever changes are allowed for by the particular constitution of the small-scale organization which they have joined; or by their being joined by, or imitated by, others. For all this to take place, it is necessary that there be a state – or some other institution which plays a similar role – which preserves individuals (and voluntary communities and associations) from aggression and overspill effects, and which also prevents individuals from being held prisoner by some community or association that they have joined. Such an authority must as far as possible be neutral between the substantive enterprises and beliefs of specific organizations or communities, but must take particular care that children – second generation members – have the opportunity to exercise choice between alternatives. Communities themselves may be as 'open' or as 'closed' as their members wish. They may exemplify different particular claims to knowledge, say, as to the character of the good life; or different constitutional theories about how social organizations should change with circumstances. In their internal organization they may be, variously, democratic, authoritarian or traditionalistic, and socialist; and among them would presumably figure, as a large-scale social experiment, Hayek's own specific ideas for the constitutional organization of a good society. Within communities, roles and property may be distributed on whatever basis its constitution or rules state. Individuals, as mentioned above, would be free to leave one community and to join or set up another – though, clearly, some community may impose conditions on new members, or conditions upon those who may wish to leave it, subject, obviously, to the broader requirements laid down by the framework authority.

All these ideas, however, also have a further role. For they offer us an opportunity to solve some problems otherwise left open by Hayek's ideas. This, however, we will explore in the next chapter.

7

KNOWLEDGE AND IMPERFECTION IN A MINIMAL STATE

A RETROSPECT AND SOME PROBLEMS

Let me sum up the situation that we have reached so far. My argument has been that Hayek, starting from concerns which might be described as broadly utilitarian, moved from an early socialism to advocate a market-based social order, under the impact of Mises and of his own development of the argument from economic calculation under socialism. This led him to a distinctive view of markets and their functions, of other institutions such as the legal system, and also of the political process. This brought him to an appreciation of the importance of individuals being free to learn, of competition as allowing for discovery and as a check upon power, and also of the inevitable imperfection of some of our major social institutions. All this, in turn, led him to the view that his early self – the person concerned with the alleviation of misery – should turn to markets as opposed to socialism and the central direction of the economy, for the pursuit of his ideals. He argued, further, that once a moral choice had been made for a market-based social order, certain other goals, such as 'social justice', could not at the same time be successfully pursued.

The younger, post-Mises, Hayek had some good arguments against central planning and forms of interventionism which did not take account of markets. Later, Hayek introduced some arguments which also hit 'market-wise' socialists: on the one side, an argument that some of their aims, such as tendencies towards corporatism, were in fact undesirable in their consequences, in that, if effected, they would prevent the operation of important checks to the power of companies in the market-place. He argued further that they also took a naive view of the political process, in the sense of assuming too lightly that their ethical aims would be realized within it. Not only is there a problem as to whether some goals can be realized at all, given individuals' freedom of action in the situations in which they find themselves, but there is also a tendency, on the part of those who ask for governmental intervention, to assume that governments with the power to realize their goals would in fact act to do so. This, in effect, leads to an important methodological point: that it is not enough for the normative theorist to offer a shopping list of what is desirable.

He also has to explain, institutionally, how it can be realized, where his account will also require that we take a realistic view of how agents within his model will behave.

All this serves to strengthen Hayek's case against those moderate socialists or corporatists with whom he was involved, such as Rathenau and Wieser. It also suggests the lines along which his ideas might be developed against his modern critics, such as David Miller. At the same time, it generates some problems.

Hayek offers some views of his own concerning the scope of governmental activity, and also some constitutional proposals as to how government might be restricted to the scope that he prefers. In his exposition of these, Hayek dissents from the view that the state should have only minimal functions. As I have suggested, his argument here is open to criticism. In my view, his constitutional proposals would not serve to limit government along the lines that he desires. There also seem to be excellent arguments, in his own work, as to why government should not be accorded more than minimal functions.

However, a difficulty of a different kind faces Hayek. During the course of his own argument, there arise three kinds of problem about social institutions concerning knowledge, to which he does not offer an adequate solution. The first is the idea, which runs through so much of Hayek's work, that our social institutions are inevitably imperfect. This poses a problem, just because it is not clear how citizens will be able to match up the disadvantages of such institutions with the benefits that they obtain from them. While this is information that might be possessed by a social theorist, it is not clear how it is supposed to be accessible to citizens. And while, to a degree, these problems may be solved in a practical way, through citizens simply being accustomed to their own societies and their institutions, Hayek's own insistence on the importance of experimentation, if citizens were to take it to heart, would have the consequence that they will question whether things must work as they do. It is not clear how Hayek's constitutional proposals can assist here, in the sense that we have any reason to believe that the citizens who serve on his legislative body, and the political forces to which they respond, will produce the appropriate results.

Second, there is a problem of expert theoretical knowledge. There is here the problem, which the younger Hayek highlighted, of how to reform our legal institutions such that they will play a better functional role within a market society. There is also a further problem, raised by the way in which, throughout Hayek's work, he offers us substantive suggestions as to what government should or should not do, which depend upon his own ideas in economics and on other matters. Again, while Hayek might be right concerning what he is suggesting we should do, it is not clear how one can expect a government or a legislative body within Hayek's constitutional arrangements, to say nothing of those who elect them, to accept and then to act upon his views – not least because of Hayek's own belief that such institutions will have ineliminable defects.

Third, a problem is posed for Hayek's own views as a consequence of his ideas about the disaggregation of decision-taking, and of the way in which social institutions are typically the products of human action but not of human design. This, for Hayek, was a useful critical tool. But it is one that can also be turned against his own ideas. For we can well ask: can the kind of social order that Hayek favours be maintained on the basis of the disaggregated decision-taking that will characterize a society of the kind that Hayek favours? That is to say, suppose that citizens indeed thought that the kind of society that Hayek depicts is a good society. We can still ask: will those citizens be able to maintain such a society in existence, given that its continued existence will be a by-product of disaggregated decision-taking?

There is also a further source of problems for Hayek's views. Hayek's argument is consequentialist in its character. But there are tendencies within his own work which suggest that there are problems about such argument. I have discussed these at some length, and in response have suggested that we can perfectly well make the kinds of comparisons about people's well-being that, in my view, his own argument demands. If we are arguing about socialism as it was traditionally understood, i.e. as an approach that would replace markets with planning, it seems to me that Hayek simply wins the argument. However, the more the live alternatives to his ideas shift from demands for full-scale socialist planning, for the pursuit of social justice in some full-fledged sense, or that we should give power to administrators to act as they think fit in the pursuit of some ideal, the less clear-cut Hayek's argument becomes. For just what does Hayek have to say to those who accept his broad case for the market and for the rule of law, but urge a case for, say, greater entitlements for the disabled than Hayek would seem to favour, within it? While one would be led by Hayek's approach to demand a full account of the institutions that are being proposed, and while the person who favours Hayek's views will examine critically their likely consequences, this exercise is hardly likely to be productive of a definitive argument for Hayek's views.

Indeed, there are two issues here. The first is that, against Hayek, it would seem as if both qualitative and quantitative knowledge about trade-offs becomes vital. I believe that Hayek is correct in thinking that there is something desirable about using general arguments if one can obtain them. I also think that he is right that we should not admit criteria for explanation which blind us to the possibility of knowledge of the qualitative or 'pattern prediction' kind that he offers us. However, Hayek himself seems to need to be able to make quantitative assessments of the costs and benefits of various proposed policies if he is to be able to engage in argument about them with those who want to use government to pursue socialist values within a market economy. This, however, leads us to a further issue. I can well imagine that Hayek could be vindicated in respect of some proposals, although this would clearly depend upon the specifics of each case. It may well turn out that those with whom he disagrees will have been proposing things which are not in fact compossible, or which turn out to be morally problematic. But in many other cases, we will simply be faced by alternatives, each with their characteristic costs and benefits, between which we would seem simply to have to make a choice.

Consider, for example, ideal types of three different kinds of society, loosely based upon idealized versions of Britain, the United States and, say, Sweden, each of which (for the sake of argument) was following policies that did not depart too radically from the concerns of the young Hayek. (These societies might, say, instantiate packages which offered, respectively, a tendency towards elitism, individualism and moderate welfare policies; anti-elitism, individualism and low welfare policies; and anti-elitism, low individualism and generous welfare policies.) It would certainly seem possible to depict someone rationally making a choice for life in one or the other of these societies, when knowing something about the distribution of wealth, of welfare and of different kinds of freedoms and of opportunities within them, and to argue that their choice was fully compatible with the kinds of concerns that had exercised the young Hayek. They would, however, recognize, and give different weights to, other values. At a certain point, it would seem to me that argument of Hayek's kind – of a character that, broadly speaking, is concerned with issues in political economy – must come to a halt, leaving us with individuals having different tastes, or possibly pursuing their disagreements by means of argument within moral philosophy. And while it may be possible to resolve some disputes as to the character of the good society through argument, or through their being tried out as experiments in living, it is not clear what, at a certain point, could be said for or against someone who favours one rather than another such society, knowing their characteristics and the distributions of different benefits within them. It starts to become a bit like arguments about the desirability of mountaineering or sitting at home reading and listening to classical music, and to relate, clearly, to the issues about values and choices raised but not resolved in our earlier discussion of welfare.

In part, our attitudes towards such matters will depend upon our view of the balance of the argument concerning the character of our obligations towards others. I have earlier advanced a line of argument which if it can be sustained would push our choices here away from some large-scale conception of social justice, and in the direction of a combination of individualism and local obligations. However, we were, in that discussion, at some way removed from Hayek's own arguments.

I would like, here, to explore another approach, which is much closer in its spirit to Hayek's work, for what it may offer concerning *all* of these problems. Before we turn to it, and to a brief exploration of some of its characteristics (a full examination would demand a separate book), I would like to recur to one other issue. For in the points that I have made in the last few paragraphs, I have stressed issues of choice and pluralism. But we should not neglect one other line of argument that has run through this volume from the very start: the *non-pluralistic* theme that someone who shared the values of the early Hayek should choose a market-orientated political economy, not the socialism of Hayek's youth. The reader will recall that I earlier gave a further twist to this argument, by suggesting that Hayek's own vision of an active state limited by his constitutional proposals was unlikely to deliver what he was after, and that the arguments that he has advanced should lead us, instead, towards a minimal state. It is, indeed, such a minimal state, and voluntary formations within it, that it is interesting to consider as a setting within which can be resolved our problems of pluralism and choice, and of the problematic character of claims to knowledge such as those made by Hayek himself.

A LIBERAL METAUTOPIA

This is not the place for me to try to set out the rationale for the adoption of the groundrules of a liberal metautopia, or to say much about its characteristics, or the problems to which it may give rise. Some of this I have attempted earlier; but any more extensive discussion clearly belongs to a project rather different from the present one. Rather, I will here suggest that, as a place-holder for a discussion of the characteristics of such a metautopia, the reader considers Robert Nozick's discussion in *Anarchy, State, and Utopia*. (I should remind the reader that this section of Nozick's work is not dependent on the rights-based approaches of the earlier chapters of his work. Rather, he suggests that one might understand it, alternatively, either in utilitarian terms, or in terms of its role as a discovery procedure.)

Essentially, our concern is with a minimal state which is liberal in its character, in the sense of being concerned with individuals' freedom from coercion, and the protection of their property rights (it would, thus, not possess the richer characteristics of Hayek's favoured constitutional order, in so far as these rest upon his substantive theories of political economy and its relation to law). Within the bounds of such a regime, individuals could choose membership of different organizations, from clubs, through residential communities, to quasi-states, which would offer their different packages of regulations, entitlements and so on. The central state would protect the autonomy of such groups from the aggression of others, and protect the freedom of exit and property rights of individual members.

One important feature of such ideas relates to the kind of freedom that they accord to individuals. Essentially, it allows them rights to their own person and property and the right to form and to exit from forms of voluntary organization upon terms that they agree.[1] What it does *not* allow is the right to change the basis upon which such forms of organization are constituted, except in so far as this is itself agreed as part of their constitution. Accordingly, while somebody might choose to live in a participatory democracy, he and his fellows would only be able to impose their will through the ballot box upon those who had also agreed to live in such a regime.

What regimes people could choose to live in would be constrained by the fact that those who wished to do so could leave any such regime, and would be protected in this right by the framework government. Such a government would, however, protect them only from the breach by individuals or associations of contractual obligations, such that if, say, they had been foolish enough to enter a democracy which then (in proper accordance with its own constitution) passed laws to seize their property, they would have no right to ask the central government to restore to them their property – although they would have the right to appeal to it to get them out with whatever was left to them. They would also have rights of exit but not of entry. Thus, say, those who had chosen 'America' but had done badly from it would have the right to exit from 'America' (although they might have to undertake some period in prison first, if they had broken any of its laws), but not to enter 'Sweden' and enjoy its welfare benefits, except under such conditions as 'Sweden' might impose. Similarly – and however much I may regret this, personally – there would be no right for the fat and balding to demand admission to groups which had been set up with some minimal standard of physical attractiveness as an entry requirement. (I should mention, however, that in my view the framework government should maintain a forum in which the desirability of such discrimination on the basis of race, sex or sexual preference, could be the topic of argument, and in which people could be called upon to answer criticism of their views and choices – and their consequences.)

Within such a regime, social experiments of various kinds could be tried out by those who had interest in so doing. It would also allow for the realization of regimes of different kinds, such that our 'Sweden', 'Britain' and 'United States' could be chosen by those who favoured them. In addition, wilder ideas could be tried out too, provided that they were tried out, and sustained, on a basis of consent amongst their members. (Although, clearly, the viability of 'Sweden' would depend upon its being preferred, even by those who would do well in 'America', and where – and perhaps against the ethical ideas that had originally inspired it – it may clearly have to limit entry from those who tried but were unsuccessful in 'America'.) Such choices would also allow for the exemplification of different views of the good life; in addition, they would serve as a learning mechanism. Hayek's concern for experimentation would be satisfied, and by such means what Hayek was hoping for in his discussion of social 'evolution', would also seem to me to be realized.

As I have indicated, I do not wish here to explore further the characteristics – and the problems – of such societies.[2] Instead, I will discuss how such an arrangement would offer a solution to some of the problems in Hayek's work which we have raised earlier in this volume. They are the (related) issues of expert knowledge, and of the disadvantages of even the best institutions to which we can aspire. I will discuss these – and present a solution to them –

through a consideration of these problems as they arise in the work of two historical figures, whose work Hayek has himself used as the vehicle for the exposition of these problems – Hume and Mandeville.[3]

HUME, COMPLEX INSTITUTIONS AND EXIT RIGHTS

In his *Treatise*, Hume argued 'tis only the concurrence of mankind, in a general scheme or system . . . which is advantageous'; and while 'the whole scheme . . . of law and justice is advantageous to . . . society', if we consider *particular* cases we may find that 'Judges take from a poor man to give to a rich; they bestow on the dissolute the labour of the industrious; and put into the hands of the vicious the means of harming both themselves and others'.[4]

Hume, that is to say, is concerned that a system of justice which bestows great social benefits may intrinsically generate certain difficult cases – cases which cannot be remedied by changing the system, without damage to the system itself. Hayek – who, as we have seen, follows Hume in this – takes the view that even the best of social institutions will have such defects, and that these institutions are in consequence vulnerable to those who demand change on the basis of the detection of such defects.

In his *Essays*, Hume writes:[5]

All general laws are attended with inconveniences, when applied to particular cases; and it requires great penetration and experience, both to perceive that these inconveniences are fewer than what result from full discretionary powers in every magistrate; and also to discern what general laws are, upon the whole, attended with fewest inconveniences.

It is, it would seem to me, plausible to suggest that it is this very thesis which lies at the root of the highly conservative views that are expressed in – for example – Hume's 'Of the Original Contract'. In this essay, in the course of his criticism of the doctrine of tacit consent, Hume takes the view that even people who leave their native land and settle in some hitherto uninhabited region are commonly – and it would seem from Hume's discussion in his view correctly – considered their King's subjects.[6]

But why should Hume endorse such a strong conception of a citizen's allegiance to his sovereign? Hume's view becomes comprehensible, it would seem to me, in the light of his view of the character of a legal system and his scepticism about the powers of human reason. For how else – one might think – could a legal system of the character that Hume has described remain in being, given that citizens can hardly appreciate its rationale intellectually, other than by their having powerful and relatively undiscriminating habits of allegiance? If we are to have such useful institutions as a legal system of the kind that Hume describes – it seems to me that Hume may have thought – citizens must be highly conservative in their habits of obedience.

Now, whether or not I am correct in my speculations about Hume's views, this problem of the maintenance of complex institutions is certainly to be found in Hayek's work – not least in his own discussion of Hume's political thought. For example, and going back to his Inaugural Address at the LSE, there is Hayek's view that the market order itself makes essential use of forms of human motivation that are unlovely. Being guided by profit and self-interest may not, in itself, be at all morally appealing; and while, as Hayek has argued, the rich play an important functional role in a liberal society, as an initial market for goods which gradually become available to us all, this does not make them and their activities any more lovely in the eyes of the rest of us.

A similar problem is posed by the functional role played in liberalism by a legal system – and a form of distribution of benefits in the market-place – that treats everyone equally, in the sense of being no respecter of those local claims and preferences which form the moral order in which we live our day-to-day lives. In addition – and as Hayek has argued at some length – the market does not reward on the basis of effort or merit, but in terms of the functional role that is played by someone's efforts and endowments, and even on the basis of where someone happens to be at some particular time.

Thus, Hayek's much-treasured market order, which he believes citizens would prefer to any alternative social formation if they could only see it in all its glory, is – like Hume's system of justice – full of particular problems. And citizens' reactions to these problems may lead them to reject what – in Hayek's view – is the best attainable framework of social institutions.

The very same kind of problem also arises – as Hayek has argued – in respect of systems of social conventions, or social roles. Here, again, the very best system may have its defects, and citizens striving to remedy these may well destroy the systems themselves.

Hayek has put this very point strikingly in a lecture:[7]

> We owe not only our prosperity, but our capacity to maintain a population as large as that to which the Western world has grown, to obeying certain traditional rules or morals, essentially the rules of property and the family, whose functions we have never understood, which people dislike because they do not understand their function, and against which the great revolutionary movements of our time, socialism and communism, are directed.

In Hayek's work, just as in Hume's, the reaction to this problem is, as we have seen, a certain kind of conservatism. As Hayek wrote in his 'Individualism: True and False':[8]

> The individual, in participating in the social processes must be ready and willing to ... submit to conventions ... whose justification in the particular instance may not be recognizable, and which to him will often appear unintelligible and irrational.

And, further, that

> It is an open question whether a free or individualistic society can be worked successfully if people ... are too unwilling to conform to traditions and conventions and if they refuse to recognise anything ... which cannot be demonstrated as rational to every individual.[9]

But as we saw earlier, this reaction clearly will not do. For Hayek has a theory of the development of such institutions, and must thus also allow for the possibility of that innovation which is a necessary condition for such development to take place. Thus, what is needed is a theory which can allow for both the conservatism needed to maintain useful complex institutions, and for innovation so as to allow institutions to develop. It must also solve this problem in such a way that innovation does not bring about the destruction of valuable institutions of a systematic character which possess the kinds of unlovely features which we have discussed, above.

To this problem the metautopian liberal ideas suggested earlier would seem to offer a solution, through the kinds of choice and of freedom they allow to the individual. For they would grant the individual freedom – but only either as is agreed within the particular institutions in which he is living, or in the form of the freedom to move or to found some other institutions. Within such a system, the restrictions of life in a particular community are not properly considered a restriction upon an individual's freedom, just because he has the opportunity to leave.

As a result, when Hume argued in 'Of the Original Contract':[10]

> And did a prince observe, that many of his subjects were seized with the frenzy of migrating to foreign countries, he would doubtless, with great reason and justice, restrain them .... Would he forfeit the allegiance of all his subjects, by so wise and reasonable a law?

he had got things completely wrong. For while a willingness, of some sort or another, to go along with the conventions and obligations of the system in which one is living may be a necessary condition for its maintenance, there would seem every reason why the freedom to migrate should be allowed. And this may mean simply moving down the road, or joining or forming a new club.

The possibilities opened up to citizens by the rights that they are granted by such a regime would also appear to allow for just those 'evolutionary' patterns of learning – by movement and imitation, without full intellectual understanding – which have so exercised Hayek in his more recent writings.

SCEPTICAL LIBERALISM AND PROBLEMS OF POLITICAL KNOWLEDGE

One weakness that would seem to be possessed by Hayek's liberalism is that it would seem to have no room for claims to political expertise – other than those that can be recognized by all citizens (whether directly, or via some mechanism such as representative government; a problem which also so concerned J. S. Mill).[11] The fundamental issue, here, is of claims to expert knowledge concerning large-scale social, moral or political issues. If someone claims expertise as a ruler, or as the maker of constitutions, or even as the possessor of knowledge as to how our existing institutions should be reformed, it might not seem as if his knowledge can be utilized by individual citizens in the same way as, say, that of the person who claims expertise as a plumber. The difficulty is that the people making the claims in question ask for power. Not only is there the problem of assessing who actually possesses knowledge in this area. But if people gain power there is the problem of how to prevent them abusing it. If one reacts to this problem by suggesting democratic decision-making, then unless the majority of the people can recognize the cogency of the claims in question, as they are put to them in the hustings, the benefits of the knowledge may be lost.

Now, it might be possible to react by saying simply that this is tough, or by denying that there could be expertise which could not be recognized by ordinary people through democratic processes and debate. But such a response poses a problem: can liberalism do without those 'statesmen' and statesmen-like figures, whose task seems to be to manipulate the situations in which citizens find themselves (whether directly or by means of constitutions), such that self-interest and 'natural' (or unreflective) forms of behaviour will then lead citizens to act in the public interest?[12]

Hayek himself, at times, seems to require such action to be taken, on the basis of theoretical knowledge that is hardly possessed by the populace at large. Consider his proposals for the denationalization of money, his plea that a new set of constitutional arrangements are needed, or his arguments for the reform of our inherited legal ideas so that they will function better for the purposes of a market-based economy. And if one looks at the history of liberal political thought – say, at the ideas of those figures whom Hayek has identified as close to his own views – a number of similar examples spring to mind.

First, there is Mandeville's manipulative statesman. In his *Letter to Dion*, his reply to Berkeley's *Alciphron*, Mandeville emphasizes that his views will be misunderstood if one simply focuses on the subtitle of his *Fable of the Bees*, namely, 'private vices, public benefits'. For, he says,

> It is evident that the words 'private vices, public benefits' make not a complete sentence according to grammar; and that there is at least a verb if not a great deal more wanting to make the sense perfect.[13]

And he continues:

> In the *Vindication of the Fable of the Bees* I have said that I understand by it that private vices, by the dextrous management of a skilful politician, might be turned into public benefits.

It may be thought that liberalism does not, generally, stand in need of such people. But consider the following comment from Lionel Robbins on classical liberalism:[14]

> So far from the system of economic freedom being something which will certainly come into being if things are just left to take their course, it will only come into being if things are not left to take their course; if a conscious effort is made to create the highly artificial environment which is necessary if it is to function properly.

But who, precisely, is envisaged as making such a conscious effort; and how are they in a position to be able to perform this task?

And as for Adam Smith – whom some might suppose an exception to all this – Rosenberg has commented that in Smith's view a particular institutional framework was required, if beneficial consequences were to be derived from a market order; one which would

> cut off all avenues (and there are many) along which wealth may be pursued without contributing to the welfare of society.[15]

If such activity is needed, it is important to ask who is performing it, and how such activity is compatible with the principles of liberalism.

Second, there is a problem concerning the specific activities of the statesman in Smith. These may be related to the problematic of the civic humanist tradition. Basically, in Smith's work there is a recognition of some 'disadvantages of commercial society', in which the complaints against commerce and cities of the civic humanist tradition are reinterpreted as problems intrinsic to commercial society and the division of labour. In the face of these, Smith usually appeals for (moderate) state action – especially in taking measures that force citizens to acquire a modicum of education. Thus, Smith writes:[16]

> Ought the publick ... to give no attention ... to the education of the people? Or if it ought to give any, what are the different parts of education which it ought to attend to in the different orders of the people? And in what manner ought it to attend to them? In some cases, the state of society necessarily places the greater part of such individuals in such situations as naturally form in them, without any attention of government, almost all the abilities and virtues that the state requires or perhaps can admit of. In other cases the state of ... society does not place the greater part of individuals in such situations, and some attention of government is necessary in order to prevent the almost entire corruption and degeneracy of the great body of the people.

Further, both Donald Winch and Knud Haakonssen have argued for the idea that an important role is played by the activities of the statesman or legislator and by politics in Smith's work.[17] But such a move brings us straight back to the problem of how, in liberalism, the possessor of this 'knowledge' is to be granted power so as to make others comply with its – his – diagnosis (a problem that is not eased by his offering to act by means of fixed constitutional principles, as opposed to discretionary means).

Third, James Mill and the public choice tradition which has followed him have raised the important problem of the motivation of the ruler – and more generally, of those in positions of power – and of how the interests of the ruler can be linked to those of the ruled.

Our suggestion offers the possibility of solutions to some of these problems. For if we are concerned with specific claims about the good life, made by some statesman – let us call him 'Plato' – they may actually be tried out, by 'Plato' and anyone whom he can convince of the *prima facie* interest of his claims, as a voluntary community. While the wider system is liberal in character, there is nothing to stop someone choosing voluntarily to enter (under certain specified conditions)[18] a system within which he does not have the full freedoms which he enjoyed under the wider system, and in which he is subject to the rule of 'Plato'. This may involve any sort of regime we may imagine – including the *specific* constitutional and other ideas which constitute Hayek's own version of liberalism.

The special advantage, here, would seem to be that the knowledge claims of 'Plato' can be tried out. So presumably, in so far as they held good and life in his community was indeed all he claimed for it, this fact would be manifest, and others might well also want to join or to imitate it. On the other hand, in so far as the claims were perceived by his followers not to work, they would be free to leave. Their right to go – and to take anything that remained of their property – would be safeguarded by the wider government. It is interesting also to note that the threat of members possibly leaving might of itself go a long way to identify the interests of the ruler and the ruled: *prima facie*, it would be very much against the interests of the ruler to lose his one-time followers in such a manner.

Indeed, it is worth noting that in our quotation from Hume about the prevention of migration, I omitted the phrase 'in order to prevent the depopulation of his own kingdom'. The ability of a ruler to use force in such circumstances removes a major constraint over his policies: that they must be such that people will wish to remain in his realm!

I will sum up this section by relating it to the contrast that Hirschman makes between 'exit' and 'voice'.[19] Hayek's argument about problems of consensus and interest groups within democracy suggests that there are severe limitations on the power of 'voice' to offer a genuine resolution of problems, if dialogue is unrestricted in its scope. Hayek's own constitutional suggestions seem to me still to give too much scope to government for voice to be effective. My suggestion gives pride of place to exit. But the fact that exit is guaranteed (and that there is a residual element of accountability by dialogue to one's external critics) means that within *particular* communities and traditions voice *may* become important and prove its worth, such that if people are interested in

209

such things, participatory democracy and loyalty to collective decisions may become an important feature of life in particular communities. But there can clearly be other communities in which voice does not play any significant role.

Hayek's substantive political thought – as opposed to the attenuated version of it which forms our metautopia – would constitute one community or tradition among other actual or possible communities. And if Hayek's theoretical ideas are in order, it would presumably attract citizens to it, in virtue of its success.

THE MINIMAL STATE

The argument in this chapter has two themes. The first, which we have explored in the preceding sections, was that some problems that are outstanding in Hayek, and others that are raised when considering what is at issue between him and some of his critics, might be resolved through the device of a liberal metautopia. But this, clearly, is also related to my second theme: that the logic of Hayek's own argument points to a minimal state, rather than to the limited state that Hayek himself favours. To issues raised by this suggestion, I now turn.

The argument that I offered, earlier, for this option, has two aspects to it. The first is that it is a conclusion that should be accepted through the consideration of Hayek's own arguments, and some critical reflection upon his own constitutional proposals. While it would constitute a strong argument for the state, for someone with the concerns of the early Hayek, if the state could, indeed, handle problems of public goods and externalities in an acceptable manner, there is no reason to suppose that *actual* states can be depended upon to do any such thing. Indeed, there is a significant but underappreciated theme within the classical liberal tradition – of the state as a vehicle of exploitation[20] – which should alert us to the possibility that it is a mistake to think of the state as an obvious instrument through which we may collectively pursue our common interests, but which is sometimes captured by particular interests. Rather, the state might be seen as a vehicle of coercive exploitation, which legitimates itself by providing 'public goods' (and to the alternative provision of which those who at any one time control the state or benefit from it are thus understandably hostile), but which can sometimes be tamed by its victims. Clearly, the merits of such contrasting views cannot be argued here. But it is certainly worth considering that there is an alternative to the view that we should think of the state as the natural vehicle for whatever ideas we consider to be conducive to the well-being of humankind.

Our second argument was that a minimal state would allow both for diversity, but also for the possibility of solving some of the knowledge-related problems that are raised by Hayek's work, as we have seen in the previous section.

Against such views, however, it could be claimed that any proposal for a minimal state would founder upon problems of community, moral identity and legitimacy. I will conclude by addressing these issues briefly. So far, I have suggested that our minimalist interpretation of Hayek's ideas will furnish solutions to problems that are raised by, but not fully resolved within, Hayek's work: the problem posed by the imperfection of social institutions, and the problem of claims to expertise.

In this section, I argue that these ideas also suggest a way in which a further problem that is often thrown at the classical liberal might be resolved: the problem of community and of moral identity. A full identification of such problems would require a historical treatment that I cannot offer here.[21] Suffice it to say that from around the end of the eighteenth century civic humanists, and subsequently some conservatives and early socialists, criticized a market-based society on the grounds that it was destructive of social institutions and relationships that had earlier provided an identity for the individual and had contributed to the constitution of his moral character. The history of the argument is wide-ranging. It includes debates among the Founding Fathers about the character of the new United States,[22] and the understanding of the disadvantages of commercial society as discussed in the work of Adam Smith and Adam Ferguson[23] and their reception and reinterpretation in Germany.[24] It may be questioned how much historical verisimilitude the premises of the entire discussion possessed;[25] but for better or worse the discussion became an important element in our own intellectual culture, and is very much a live issue today.[26]

There are, as I understand it, two central criticisms involved of a liberal, market-orientated society. The first is that such a society is atomizing in its consequences, destructive of intermediate institutions and in consequence destructive of the individual's socially constituted moral character. The second is that, as a further consequence, such a society faces a legitimacy problem, in that it cannot produce, from its own resources, the moral capital needed to legitimate itself to its citizens.

First, let us look at the problem of morality. There are several different strands to the problem about morality that a market-based society is understood as facing. The most powerful rests upon the view that our moral characters are a social product and depend upon the presence of appropriate institutions and social monitoring. The idea is that the content of our moral conduct is bound up with particular social roles or identities sustained by particular ways of life, and thus with particular social institutions. Such a social role, and such institutions, give a specific content to moral responsibility, and provide objects for its exercise; other members of such institutions – and more generally of one's community – socialize one into such a character, and sustain one in it through their monitoring, and their approval or disapproval of one's conduct.

Commercial society is seen as morally destructive because it is seen as destructive of these institutions and of the patterns of socialization and of monitoring that are based upon them. The most plausible reason why commercial society is seen as having such effects would seem to be that received patterns of behaviour are set within traditions that have economic components, and in a market-based society these economic components are, in principle, open to competition. Yet there is no special reason to suppose that those institutions that are economically successful in such competition will bring with them roles and new patterns of behaviour that will sustain the old patterns of moral behaviour, or anything else that can play a similar role. Market-based societies also bring with them possibilities for mobility that can free individuals from authority figures and from monitoring – notably, life in a big city – and which in consequence limit the authority that institutions exercise over those who stay (because they now have the option of going). In addition, increased choice and opportunities for profitable activity give individuals the opportunity to scrutinize existing institutions and ways of spending their time, from the point of view of immediate personal satisfaction. And this may lead to a reduction of time put into the sustaining of older obligations.

A second, and venerable, line of argument goes back to the distrust of commerce exhibited in Plato and Aristotle, and to civic humanism's concerns for the dangers of wealth. The idea here (in its modern reworking) is that morality – and especially the morality required of a citizen in a democracy – requires a certain toughness of character and willingness to avoid self-indulgence. Yet wealth – and the (mixed) blessings that go with it – are, if the advocates of a market-based society are to be believed, the natural products of such a society. It might further be argued that a person whose character is shaped by commercial society, and by advertising within it, is a sorry creature, yet its siren voices, projected with great sophistication, outweigh the moral council of family and friends.

One additional argument which has considerable appeal but which is much less powerful is a collectivist version of our first argument. This is the view that, in some sense, communities have rights *per se* and that these are called into question within a market-based society. But here, the premise is so dubious as to render the argument extremely weak. For it is not clear why a community should be accorded rights over and above those of its members; not least as to do so would typically bring with it the imposition of the preferences of one set of people – those who benefit from membership of the community – upon those of others: those who are members of the community but who do not wish to continue their membership, or those whose activity has sustained the community but who no longer wish to continue the relationship. In so far as there are genuine problems here, they would seem to be problems of expectations; most radically of the person who contributes to the life and welfare of a community under the expectation that he will benefit in his turn, only to discover that there is nothing there to give him assistance when the time comes to ask for help, instead of receiving it.

In so far as such problems are a product of a distinctively commercial society, however, they would seem to me open to solution within it. The fact that informal arrangements are labile within such a society may be handled by spelling out obligations in contractual terms[27] and the taking out of insurance to cover contingencies. Indeed, such instabilities are not just a product of commercial society: the difference, rather, is that it is only commercial society that offers such remedies.

As to the more general problem of intermediate institutions, I would accept that inherited institutions may indeed wither in such a society. But we should not be too ready to blame commercial society for atomization. For within such a society, the loss of intermediate institutions is open to an attractive solution: the formation of new ones, better adapted to mobility and social change. These can be an important vehicle for the individual's choice of his identity, in the sense of choosing what, of his background and of the options open to him, will be important for him. And it can also become an important vehicle for the provision of welfare and other forms of assistance, too. The absence or decline of such institutions in modern 'commercial societies' could be a consequence of the state provision of medical and welfare services which has been accompanied by a spectacular decline in forms of mutual aid.[28] If this is correct, and I offer it as a suggestion which demands further research rather than something for which I can here offer convincing arguments, it would suggest a reason as to why the state should not be involved in the provision of welfare at all: that *this* contributes to social atomization, by removing from citizens the incentive to form and sustain moral communities.

Second, it has been argued further that a liberal society faces a particular problem about legitimacy.

The argument might be developed as follows. Even if one were to grant Hayek's general claims about a market-based social order, it is not clear that it would be found acceptable by its citizens. For, as Hayek has himself stressed, there is no clear relationship between the rewards offered by such a society and an individual's merit. It is not the case that if an individual works hard and does all that he can to better himself, he will meet with success. Accordingly, while liberalism may inherit a habit of compliance with its institutions – notably, property rights – from a pre-capitalist era, it cannot offer an acceptable rationale for these to its citizens. In addition, markets and their associated legal orders may generate many situations that are very tough on particular individuals and which are resented by them and by those who know their situation. In the face of this, they may seek for political redress. But as Habermas has argued in his *Legitimation Crisis*, using arguments that in some ways parallel those offered by Hayek,[29] it is not clear that the state can meet their expectations, either.

In my view, the kind of arrangements that we have explored in this chapter offer ways in which such problems can be solved. Essentially, the path to their solution has two branches. At one level, it requires the defence of a minimalist liberal society – of our framework – upon a rationalistic basis. (Compare, in this context, Hayek's own comment, in *Law, Legislation and Liberty*, in which he writes: 'It must...in the last resort be our intellect and not intuitive perception of what is good which must guide us'.)[30] Such a regime, and the bare institutions of private property, would require legitimation through argument; argument that, above all, emphasizes their role as a vehicle for individuals to express their own judgements about their lives and the kind of societies in which they wish to live. The second level of legitimation is one of choice: people have the freedom to choose what kinds of social institution they wish to participate in, on both a large and a small scale. In making such choices, they choose to take the rough with the smooth, and the imperfections of commercial society, and of the legal system and of other institutions that Hayek has done so much to highlight, are chosen along with the large-scale and desirable consequences with which they are associated.

To be sure, people may make bad choices. And even those who choose the best of societies may find that they do not prosper within them. But because their situation is one that they have chosen, it seems to me that there need be no special problems of legitimation associated with it. And as for community, I would suspect that, if individuals are responsible for their own welfare provision, the problem in commercial society is going to be not too little community, but too much, and that John Stuart Mill's concerns about social pressure upon individuality will be more real than will worries about *anomie*. But all this, and any further exploration of these admittedly speculative ideas (and of the problems to which, in their turn, they lead), must await another occasion.

CONCLUSION

What, after all this, is the task that faces those attracted to Hayek's approach to liberalism? I would see this as having three dimensions.

First, there is the need to develop, clarify and defend the value basis of such a view. Just what is it about a classical liberal social order that is supposed to make it so attractive? And just what do each of us, within it, owe to one another and why? To this task I believe that I have here made some contributions, both critical and positive, although I have no illusions as to the strength of such positive arguments as I have been able to offer. All that I would say in this connection, is that I have at least attempted to address a problem that faces all liberals, whether classical or 'modern', and more generally all those who have an underlying concern for the rights or the well-being of all people even when their explicit formulations might give one reason to suppose otherwise;[31] namely, of trying to explain what secular rationale there might be for the universalism of the liberal tradition. This is something that is in urgent need of argumentative support, rather that something on the correctness of which we can simply presume. And if – as would not surprise me – my efforts in this volume are judged less than successful, I would hope that they might serve to stimulate those more able than myself to do rather better.

Second, there is the development of a political economy of the kind needed to argue the case for classical liberalism, against its market-wise critics. Here, I would see my contribution as having been to set out some of the problems, and also to have argued against certain assumptions which seem to me widely shared among economists inclined towards classical liberalism. These, in my view, have prevented the very people best equipped to address such issues from doing what would be required if Hayekian arguments are to progress from interesting sketches of what telling arguments might look like, to actually delivering the goods.

Third, relating to the concerns of this final chapter, there is the theoretical and practical task of developing forms of life which would be both satisfactory as a basis for people's day-to-day lives, and more specifically for the kinds of lives that we, variously, wish to live, and which would also sustain the institutions of a free society. One could see such a task as being that of the development of a variety of *Sittlichkeiten* which would both be sustainable within a liberal, market-based social order, and which would also generate or sustain the institutions of that social order.

What is required here is a delicate and difficult task. For, as I have suggested, a free society seems to require the cultivation and enjoyment of specific forms of life which are satisfying to us as people, in our different situations and at different stages of our lives, but which can also serve to support the institutions of such a society itself. This may be problematic in one of two ways. On the one hand, there is the problem of how, from the perspective of particular forms of life, support for the broader institutions of such a society – including a market order, its associated legal system and property rights; and also, as I have suggested, a public forum – is to be forthcoming. May not the patterns of ideals, routines and obligations of such societies, and the dispositions and prejudices that people acquire within them, lead them to indifference or even hostility towards the larger framework within which they are living, and the duties required to sustain it?

On the other hand, may not the very institutions of this wider society have an adverse impact upon those things which make people's day-to-day lives viable and intelligible? The economic basis of some form of life may be undermined, when, say, people on the other side of the globe start producing, and at prices that cannot be matched, whatever had hitherto sustained it. And people also may find themselves faced, through the direct commodification of what had previously not been as starkly market-based arrangements, with choices which they would rather that they did not have to face. There may also be problems concerning how what is required, locally, to sustain some day-to-day way of life, relates to critical rationalist concerns for scrutiny in a public forum. For there may surely be a sense in which specific forms of life may depend upon the exclusion of alternatives without having good reason for so

215

doing, and may also depend on ideas which could not withstand the full light of universalistic public scrutiny. (The reader might well here consider – as I did – how they would live their life if they were not allowed any illusions at all; say, about their character and motives, or the wider importance of virtually anything that they did.) Further, even if what they were doing was defensible, the problem of the moral imperfections of any social order, which we have encountered so extensively in the course of the discussion of Hayek's work, is likely to mean that virtually no one would be in a position to offer a cogent defence of their actions or of the society in which they were living, even if one did exist.

In the face of all this, my tentative suggestion is that we might look at these matters by considering proprietorial communities, which might range from a housing development, through a village to a city and its hinterland, to something which (if people were interested) would have a much more strongly communitarian flavour to it. Just as, at present, certain kinds of theoretical knowledge are packaged into the physical design of buildings, so, I would suggest, could be ideas about social organization into the design of such communities. Potential inhabitants would be offered arrangements which, while aiming to satisfy the requirements of our day-to-day lives, would also address the issue of the emergent qualities of a social order, by way of their arrangements being tailored to produce specific such effects.

What might any of this look like? I will conclude with a brief illustrative discussion of this theme.[32]

To get an initial picture of how this might work, consider the kind of knowledge about what works and what does not work in a city environment, as discussed by Jane Jacobs in her *Death and Life of Great American Cities*.[33] In this book, she considers the kinds of practical arrangements which did – and those that did not – give rise to an effective and pleasant community, as, in the terms we have been using here, an emergent property. Now, it would surely be possible for entrepreneurs, if they were free to do so, to take up such ideas, and to offer people an environment in which not only would their immediate day-to-day requirements be met, but which was also geared to the production of other emergent properties that they might value, but not know how, directly, to produce. This would, doubtless, involve the imposition of rules which, if imposed within a non-proprietorial political setting, might seem highly intrusive upon people's freedom. For, in such a setting, there may not be agreement that the overall emergent order is desirable; and people also would not necessarily be able to understand the connection between the rules and the overall product. In addition, it would doubtless be necessary to exclude those who would not comply with the rules, or – in so far as the community functioned on a basis that was significantly different from that which was more common within the wider society – to exclude the general public, other than under specified circumstances.

One might, further, envisage such communities operating not just in respect of limited services in a limited location, but as being both extensive, and all-encompassing, in the sense of covering the full range of people's lives. They would, in effect, form private governments, geared up to the production and maintenance of certain valued characteristics. This would include not only characteristics of the community considered in itself, but also those that relate to compatibility between its operations and those of the framework government within which it is operating. The rules involved might have a number of interesting features. For example, in so far as a particular community itself favoured rugged individualism, it might require, as a condition of membership, that members be insured against problems that might otherwise render them charges upon the rest of the community. Alternatively, they might also incorporate restrictions upon people's behaviour which are more reminiscent of contemporary Singapore than they are of life in most Western democracies.

The fact that there were such restrictions, however, would be balanced by the fact that there would be genuine choice in respect of membership. Everyone would, in effect, be in a position similar to that of a Resident Alien; although they would have greater protections against governmental predation, in that the terms of their relations with the community within which they were living would be restricted by contractual arrangements made subject to the jurisdiction of the framework government. (In respect of these, there would, presumably, be provision for various kinds of changes under specified conditions; not least because of the need of communities to remain viable, to make corrections to their procedures if they did not produce the effects that they were after, or to make some response in the event of their starting to lose members in ways that would affect their overall viability.) There need be no bar to migration, although in many communities membership would involve the keeping of specific rules. This would mean that immigrants would have no right to assert their distinctive customs against the rules of the community that they joined; not least because those rules would have been designed with the idea of bringing about certain large-scale consequences.

Two immediate problems that might seem to arise, are the following. First, what about discrimination? One must say here, at the outset, that discrimination of some kinds is essential: the production of an overall order of a particular sort will depend on the enforcement of certain kinds of conduct. (And clearly, different arrangements are likely to be tried, by those who think that a good society can function with only minimal restrictions, and those who believe that relatively rigid specification of permitted forms of conduct is required.) But what of discrimination of other kinds? This is something that would be moderated to a degree by the existence of a public forum, in which the practices of particular communities could be submitted to critical scrutiny. Such scrutiny would not have political force behind it, other than if it should turn out that the practices of some

217

community were in breach of the minimalist liberalism of the framework community. It would also not necessarily be institutionalized into people's day-to-day lives within individual communities. There would, there, be something specific and often restrictive into which people could be socialized or acculturated.

However, such criticism of the conduct of communities in a public forum would play an important role. In such a setting, complaints could be voiced, and spokespersons for different individual communities could do their best to meet them, and also to explain the rationale behind their day-to-day practices. It is in such a context that one might imagine that such communities might be questioned very closely as to whether the patterns of discrimination associated with them genuinely had the role of bringing about some desirable overall goal (or at least one that they could plausibly defend as desirable in a public forum, even if others could not necessarily share in the judgement as to its desirability).

The existence of such a forum would also meet a second problem. For, one might well say, to enter into such arrangements as an adult is one thing; to be brought up in them is another. In what sense can such people exhibit choice, or, if they can, would their capacity to do this not be disruptive of the dispositions needed to enjoy life within a specific such community? My suggestion would here be that introduction to such a public forum, and to the discussions within it, should serve as something like an initiation ceremony, to indicate a person's transition to adulthood. Prior to this, there would be people within the community – in effect, its spokespersons in the public forum – to whom young members could be referred for explanations as to why particular customs etc. are mandatory; something that could not necessarily be explained cogently by just *any* adult. But it would serve to keep such spokespersons honest to know that, at the point of adulthood, their young people will be exposed to the full force of debate within a public forum; such that if what a community's spokespersons had told their young people could not withstand such critical scrutiny, it would be exposed as such.

I could continue discussing such ideas, their pros and cons, and how possible problems might be met, at great length. But I will not do so here, because my concern is simply to float the idea, and also because their detailed elaboration would not be appropriate for the present volume. I will, however, conclude with a brief discussion of three points.

First, what of economic change, and the threat that this may pose to some community and its way of life? This is an important problem, and one the importance of which is likely to grow with the globalization of a market economy. Here, I would suggest that the company that owns the community would have an interest in monitoring for changes that might affect the well-being of its residents in ways that affect its viability (or, bearing in mind the possibility of mobility, its attractions *vis-à-vis* other communities). Consider, say, a company that owned a community that depended heavily upon some form of mining. They would have every interest in information about the viability of the community, and about possible alternative forms of employment for its residents, should the mine fail. One would expect there to grow up various specialized agencies which would monitor and supply information about such things.

Second, what about those who, for one reason or another, are excluded from specific communities, or who simply prefer freedom in the more ordinary sense to life in a community? Exit from any specific community in which they might happen to be living is open to them; and if for some reason or another they could not form a minimalist community of their own, there would seem to be nothing to stop them living their lives independently, or with others who would prefer to be free from any specific form of order, over and above that of the framework community (under the rules of which, individuals could hold property). Life, however, might be difficult for members of particularly unpopular and small minorities; but they would have the security of the framework government's property rights; and, historically, trade has often overcome prejudice. In an extreme situation – where, say, their survival was being put at risk because of an effective boycott against trade with them – the framework government might invoke measures like those suggested by Hayek to handle problems of monopoly power.

Finally, it might be questioned whether this is not just all an absurd fantasy. Surely all this is so remote from conditions which face any of us, as to be pointless even to think about? I am not so sure. For with the growth of a global market economy, and under the impact, also, of modernizing political regimes, many people may find themselves in conditions not too far removed from the starting-point of such ideas.

There would seem to me room for an alliance between would-be communitarians or 'republicans' (if only they can be persuaded to give up their wish to coerce those who do not agree with them) and libertarians, to build, upon the havoc that has been wrought upon much about which we care, new forms of life within which people can live in the different kinds of setting that they find attractive, and within which they can flourish throughout the different phases of their lives.

Accordingly, I would argue for the importance of the ideas discussed here, not just as the objects of exploration and debate among academics, but also as something that might be tried out in practice. For example, we might allow such 'communities' to remove themselves, initially, from the provision of services by local government, and from local governmental regulation except in so far as this involved the imposition of externalities upon others. Should such experimentation prove fruitful, the freedom of such groups might then be extended to freedom from central government control, too, over and above what would be involved in the minimalist ideas which I have discussed, earlier, and, at least initially, taxation in respect of certain responsibilities to others which is a product of the existing political systems within which they have been living.

To such suggestions, the reader might well object. This book will have been successful to the degree to which it is clear why I am making such suggestions – and also in so far as the reader is provoked to think through exactly what they think is wrong with them, and how these matters might be handled better, by other means.

NOTES

1 INTRODUCTION

1 See, for a further development of this argument in a slightly different way, J. Shearmur, 'Consumer Sovereignty, Prices and Preferences for Higher-Order Goods', *Political Studies*, 39(4), December 1991, pp. 661–75.

2 Compare, for example, Macur Olson's *The Logic of Collective Action*, Cambridge, MA: Harvard University Press, 1965.

3 See, for example, Hayek's 'The Pretence of Knowledge', in his *New Studies*, London: Routledge & Kegan Paul, 1978.

4 Compare *Hayek on Hayek*, ed. Stephen Kresge and Leif Wenar, Chicago: University of Chicago Press and London: Routledge, 1994, p. 110, where in a transcription of Hayek's remarks in a radio broadcast in April 1945, Hayek said, when asked to sum up the main thesis of his *Road to Serfdom*: 'It is not really an attack on socialists; it is rather an attempt to persuade socialists, to whom I have dedicated my book. My main thesis is that they are mistaken in the methods for getting what they want to achieve.'

5 For discussion of this, and of more general issues relating to the ideas discussed in the text, see J. Shearmur, 'Popper, Lakatos and Theoretical Progress in Economics', in N. de Marchi and M. Blaug (eds) *Appraising Economic Theories*, Aldershot: Edward Elgar, 1991, pp. 35–52.

6 See Jon Elster, 'Marxism, Functionalism, and Game Theory' and G. A. Cohen, 'Reply to Elster', in A. Callinicos (ed.) *Marxist Theory*, Oxford: Oxford University Press, 1989, pp. 48–104.

7 Compare, on this, Michael Ignatieff's brief comment on page 7 of his *Blood and Belonging*, London: Vintage, 1994.

8 See, for further discussion, chapter four of J. Shearmur, *The Political Thought of Karl Popper*, London: Routledge, 1996.

9 A response which parallels Adam Smith's response to the 'disadvantages of commercial society'.

10 See, on this, J. Shearmur and D. Klein, 'Good Conduct in a Great Society', in D. Klein (ed.) *Reputation*, Ann Arbor: University of Michigan Press, forthcoming.

11 Although see Shearmur and Klein, 'Good Conduct', as well as other articles in Klein's *Reputation*, for some examples.

12 More easily than if we were dealing with social formations which could claim that they are sovereign, or involved in some form of self-determination.

13 Compare K. R. Popper, *The Logic of Scientific Discovery*, London: Hutchinson, 1959; and Imre Lakatos, *Philosophical Papers* (*The Methodology of Scientific Research Programmes* and *Mathematics, Science and Epistemology*), ed. John Worrall and

NOTES

Gregory Currie, 2 volumes, Cambridge: Cambridge University Press, 1978; and *Proofs and Refutations*, ed. John Worrall and Eli Zahar, Cambridge: Cambridge University Press, 1976; and W. W. Bartley III, *The Retreat to Commitment*, 2nd edn, La Salle, Ill.: Open Court, 1984.

14 *Pace* Richard Rorty, *Philosophy and the Mirror of Nature*, Princeton: Princeton University Press, 1980. But for some reservations, compare J. Shearmur, 'Harris, Relativism and the Limitations of Method', *Journal of Economic Methodology*, 1(2),1994, pp. 335–9.

15 Such appraisal rests on an open-ended intersubjective consensus as to what is the case. Compare Popper's discussion of the 'empirical basis' in his *Logic of Scientific Discovery*, and for some discussion of this point my contributions to 'Making Sense of History' (with M. H. Nielsen), *Inquiry* (Norway), 22, 1979, pp. 459–89, and J. Shearmur, 'Popper, Lakatos and Theoretical Progress in Economics'.

16 See J. Shearmur, 'Popper, Lakatos and Theoretical Progress'.

17 Compare Pierre Duhem, *The Aim and Structure of Physical Theory*, Princeton: Princeton University Press, 1954, and for detailed argument about the need to proceed in a systematic manner within philosophical argument, J. Shearmur, 'Philosophical Method, Modified Essentialism and the Open Society', in I. C. Jarvie and N. Laor (eds) *Critical Rationalism: The Social Sciences and the Humanities*, Dordrecht: Kluwer, 1995, pp. 19–39.

18 Compare Imre Lakatos, 'The Method of Analysis-Synthesis' in his *Mathematics, Science and Epistemology*, and his references there to A. Szabo's *Anfaenge der Griechischen Mathematik*, Budapest: Akademiai Kiado, 1969.

19 Compare, for example, some of the contributions to J. Paul (ed.) *Reading Nozick*, Oxford: Basil Blackwell, 1981.

20 Compare Robert Nozick, *Philosophical Explanations*, Oxford: Clarendon Press, 1981.

21 These will have a tentative character, so that the discovery that our best such theories clash with our normative ideals may give us a strong incentive to see whether, perhaps, it is not the theories that are incorrect.

22 Compare Ronald Coase, 'The Lighthouse in Economics'; for example, in T. Cowen (ed.) *The Theory of Market Failure*, Fairfax, VA: George Mason University Press, 1988, pp. 255–77.

23 The discernment of presuppositions and power relationships is not, in itself, a sufficient ground to reject some substantive conclusion. There seems no reason to suppose that we can get away from either. What, rather, is to the point is whether there is some alternative open to us that will better serve whatever our purposes are in the activity in question.

24 A view shared by theorists as otherwise diverse as Durkheim and Winch. I should stress, however, that I am not here proposing an a-social psychologism or view based upon the activities of rational economic man. My argument, rather, is that we should not simply presume that what is social is shared across a society, or that shared concepts necessarily illuminate what is going on in those social events to which they pertain.

25 Compare on this John Gray, 'On Negative and Positive Liberty', in his *Liberalisms*, London and New York: Routledge, 1989, pp. 45–68.

26 I am, thus, defending the approach that Felix Oppenheim criticizes in connection with Paul Feyerabend, in his *Political Concepts: A Reconstruction*, Oxford: Blackwell, 1981.

27 I do not wish to rule out that how we interpret what we had taken as 'premises' may well change as our argument unfolds. Compare, on this, Imre Lakatos, *Proofs and Refutations*.

222

28 In this respect, one generates a view that is somewhat Kantian in its character, albeit from arguments that derive from the first and third critiques, rather than the second. Compare J. Shearmur, 'Epistemological Limits of the State', *Political Studies*, 38, 1990, pp. 116–25, and also chapter six, below.

29 Plant made this point in an unpublished paper delivered to the Carl Menger Society in London in the early 1980s. A similar argument has been developed by M. Golding in 'The Primacy of Welfare Rights', *Social Philosophy and Policy*, 1, 1984, pp. 119–36.

30 Compare, in this connection, the work of 'analytical Marxists' such as Jon Elster and Gerry Cohen, and, for some discussion, my review of Jon Elster and Karl Ove Moene (eds), *Alternatives to Capitalism*, in *Philosophy of the Social Sciences*, 22, September 1992, pp. 381–4.

31 Historically, the Scottish Enlightenment is of great importance in providing a group of problems and issues in terms of their relation to which one can understand and render commensurable many of the disparate intellectual traditions which have subsequently been of importance in political thought.

32 Compare J. Shearmur, 'Subjectivism, Falsification and Positive Economics', in J. Wiseman (ed.) *Beyond Positive Economics?*, London: Macmillan, 1983; 'From Hayek to Menger', in B. Caldwell (ed.) *Carl Menger and his Legacy in Economics*, Durham NC and London: Duke University Press, 1990; 'Common Sense and the Foundations of Economic Theory: Duhem versus Robbins', *Philosophy of the Social Sciences*, 21(1), March 1991; 'Schutz, Machlup and Rational Economic Man', *Review of Political Economy*, 5, 1993, pp. 491–507; and 'Subjectivism, Explanation and the Austrian Tradition', in S. Boehm and B. Caldwell (eds) *Austrian Economics: Tensions and New Directions*, Boston, Dordrecht and London: Kluwer, 1993, pp. 103–27.

33 Compare Norman Barry, *Hayek's Social and Economic Philosophy*, London: Macmillan, 1979; John Gray, *Hayek On Liberty*, 2nd edn, Oxford: Blackwell, 1986; Chandran Kukathas, *Hayek and Modern Liberalism*, Oxford: Clarendon Press, 1989; and Roland Kley, *Hayek's Social and Political Thought*, Oxford: Clarendon Press, 1994.

2 FROM SOCIALISM TO *THE ROAD TO SERFDOM*

1 W. W. Bartley III and Stephen Kresge (eds) *The Trend of Economic Thinking*, London: Routledge, 1991, p. 19.

2 *Ibid.*, p. 123, quoting from A. C. Pigou, *The Economics of Welfare*, 4th edn, London: Macmillan, 1948, p. 5. The reference to 'wonder' is presumably an implicit contrast with the role given to wonder in the development of knowledge in the natural sciences by Adam Smith in his *History of Astronomy*.

3 F. A. Hayek, Foreword to Ludwig von Mises, *Socialism*, Indianapolis: Liberty Classics, 1981, p. xix.

4 Compare *Hayek on Hayek*, p. 47: 'Walter Rathenau, from . . . whom I derived most of my first economic ideas'. Hayek here indicates that this interest in such material went back to his seventh form in the Gymnasium, in 1916.

5 Walther Rathenau, *In Days to Come*, London: Allen & Unwin, 1921, p. 41.

6 *Ibid.*, p. 44.

7 *Ibid.*, p. 59.

8 *Ibid.*, p. 72.

9 *Ibid.*, pp. 113–17.

10 Compare Rathenau's discussion (*ibid.*, p. 87) of the contrast between a world monopolist and a multiplicity of owners.

11 *Ibid.*, p. 91.

12 *Ibid.*, p. 125.

13 Compare James Joll, *Intellectuals in Politics*, London: Pantheon, 1960, p. 92.

14 David Felix, *Walther Rathenau and the Weimar Republic*, Baltimore and London: Johns Hopkins University Press, 1971, p. 47.

15 *Ibid.*

16 *Ibid.*, p. 58.

17 On Spann, compare *Hayek on Hayek*, p. 54. On Wieser, compare Hayek's, 'Coping with Ignorance', in his *Knowledge, Evolution and Society*, London: Adam Smith Institute, 1983, p. 17.

18 Compare, for example, J. R. Hicks and W. Weber (eds) *Carl Menger and the Austrian School of Economics*, Oxford: Clarendon Press, 1973; *Atlantic Economic Journal*, September 1978, special issue on 'Carl Menger and Austrian Economics'; W. Grassl and B. Smith (eds) *Austrian Economics: Historical and Philosophical Background*, London: Croom Helm, 1986, and B. Caldwell (ed.) *Carl Menger and his Legacy in Economics*, Durham, NC and London: Duke University Press, 1990.

19 Compare T. W. Hutchison, 'Carl Menger on Philosophy and Method', in his *The Politics and Philosophy of Economics*, Oxford: Blackwell, 1981, pp. 176–202.

20 But compare Erich Streissler, 'The Influence of German Economics on the work of Menger and Marshall', in B. Caldwell (ed.) *Carl Menger and his Legacy in Economics*, pp. 31–68.

21 The situation was, in fact, more complicated than this might indicate. Compare Ludwig von Mises, *Notes and Recollections*, South Holland, Ill.: Libertarian Press, 1978 and *The Historical Setting of the Austrian School of Economics*, New York: Arlington House, 1969, with Hayek's recollections in *Hayek on Hayek*.

22 Friedrich von Wieser, *Social Economics*, London: Allen & Unwin, 1927, p. 207.

23 *Ibid.*, p. 153.

24 *Ibid.*, p. 151.

25 *Ibid.*, p. 413.

26 *Ibid.*, p. 412.

27 *Ibid.*, p. 414.

28 *Ibid.*

29 *Ibid.*

30 Ludwig von Mises, *Die Gemeinwirtschaft*, 1922; the most recent English edition is *Socialism*, Indianapolis: Liberty Fund, 1981.

31 Hayek, 'Coping with Ignorance' in *Knowledge, Evolution and Society*, London: Adam Smith Institute, 1983, pp. 17–27. The biographical information in the text is also extracted from this paper.

32 See E. Butler, *Hayek*, London: Temple Smith, 1983, p. 2, and Hayek, Introduction to R. McCloughry (ed.) *F. A. Hayek, Money, Capital and Fluctuations*, London: Routledge and Kegan Paul, 1984.

33 See Hayek, 'Coping with Ignorance', pp. 17–18. For some interesting discussion of this institute and the circumstances of its founding, see Paul Silverman, *Law and Economics in Interwar Vienna*, University of Chicago Ph.D. dissertation, 1984, and also *Hayek on Hayek*.

34 Hayek, 'Coping with Ignorance', p. 18.

35 Hayek, 'Foreword to Mises', *Socialism*, p. xix.

36 *Ibid.*

37 Mises, *Notes and Recollections*, South Holland, Ill.: Libertarian Press, 1978, p. 2.

38 *Ibid.*, p. 6. The work was *Die Entwicklung der gutsherrschaftlichbaeuerlichen Verhaeltnisses in Galizien, 1772–1848*, Vienna and Leipzig: Deuticke, 1902.

39 *Ibid.*, p. 6. The study to which Mises refers presumably formed the basis of two articles on the Austrian textile industry in *Zeitschrift fuer Volkswirtschaft*, XIV, 1905 and XVI, 1907. See, for details, David Gordon, *Ludwig von Mises: An Annotated Bibliography*, Auburn, Al.: Ludwig von Mises Institute, 1988.

40 Compare Mises, *Notes and Recollections*, p. 16: 'When I entered the university I . . . was a thorough statist'.

41 Hayek, 'Foreword', p. xx.

42 Mises, *Notes and Recollections*, p. 93.

43 'Die Wirtschaftsrechnung im sozialistischen Gemeinwesen', *Archiv fuer Sozialwissenschaft and Sozialpolitik*, 47, 1920–1, pp. 86–121; subsequently translated in F. A. Hayek (ed.) *Collectivist Economic Planning*, London: Routledge, 1935, as 'Economic Calculation in the Socialist Commonwealth'.

44 Mises, *Notes and Recollections*, p. 113.

45 See 'Economic Calculation in the Socialist Commonwealth', p. 88. It was provoked, more particularly, by Otto Neurath's *Durch die Kriegeswirtschaft zur Naturalwirtschaft*, Munich: Callwey, 1919.

46 See, on this dispute, Don Lavoie's study of the economic calculation debate, *Rivalry and Central Planning*, Cambridge: Cambridge University Press, 1985. As I was in the final stages of revising the manuscript of this section, I received David Ramsay Steele's, *From Marx to Mises*, La Salle, Ill.: Open Court, 1992, which would seem particularly valuable on Mises' work and its significance. I have gained greatly from discussing these issues with Steele, and from an earlier version of his manuscript, but I have not been able to make use of the published version of his work.

47 Hayek, 'Foreword', p. xxi.

48 *Ibid.*, p. xxiii.

49 'The Trend of Economic Thinking', *Economica*, May 1933, pp. 121–137. The essay is reprinted in F. A. Hayek, *The Trend of Economic Thinking: Essays on Political Economists and Economic History. The Collected Works of F. A. Hayek, Volume 3*, ed. W. W. Bartley III and Stephen Kresge, Chicago: University of Chicago Press, 1991, pp. 17–34. See, on this essay, Bruce Caldwell's 'Hayek's "Trend of Economic Thinking" ', *Review of Austrian Economics*, 2, 1987, pp. 175–8 and his 'Hayek's Transformation', *History of Political Economy*, 20, winter 1988, pp. 513–44.

50 Subsequently published as *Prices and Production*, London: Routledge, 1931.

51 On whom compare Max Weber, *Roscher and Knies: The Logical Problems of Historical Economics*, tr. Guy Oakes, New York: The Free Press, 1975.

52 See, for example, Streissler, 'The Influence of German Economics'.

53 See Carl Menger, *Investigations into the Method of the Social Sciences with Special Reference to Economics*, New York and London: New York University Press, 1985.

54 Hayek, 'Trend', p. 23.

55 *Ibid.*, p. 22.

56 *Ibid.*, p. 19.

57 Compare 'Repercussions of Rent Control' in A. Seldon (ed.) *Verdict on Rent Control*, London: Institute of Economic Affairs, 1972, pp. 3–16 (the quotation is from page 14). This paper is an English translation of a lecture first published in *Schriften des Vereins fuer Sozialpolitik*, 182, 1930, which itself draws on a fuller study, *Das Mieterschutzproblem: Nationaloekonomische Betrachtungen*, Vienna: Steyermuehl-Verlag, Bibliotek fuer Volkswirtschaft und Politik, 2, 1929.

58 Hayek, 'Trend', pp. 26–7.

59 *Ibid.*, p. 30.

60 *Ibid.*, p. 26.

61 See *ibid.*, p. 22 and *The Constitution of Liberty*, London: Routledge & Kegan Paul, 1960, p. 445. It is striking, however, that there is also a strongly contrasting theme, in Hayek's work, of the importance of custom and tradition, and of the role played by rules of which we do not have a conscious knowledge.

62 Hayek, 'Trend', p. 24.

63 *Ibid.*, pp. 32–3.

64 Hayek, 'On Being an Economist' in *The Trend of Economic Thinking*, pp. 35–48; see p. 40.

65 *Ibid.*, p. 46.

66 Hayek, 'Trend', p. 34.

67 *Ibid.*, pp. 27–8.

68 *Ibid.*, p. 31.

69 Cf. *ibid.*, p. 27.

70 See, for more general discussion of this theme, J. Shearmur, 'The Austrian Connection: Hayek's Liberalism and the Thought of Carl Menger', in W. Grassl and B. Smith (eds) *Austrian Economics*, pp. 210–24, which was based on a paper given in London in 1980.

71 See, for example, the reprint of that introduction as the Introduction to Carl Menger, *Principles of Economics*, New York: New York University Press, 1981, p. 13.

72 *Ibid.*, p. 23.

73 See Erich Streissler, 'Carl Menger on Economic Policy: The Lectures to Crown Prince Rudolf', in Caldwell, *Carl Menger and his Legacy in Economics*, pp. 107–30.

74 Menger, *Investigations*, pp. 176–7. The next two references in the text are to the same two pages.

75 *Ibid.*, p. 177. To attribute such views to Smith himself would be to do him a grave injustice. Hayek has quoted the end of this passage, on socialism, on several occasions.

76 *Ibid.*, p. 233.

77 *Ibid.*, p. 234. Compare, for a similar view, Hayek, *Law, Legislation and Liberty, Volume 1*, London, Routledge & Kegan Paul, 1973, p. 88. 'Calling' must be understood as a critical reference to Savigny's *Vom Bereufe unsere Zeit*. See, on this, chapter three, below.

78 I should stress that I have no specific evidence of the influence of Menger's treatment of Savigny upon Hayek's conception of his intellectual research programme.

79 Compare Roy Harrod's review of Hayek's *Individualism: True and False*, *Economic Journal*, 1, 1946, p. 439, and Lionel Robbins, 'Hayek on Liberty', *Economica*, 1961, pp. 66–81.

80 See Oskar Lange, 'On the Economic Theory of Socialism' and F. M. Taylor, 'The Guidance of Production in a Socialist State', in B. Lippincott (ed.) *On the Economic Theory of Socialism*, Minneapolis: University of Minnesota Press, 1938, pp. 55–142.

81 See Lange, 'Economic Theory', p. 65.

82 For a useful survey of such opinions, see Lavoie's *Rivalry and Central Planning*. David Ramsay Steele, however, has subsequently made the devastating point, against Lange, that it achieves nothing to say that planners must simulate market solutions, unless one also explains exactly how this is to be accomplished.

83 Compare, in this connection, Marx's remarks on the Paris commune in 'The Civil War in France', and 'First Draft of "The Civil War in France"', in D. Fernbach (ed.) Karl Marx, *The First International and After*, Harmondsworth: Penguin Books, 1974, and Lenin's *The State and Revolution*. Marx's own blindness to

problems of this sort, as raised against him by Bakunin, for example, is beautifully illustrated by his 'Conspectus of Bakunin's *Statism and Anarchy*', also included in Fernbach's collection.

84 Compare Hayek's own discussion in his *Individualism and Economic Order*, London: Routledge & Kegan Paul, 1949.

85 Compare Mises' critical comment, in his *Notes and Recollections*, that Wieser stood nearer to the Lausanne (general equilibrium) than to the Austrian School.

86 Notably in Lavoie's *Rivalry and Central Planning*.

87 Don Lavoie, 'A Critique of the Standard Account of the Socialist Calculation Debate', *Journal of Libertarian Studies*, 5, 1981, p. 42.

88 See his *Rivalry and Central Planning, passim*.

89 See his Editor's Introduction to *Money, Capital and Fluctuations*, p. x; Stephan Boehm, 'The Private Seminar of L. von Mises', delivered to the meeting of the History of Economics Society, Pittsburgh, May 22–4, 1984, and *Hayek on Hayek*.

90 Adam Klug, *Historical Precedent in the Theory of International Trade*, Ph.D. dissertation, Tel-Aviv University, 1990. I have benefited greatly from discussion with Klug, who kindly made available to me the manuscript of an article, 'The Research Tradition in Intertemporal Trade' based on part of his dissertation. Magnad Desai also spoke of the importance of this early work of Hayek's, in similar terms, in an unpublished paper delivered at the American Economic Association in Washington DC in 1990. Klug's work would suggest that there is another entire dimension to this story, relating to Hayek's *Monetary Nationalism*, but this raises issues which cannot be pursued here.

91 In which connection one should note, in Mises' 'Economic Calculation in the Socialist Commonwealth', remarks about individuals' 'estimation of economic facts' (p. 107); the 'inconveniences' and 'serious defects' of monetary calculation (p. 109); and the 'mistakes [which] arise from the necessity of calculating with what are not from many points of view rigorously ascertainable data' (pp.110–11). The themes of human activity and subjective estimation, which were to become the hallmark of the distinctively 'Austrian' approach, are clearly there; though just what significance this has is clearly a matter for the specialist in the development of Mises' ideas.

92 They were subsequently reprinted in Hayek's *Individualism and Economic Order*.

93 See *ibid.*, p. 152.

94 *Ibid.*, p. 153.

95 A theme that is extensively developed in Hayek's subsequent work.

96 *Ibid.*, p. 155.

97 See 'Socialist Calculation III: The Competitive "Solution" ', 1940, reprinted in *Individualism and Economic Order*.

98 As was stressed to me in discussion of this material by Larry Briskman.

99 'Socialist Calculation III', p. 156.

100 See 'Competition as a Discovery Procedure', in his *New Studies*.

101 *Ibid.*, p. 167.

102 *Ibid.*, p. 150.

103 *Ibid.*

104 See, for example, his *Individualism and Economic Order*. See also, on the importance of this move, Bruce Caldwell, 'Hayek's Transformation', *History of Political Economy*, 20, 1988, pp. 513–41; E. Thomsen, *Prices and Knowledge*, London and New York: Routledge, 1992; and, in an essay which reached me too late to take into account in the text of this volume, M. Desai, 'Equilibrium, Expectations and Knowledge', in J. Birner and R. van Zijp (eds) *Hayek, Co-ordination and Evolution*, London: Routledge, 1995.

105 See *Individualism and Economic Order*, p. 50.

106 The role of market prices in transmitting knowledge, and the problems caused by their distortion by monetary factors, are also themes of his earlier writings on the trade cycle.

107 'Economics and Knowledge' in *Individualism and Economic Order*, p. 48.

108 See, for a recent useful overview, Stephan Boehm, 'Hayek on Knowledge, Equilibrium and Prices', *Wirtschaftspolitische Blaetter*, 36, 1989, No. 2, pp. 201–13.

109 'Economics and Knowledge' in *Individualism and Economic Order*, p. 48.

110 There were in fact two such pieces 'Freedom and the Economic System', in *Contemporary Review*, 1938; and *Freedom and the Economic System*, University of Chicago Press, Public Policy Pamphlet No. 29, 1939, an expanded version of the earlier piece. In *Hayek on Hayek*, p. 102, he indicates that they started life as a memorandum to Beveridge.

111 *Freedom and the Economic System*, 1939, pp. 8–9.

112 *Ibid.*, p. 9.

113 *Ibid.*, p. 10.

114 *Ibid.*

115 *Ibid.*

116 *Ibid.*, pp. 10–11.

117 For example, James Buchanan, *The Limits of Liberty*, Chicago: University of Chicago Press, 1975; David Gauthier, *Morals by Agreement*, Oxford: Oxford University Press, 1986. See also John Gray's *Liberalism*, Milton Keynes: Open University Press, 1986.

118 *Freedom and the Economic System*, pp. 11–12.

119 Hayek, *The Road to Serfdom*, p. 13.

120 *Ibid.*, p. 27.

121 Now in Hayek's *Individualism and Economic Order*.

122 *Ibid.*, p. 22.

123 See Harrod's review of Hayek's pamphlet in *Economic Journal*, 1, 1946, p. 439.

124 'Individualism: True and False', p. 17.

125 *Ibid.*, p. 19.

126 *Ibid.*, p. 20.

127 *Ibid.*, p. 20.

128 *The Political Ideal of the Rule of Law*, Cairo: National Bank of Egypt, 1955.

129 *Ibid.*, p. 5.

130 *Ibid.*, p. 10.

131 *Ibid.*, p. 11.

132 *Ibid.*, p. 13.

133 *Ibid.*

134 *Ibid.*

135 'Individualism: True and False', p. 26.

136 *The Political Ideal*, pp. 15–16.

137 *Ibid.*, p. 20.

138 *Ibid.*, p. 19.

139 For discussion of this issue, see chapter three, below.

140 *The Road to Serfdom*, p. v.

141 It is striking that the central points of Nove's criticisms of Marxist ideas about economic planning in his *The Economics of Feasible Socialism,* London: Allen & Unwin, 1983 (of whose phrasing I have made use in the text) reproduce, and elaborate upon, Hayek's main arguments. It is even more striking that Nove did not seem to be aware of this fact.

142 *Freedom and the Economic System*, p. 21.

143 *Ibid.*

144 See Hayek, *Pure Theory of Capital*, London: Macmillan, 1941, p. 27.

145 In addition, the advocate of such a theory could argue that he would be able to make adjustments, such that there is a greater equality in disposable resources, so that individuals' preferences are more evenly weighted than is the case in a market economy. Such a view, however, in addition to hitting the problems raised below, would also be faced with Hayek's ideas about whether their preferred arrangements could simulate other functions of the market which we have met earlier, and about the problems of the concentration of power in the hands of those who are responsible for the allocations involved.

146 *The Road to Serfdom*, p. 11.

147 *Ibid.*

148 H. Finer, *The Road to Reaction*, London: Dobson, 1946.

149 In his essay 'The Rule of Law and its Virtues' in R. Cunningham (ed.) *Liberty and the Rule of Law*, College Station: Texas A & M University Press, 1979, pp. 3–21.

150 There is also the problem that Hayek, while he tells a story of the development of the ideal of the rule of law that makes reference to such moralists as Rousseau and Kant, himself – in *The Constitution of Liberty* – seems to be after a formal explication of freedom under the rule of law, although he is doubtful if it can be achieved. Not only do his ideas here not work (cf. John Watkins, 'Philosophy', in A. Seldon (ed.) *Agenda for a Free Society*, London: Hutchinson, 1961), but this very move to making the rule of law a formal matter is one which Hallowell argued was fatal to the *Rechtsstaat* tradition. Hayek, in *Law, Legislation and Liberty*, volume 2, recognizes this problem, which he discusses with reference to Hallowell's work; but Hayek lays the responsibility at the door of legal positivism.

151 Other than that he came to doubt – mistakenly, as I will argue in chapter five – whether one can make interpersonal comparisons of utility.

152 Although clearly there is some ambiguity about just what should count, here. For as Lionel Robbins argued in his *Theory of Economic Policy in Classical English Political Economy*, London: Macmillan, 1952, one group of people to whom it would be difficult to deny the name 'liberal' had a fairly extensive view as to what forms of governmental activity were appropriate.

153 Compare, on Hayek's view of government at the time, his remarks in the transcript of the radio discussion on *The Road to Serfdom*, in *Hayek on Hayek*, pp. 108–23.

154 To the extent that he had the dates on which he had completed the manuscript of his *Open Society* added to the text, to ensure that it did not look as if he had made use of Hayek's ideas in *The Road to Serfdom* without acknowledgement. See, on this, Popper/Gombrich correspondence, Popper to Gombrich 5 June 1944, Popper archive, Hoover Institution, Stanford University, 300.3.

155 See, in this connection, the Popper/Gombrich correspondence, Popper to Gombrich 27 June and 8 August 1944, 300.3 and also some notes of Popper's on *The Road to Serfdom*, which appear to be a draft of a letter to Hayek, in Popper archive, 305.11.

156 Compare Popper to Hayek, 15 March, 1944, Popper archive, 305.13. See also, in this connection, a manuscript of Popper's, 'Public and Private Values', Popper archive, 39.17, which must have been written shortly after Popper took up his position at the LSE, in which he urges liberals and socialists to drop their differences in favour of his minimalist agenda for social reform.

NOTES

157 See Popper/Hayek correspondence in the Popper archives at the Hoover Institution, Popper to Hayek, 11 January 1947, 305.13.
158 Chandran Kukathas, 'Hayek and Modern Liberalism', unpublished manuscript, 1993.

3 HAYEK'S LATER THOUGHT

1 *Constitution of Liberty*, p. 11.
2 *Ibid.*, pp. 20–1.
3 *Ibid.*, p. 21.
4 *Ibid.*
5 John Locke, *Second Treatise of Government*, paragraph 93.
6 *Constitution of Liberty*, p. 135.
7 *Ibid.*, pp. 135–6.
8 *Ibid.*, p. 121.
9 *Ibid.*, p. 138.
10 *Ibid.*, p. 136.
11 Since writing an initial version of this argument, I have discovered that John Gray has argued along similar lines, in his *The Moral Foundations of Market Institutions*, London: IEA Health and Welfare Unit, 1992 (see p. 22); and also, for a response in the same volume, Chandran Kukathas, 'Freedom versus Autonomy', pp. 101–14.
12 *Constitution of Liberty*, p. 137.
13 I would like to thank Stanford Ikeda for useful discussions on the topic of Hayek and coercion, at the Institute for Humane Studies in 1982. I have benefited from reading a paper by him on this topic, written when he was a fellow there, although I have not drawn specifically upon it in writing this material.
14 Cf. Hayek, *Constitution of Liberty*, p. 41.
15 *Ibid.*, p. 29.
16 *Ibid.*, p. 145. The singling out of the theme of 'data' in relation to freedom is not an aberration. Compare the following comment on 'free action' which occurs earlier in this work: 'free action, in which a person pursues his own aims by the means indicated by his own knowledge, must be based on data which cannot be shaped at will by another' (pp. 20–1).
17 See Adam Smith, *Wealth of Nations*, Oxford: Clarendon Press, 1976, V.i.f (pp. 781–2); *Lectures on Jurisprudence*, Report dated 1766, Oxford: Clarendon Press, 1978, 328–30 (pp. 539–40). Compare also Hont and Ignatieff, 'Needs and Justice in the *Wealth of Nations*', in *Wealth and Virtue*, Cambridge: Cambridge University Press, 1983, pp. 1–44.
18 Although his views are close to those of other contemporary writers in the 'Austrian' tradition.
19 Compare Robert D. Willis, 'Contestable Markets', in *The New Palgrave*, ed. J. Eatwell, M. Milgate and P. Newman, London: Macmillan, 1987, volume 1, pp. 618–22.
20 Which we have good reason to suppose cannot be the case.
21 See John Gaventa, *Power and Powerlessness: Quiescence and Rebellion in an Appalachian Valley*, Oxford: Clarendon Press, 1980. My examples are drawn from chapters three and four.
22 Compare Steven Lukes, *Power: A Radical View*, London: Macmillan, 1974; John Gaventa, *Power and Powerlessness*, chapter one.
23 Hayek, *Constitution of Liberty*, p. 136.
24 Gaventa, *Power and Powerlessness*, pp. 86–9.

25 Hayek makes several references to Mancur Olson, *The Logic of Collective Action*, Cambridge, MA: Harvard University Press, 1965. For further discussion, compare J. Shearmur, 'Hayek and the Wisdom of the Age', in N. Barry *et al.*, *Hayek's 'Serfdom' Revisited*, London: Institute of Economic Affairs, 1984, pp. 66–85.

26 See Hayek, *The Denationalization of Money*, London: Institute of Economic Affairs, 1976.

27 Compare, for example, T. Lowi, *The End of Liberalism*, New York: Norton, 1969.

28 Compare his *Das Gesetz der Macht*, 1926; my hypothesis about the implications of this work (for which he has no responsibility) draws upon an informal remark of Erich Streissler's.

29 For some brief discussion and references, see J. Shearmur, 'Epistemological Limits of the State', *Political Studies*, 38, March 1990, pp. 116–25.

30 David Miller, 'The Fatalistic Conceit', *Critical Review*, 3(2), pp. 310–23; the quotation is from p. 322. Cf., however, Hayek's 'Preface to 1976 Edition' of *The Road to Serfdom*.

31 Hayek, *The Fatal Conceit*, p. 36.

32 *Ibid.*, pp. 103–4.

33 Compare Hayek's discussion of the influence of ideas from Aristotle, with which he disagrees, through the Roman Catholic Church, in *The Fatal Conceit*, p. 47 with his argument in chapter nine.

34 *Ibid.*, pp. 61–2.

35 *Ibid.*, p. 69. I do not know the extent to which references to Popper and Bartley were made at the suggestion of Bartley.

36 *Ibid.*

37 *Ibid.*, p. 70. Part of the passage quoted is in italic in Hayek's text.

38 I would like to thank Leif Wenar, who in the course of detailed comments on the entire text raised this point as an objection to the present material.

39 Compare, for example, John Gray, *Hayek on Liberty*, p. 69; L. P. Liggio and T. G. Palmer, 'Freedom and the Law: A Comment on Professor Aranson's Article', *Harvard Journal of Law and Public Policy*, 11(3), summer 1988, p. 716, n. 121.

40 Compare Peter H. Aranson, 'Bruno Leoni in Retrospect', *Harvard Journal of Law and Public Policy*, 11(3), summer 1988, pp. 661–712, and also, for an extended discussion from which I have not been able to benefit because of my linguistic inadequacies, R. Cubeddu, 'Friedrich A. von Hayek e Bruno Leoni', *Il Politico*, 1992, LVII, 3, pp. 393–420.

41 Bruno Leoni, *Freedom and the Law*, Los Angeles: Nash Publishing, 1961, p. 21.

42 *Ibid.*, p. 17.

43 *Ibid.*, pp. 131–2. This is worth mentioning, as Hayek, in *Law, Legislation and Liberty*, when he refers to Leoni, says that Leoni has not convinced him that one can dispense with legislation (vol. 1, p. 168). However, Hayek's view of the proper role of legislation, even in his later writings, is more extensive than what Leoni would seem to have in mind.

44 Cf. Hegel, *Philosophy of Right*, paragraphs 211 and 212.

45 See Hayek to Leoni, 4 April, 1962, in Hayek archive, Hoover Institution, 77–8, in which Hayek also refers to his having heard Leoni deliver the lectures upon which *Freedom and the Law* was based, at Claremont College. See also Leoni's letter to Hayek of 8 May, 1963 (Hayek archive, 77–9), in which he suggests, on the basis of an article of Hayek's, that 'the conclusions of *Freedom and the Law* have been by and large accepted by you', and Hayek's letter to Leoni of 3 June, 1963 (Hayek archive, 77–9) for some criticism by Hayek of the idea that one could rely

just on judge-made law, along lines similar to his argument in *Law, Legislation and Liberty*.

46 Hegel, *Philosophy of Right*, paragraph 212.

47 Savigny, *Of the Vocation of our Age*, London: Littlewood, 1831, pp. 28–9.

48 Compare, on this, John Gray's discussion of natural law in his *Liberalisms*, London: Routledge, 1988.

49 '[A] cosmos has no purpose.' See 'The Confusion of Language in Political Thought', in *New Studies*, p. 74.

50 *Ibid.*, p. 77.

51 *Ibid.*, pp. 74–5.

52 The grounds for accepting which would seem to combine indirect utilitarian argument with – in Hayek's later writings – an appeal (in respect of their universality) to ideas from the Christian and Stoic traditions. See the discussion in chapter six.

53 *Law, Legislation and Liberty*, volume two, p. 17.

54 *Ibid.*, p. 9.

55 In the sense of a theory that says that there is no legitimate standard for the appraisal of the law, other than whether it is the command of the sovereign.

56 Of which they may not be explicitly aware. Compare Hayek's 'Rules, Perception and Intelligibility', in his *New Studies*.

57 *Law, Legislation and Liberty*, volume two, p. 41.

58 See *ibid.*, p. 35; this is implicitly a reply to Watkins' criticism of his ideas about freedom and the formally universal character of law in *The Constitution of Liberty*. Compare J. W. N. Watkins, 'Philosophy' in A. Seldon (ed.) *Agenda for a Free Society*, London: Hutchinson, 1961.

59 See *Law, Legislation and Liberty*, volume two, p. 52.

60 *Ibid.*, p. 55.

61 *Ibid.*, p. 54.

62 *Ibid.*, p. 41.

63 *Ibid.*, pp. 41–2.

64 *Ibid.*, p. 40.

65 *Ibid.*, p. 54.

66 The 'negative' emphasis of this material in Hayek coheres with a deep-seated theme in Popper's work concerning perception as the correction of prior expectations. Indeed, Hayek on one occasion wrote to Popper, stressing what he saw as common themes in their work, suggesting that they might use, as a common label for it, 'negativism' – as contrasted with positivism. See Hayek to Popper, 21 October 1964, Popper archive, Hoover Institution, 305.15.

67 *Law, Legislation and Liberty*, volume two, p. 43.

68 *Ibid.*

69 Or, rather, a variety of such systems; see *ibid.*, p. 54

70 Cf. Hayek's Cairo Lectures.

71 Notably in the appendix to volume three of *Law, Legislation and Liberty*.

72 Cf. *Law, Legislation and Liberty*, volume two, p. 54.

73 W. Landes and R. Posner, 'Adjudication as Private Good', *Journal of Legal Studies*, 8, 1979.

74 See Larry Briskman, *Problems and their Progress*, University of Edinburgh Ph.D. dissertation, 1983, and 'Articulating our Ignorance', *etc* 42, 1985; and also Jagdish Hattiangadi, *How is Language Possible?*, La Salle, Ill.: Open Court, 1987.

75 Compare, in this respect, the institutions through which law was transmitted in pre-literate societies; for example, that of Iceland. See, for references to a wide range of literature relevant to this issue, Bruce Benson, *The Enterprise of Law*, San

Francisco: Pacific Research Institute, 1990. For historical material on the problem of complexity in relation to the learning and transmission of law, compare J. H. Franklin, *Jean Bodin and the Sixteenth Century Revolution in the Methodology of Law and History*, New York: Columbia University Press, 1963.

76 Cf. Ernst Mach, *The Analysis of Sensations*, New York: Dover, 1959, and P. Duhem, *The Aim and Structure of Physical Theory*, New York: Atheneum, 1974.

77 See *Law, Legislation and Liberty*, volume two, p. 53.

78 For example, to 'the self-maintaining character of the social cosmos' (*ibid.*, p. 55); to 'the system of generic rules which ... became the foundation and preserver of the developing spontaneous order' (p. 54); to the social division of knowledge, and to 'the importance of [the] freedom of the individual within his protected domain' (p. 57) and the role of this, in its turn, in learning by trial and error.

79 *Ibid.*, pp. 24ff.

80 I have in mind unpublished work by the historian Leonard P. Liggio and the anthropologist Grace Goodell.

81 Compare, for example, Andrew Belsey, 'The New Right, Social Order and Civil Liberties' in Ruth Levitas (ed.) *The Ideology of the New Right*, Cambridge: Polity Press, 1986, pp. 169–97, who as a result of what seems to me a complete misunderstanding of what Hayek means by order, presents Hayek as an authoritarian enemy of civil liberty.

82 Hayek, *Law, Legislation and Liberty*, volume three, p. 41.

83 *Ibid.*, chapter 14.

84 *Ibid.*, p. 44. Compare, however, T. Cowen (ed.) *The Theory of Market Failure: A Critical Examination*, Fairfax, Va.: George Mason University Press, 1988.

85 The street on which I lived in the United States was owned by the 'community association' of the housing subdivision, a body initially set up for this purpose by the subdivision's developers. It also ran common areas, a swimming pool, arranged for a commercial company to collect rubbish, and also developed and policed regulations to make sure that we did not keep chickens, excessive numbers of cats, leave broken cars about, or paint our house in colours which would be offensive to neighbours. For some of the (growing) literature on this possibility, as well as for documentation of the extent to which it actually took place in the past, see Stephen Davies, 'Edwin Chadwick and the Genesis of the English Welfare State', *Critical Review*, 4, fall 1990, pp. 523–36; Bruce Benson, *The Enterprise of Law*; and David Beito, 'Mutual Aid for Social Welfare: The Case of American Friendly Societies', *Critical Review*, 4, fall 1990, pp. 709–36, and 'The Formation of Urban Infrastructure through Non-government Planning: The Private Places of St Louis', *Journal of Urban History*, 16, May 1990, pp. 263–303.

86 Either because one is involved with a so-called 'natural monopoly' (the idea of which is surely more problematic than it might seem, given that innovation and improvement are typically possible in respect of the provision of what is supposed to be a natural monopoly, and its character as a monopoly typically has to be secured by legislation), or because government enterprises operate under privileged financial conditions (for example, because their borrowing is under-written by taxation).

87 Compare Hayek's 'Rules, Perception and Intelligibility' in his *Studies in Philosophy, Politics and Economics*.

88 See 'Ernst Mach and the Social Sciences in Vienna' in Hayek, *The Fortunes of Liberalism* ed. P. Klein, London: Routledge, 1992, pp. 172–5.

89 See 'Rules, Perception and Intelligibility' and 'Notes on the Evolution of Systems of Rules of Conduct' in *Studies* and 'The Primacy of the Abstract' in *New Studies*.

90 See *Law, Legislation and Liberty*, volume three, p. 157.

91 *Ibid.*, pp. 157–8.

92 See 'The Presumption of Reason', 1986. Lest these ideas should seem merely a phenomenon of Hayek's very old age, it is worth noting that similar themes may be found in his 'Freedom, Reason and Tradition', an initial version of which was published in 1958.

93 Consider, for example, how, in 'The Confusion of Language in Political Thought', Hayek, after introducing the distinction between 'a spontaneous order or *cosmos* and an organization (arrangement) or *taxis* (p. 73) and describing how 'A *taxis* . . . is determined by an agency which stands outside the order', also writes 'such an external factor may induce the formation of a spontaneous order'.

94 Compare Hayek's 'Three Sources of Human Values', which forms the appendix to *Law, Legislation and Liberty*, volume three.

95 *Law Legislation and Liberty*, volume one, p. 88.

96 Compare Hayek's critical references to Descartes in his 'Individualism: True and False', and also *Law, Legislation and Liberty*, volume one, chapter one.

97 Cf. *Law, Legislation and Liberty*, volume one, chapter one, note 45 and text, and 'Dr. Bernard Mandeville', in *New Studies*, p. 263.

98 See, notably, *Law, Legislation and Liberty*, volume one, chapter one.

99 'Reconstruction' in the sense that I will take issue with some of what Hayek has written.

100 Compare Karl Popper's 'Towards a Rational Theory of Tradition' in *Conjectures and Refutations*, London: Routledge & Kegan Paul, 1963, pp. 120–35.

101 Compare, on all this, the role of 'background knowledge' in Popper's epistemology (on which see 'On the Sources of Knowledge and of Ignorance', in his *Conjectures and Refutations*); the interplay between 'dogmatism' and 'criticism' as discussed in his *Unended Quest*, London: Fontana, 1976, sections 10–12, and – in social philosophy – his 'Towards a Rational Theory of Tradition' rather than the more rationalistic parts of his *Open Society*.

102 As Larry Briskman has suggested to me in discussion. For another approach which links Popper and Menger, compare Karl Milford, 'Menger's Methodology' in B. Caldwell (ed.) *Carl Menger and his Legacy in Economics*, Durham, NC and London: Duke University Press, 1990, pp. 215–39.

103 There are, however, certain differences in the character of their views. Briefly (for I cannot do justice here to *The Sensory Order*), Hayek, while starting from a 'realist' picture of human beings, is concerned with the Machian problem of the 'order' of experience. He offers what, in Popper's terms, is an inductivist account of the development of a classificatory system within which the character of our perceptions is determined by the way in which they are contrasted with or differentiated from one another (the idea is reminiscent of Saussure). The classificatory system itself then serves to structure our experience, but is also modified by it, and is in large part also inherited (the overall account thus in some ways resembles the 'evolutionary' views on perception of Herbert Spencer). In Popper, by contrast, our perceptual mechanisms are seen as the products of (evolutionary) trial and error, but where this is understood as a selective process, rather than as the product of a form of instructive learning. On the 'instruction'/ 'selection' contrast, compare Popper's 'The Rationality of Scientific Revolutions' in R. Harre (ed.) *Problems of Scientific Revolution*, Oxford: Clarendon Press, 1975, pp. 72–101.

104 Cf. W. V. O. Quine, *Word and Object*, New York: MIT Press, 1960. On differences between Popper and Quine's views, and more general discussion of the criticizability of logic, see W. W. Bartley III, *Retreat to Commitment*, 2nd edn, La Salle, Ill.:

Open Court, 1984, Appendix 5; and Larry Briskman, 'From Logic to Logics and Back Again', *British Journal for the Philosophy of Science*, 33, 1982.

105 Since I first developed this argument, I have discovered that John Watkins raised essentially the same point with Hayek in private correspondence. See, on this, Watkins to Hayek, 24 January 1964, in the Hayek archive, Hoover Institution, 57.12.

106 'Rules, Perception and Intelligibility', pp. 60–1.

107 *Ibid.*, p. 62.

108 R. G. Collingwood, *An Essay on Metaphysics*, Oxford: Clarendon Press, 1940. See also, for some useful discussion, S. Toulmin, *Human Understanding,* volume one, Oxford: Clarendon Press, 1972.

109 Compare, on this, Eugene Miller's 'The Cognitive Basis of Hayek's Political Thought' in R. Cunningham (ed.) *Liberty and the Rule of Law,* College Station, Tx.: Texas A & M University Press, 1979, pp. 242–67.

110 In comments on an earlier version of this material, Leif Wenar objected to my use of the term 'arbitrary', on the grounds that Hayek might be understood as taking the view that such presuppositions are hard-wired into us, and suggested that, at that point, Hayek's views might resemble those of Popper on 'evolutionary epistemology'. Such an argument, however, would not in my view assist Hayek. His own 'evolutionary epistemology', if one can refer to the *Sensory Order* in such terms, seems to me to mix the arbitrary, the inductivist and the structuralist. For Hayek, sensory categories are to be understood as products of experience-generated differentiation. They are arbitrary, in the sense that the content of the qualities is genuinely arbitrary (provided that it can play its appropriate functional role); while what the categories are is, on Hayek's account, the dual product of our physiology and our experience.

111 Hayek himself noted the possibility of making use of machines in *The Sensory Order,* which in this respect is closer to Popper's views than is 'Rules, Perception and Intelligibility'.

112 Compare, on this, Hayek's reference to 'so many falls from grace', in *Law, Legislation and Liberty,* volume three, p. 161.

113 Cf. *The Constitution of Liberty*, pp. 62–3.

114 *Law, Legislation and Liberty*, volume three, p. 171.

115 Involving a sort of cultural fatalism of a sort suggested, perhaps, by Maine and by Macfarlane's reading of the character of English individualism (see Alan Macfarlane's *The Origins of English Individualism*, Oxford: Blackwell, 1978).

116 Compare, on this, Hayek's presentation of *The Constitution of Liberty* as a restatement of liberal ideas, and the Introduction to *Law, Legislation and Liberty,* volume one.

117 See also, on this issue, J. Shearmur, 'Abstract Institutions in an Open Society'.

118 See, on this general issue, Norman Barry's survey article, 'The Tradition of Spontaneous Order', *Literature of Liberty*, summer 1982, and also the discussion of Barry's work in the winter 1982 issue.

119 I will be concerned here only with this theme in the context of Hayek's political philosophy.

120 See 'The Confusion of Language in Political Thought', pp. 74–5.

121 See section 8.59. A dictator who gives directions to a slave will do so only in general terms, rather than indicate the precise movements that have to be made, such that there will always be different ways in which such directions could be complied with.

122 See *Choice in Currency*, 1976, also in *New Studies*, and *The Denationalization of Money*, London: Institute of Economic Affairs, 1976.

123 *The Constitution of Liberty*, p. 324.
124 *Ibid.*, p. 335. He had previously written on 'A Commodity Reserve Currency' in 1943.
125 See *New Studies*, p. 223.
126 Hayek's constitutional views would, I think, only work if there were already a high degree of consensus that liberal views, of the kind that he favours, are correct. For it is only from such a perspective that we would willingly impose such views upon ourselves for our own well-being – rather than perceiving them as something that others are trying to impose upon us because it is in their interest so to do. See also Robert Michels, *Political Parties*, Glencoe, Ill.: Free Press, 1949.

4 COMMERCIAL SOCIETY, SOCIAL JUSTICE AND DISAGGREGATION

1 I have in mind not only the general dangers of projecting otherwise-inspired images back onto the prehistory of humankind (cf. Adam Kuper, *The Invention of Primitive Society*, London and New York: Routledge, 1991), but also the more specific historical challenges to the kind of theorizing that one finds in Adam Smith, raised by Alan Macfarlane's *Origins of English Individualism*, Oxford: Blackwell, 1978.
2 See, for discussion and commentary, Hont and Ignatieff, 'Needs and Justice in the *Wealth of Nations*'.
3 See, in this context, 'The Moral Economy of the English Crowd in the Eighteenth Century' and 'The Moral Economy Reviewed' in E. P. Thompson, *Customs in Common*, Harmondsworth: Penguin Books, 1993. I would like to thank members of the Honours Seminar on Adam Smith in 1993, and especially my colleague Knud Haakonssen, for discussion of the issues that have gone to form this chapter. I suspect, indeed, that any good sense about Smith that may be here will have come from Haakonssen; but I must stress that neither he nor any of the other participants should carry any of the blame for what follows.
4 Cf. Karl Marx and Friedrich Engels, *Manifesto of the Communist Party*; for example in Karl Marx and Friedrich Engels, *Selected Works*, London: Lawrence & Wishart, 1968, pp. 31–63. See, for the quotation, p. 40.
5 Compare T. H. Marshall, 'Citizenship and Social Class' in *Citizen and Social Class and Other Essays*, Cambridge: Cambridge University Press, 1950, with Robert B. Reich, *The Work of Nations*, New York: Knopf, 1991.
6 See, on this, Hont and Ignatieff, 'Needs and Justice'.
7 See, notably, James C. Scott, *The Moral Economy of the Peasant,* New Haven: Yale University Press, 1976, and the literature to which it has given rise. I do not wish to involve myself here in the debate about the correctness or otherwise of Thompson or Scott's views, but will *for the sake of argument* treat these issues as if their ideas were correct.
8 See Jeremy Waldron, *The Right to Private Property*, Oxford: Clarendon Press, 1986.
9 This, of course, does not mean that they are to assess this just in terms of their own personal interests.
10 Compare here the immense moves towards the achievement of racial equality within the US armed forces, and Betty Friedan's discussion of what has been achieved there in respect of women, in her *The Second Stage*, London: Michael Joseph, 1982. Compare also the way in which the quasi-military organization of the US Forest Ranger service enables them to overcome what would otherwise seem insuperable obstacles to the achievement of their declared tasks. See Herbert Kaufman, *The Forest Ranger*, Baltimore: Johns Hopkins University Press, 1967. I

would like to thank my colleague David Adams for drawing this work to my attention.

11 There will be an element of this, even, say, with respect to how explicit orders are followed by someone who, for one reason or another, is bound to follow those orders.

12 What someone considers to be morally reasonable will to some extent be, and in my view should be, the product of intersubjective scrutiny of their moral judgements in those situations, where, of course, the character of the institutions within which those judgements are being made, and the consequences upon us of those institutions, may themselves be made the subject of further such scrutiny, upon a piecemeal basis.

13 See, on this, J. Shearmur, 'Consumer Sovereignty and Preferences for Higher-order Goods', *Political Studies*, December, 1991, pp. 661–75.

14 In part, for reasons of self-interest, as discussed by Mancur Olson in *The Logic of Collective Action*, Cambridge, MA: Harvard University Press, 1965, in part for reasons relating to moral judgement that I have discussed above.

15 If, indeed, we can talk in such terms with respect to the activities of modern government; compare my discussion later in this chapter.

16 Although it seems to me important that people be honest and conscientious; indeed, one important objection against states in Western countries is that they have, through the imposition upon individuals and small businesses of regulations of a complexity that they cannot be expected to master, and which would be difficult for anything but a large business organization to follow, served to undermine the moral practices and moral integrity of individuals within the societies upon which they are parasitic.

17 Compare, in this context, the interesting defence of the welfare state on just such a basis by Robert Goodin and Julian Le Grand, *Not Only the Poor*, London: Allen & Unwin, 1987.

18 This is an idea that I explore more fully in my final chapter.

19 Compare, for discussion of this by people who would seem attracted to it as a more general model, Betty Friedan, *The Second Stage*, and Randy Shilts, *Conduct Unbecoming*, New York: Fawcett Columbine, 1994.

20 Compare, on this, J. Shearmur, 'Schutz, Machlup and Rational Economic Man', *Review of Political Economy*, 5(4), October 1983, pp. 491–507. It would seem to me that there are two different arguments involved in the discussion about the use of economic models in politics. One is about egoism and altruism. The other concerns whether or not – and when – one needs to invoke the specific content of people's motives, including their theoretical ideas, as opposed to working with a model of them as motivated by a few, relatively simple, preferences. In so far as the latter idea has been championed, it seems to have been done on the basis of a conception of people's normative concerns which would seem to me to be over-socialized (and which, in my view incorrectly, depicts people as typically following shared social norms or rules; see, in this context, Brian Barry's discussion of Talcott Parsons in his *Sociologists, Economists and Democracy*, Chicago: University of Chicago Press, 1978; and Amati Etzioni, *The Moral Dimension*, New York: Free Press, 1988). I would argue, in preference to this, for a view which sees people as acting in ways that seem to them morally reasonable in the specific situations in which they are acting, and to which I have referred, briefly, in earlier parts of this chapter.

21 Compare, on this, Christopher Ham and Michael Hill, *The Policy Process in the Modern Capitalist State*, Brighton: Wheatsheaf, 1984, and Brian Hogwood and

Lewis Gunn, *Policy Analysis for the Real World*, Oxford: Oxford University Press, 1984.

22 See Albert Weale, 'Nature Versus the State?' *Critical Review*, 6(1–2), pp. 153–70.

23 In this respect, the device of ministerial responsibility to the feeling of the British House of Commons seems to me very important, and immensely superior to the purely legal and political controls that operate in the United States.

24 Robert Goodin, 'The Political Science Contribution' in R. Goodin and P. Pettit (eds) *A Companion to Contemporary Political Philosophy*, Oxford: Blackwell, 1993, pp. 158–83.

25 See, for discussion, J. Shearmur, 'Hayek's Case for Markets'.

26 It is, for this purpose, completely beside the point as to whether economists can show that the initial adoption of such rules was rational for *homo economicus*. What matters is that, as we encounter them, we find people acting on the basis of particular such rules and customs, rather than as might rational economic man, in general.

27 See A. Sen, *Poverty and Famines*, Oxford: Clarendon Press, 1981; and, further, Jean Dreze and A. Sen, *Hunger and Public Action*, Oxford: Clarendon Press, 1989. Thompson himself makes use of Sen, in his argument in his 'Moral Economy Reviewed'.

28 One interesting example that has been reported upon just as I write, and which if it were correct would be an interesting illustration of my point, is the claim that lower levels of male sperm counts that have been detected recently may be the product of oestrogen-like substances which are, as it were, the emergent products of a variety of human activities within industrialized societies, rather than something that has one single clearly identifiable cause.

29 Compare J. Shearmur, 'Consumer Sovereignty'.

30 In particular, I will not on this occasion even attempt to grapple with the problems of the transition from the religious ideas which underlay, say, Locke's ideas about property rights, and what would be required of a fully secular liberal theory.

31 See Locke, *First Treatise*, paragraph 42.

32 On which, see Thompson's criticism of Hont and Ignatieff, in his 'Moral Economy Reviewed'.

33 See Hont and Ignatieff, 'Needs and Justice' and Thompson's 'Moral Economy' and 'Moral Economy Reviewed'.

34 See, for some further discussion, J. Shearmur, 'The Right to Subsistence in a "Lockean" State of Nature', *Southern Journal of Philosophy*, 27(4), winter 1989, pp. 561–8.

35 I do not mean that the undeserving will get nothing, so much as that the deserving may be singled out for special assistance.

36 For an account of which, see Hont and Ignatieff, 'Needs and Justice'.

37 Consider the easy access to a plethora of interesting material on radio and television; the high-quality recordings of classical music at surprisingly low prices, to say nothing of the kind of access to information that will, presumably, soon be widely available through computer networks.

38 I am not here concerned with the substitution of state-imposed paternalism for freedom of contract, so much as with the idea that the establishment of contracted relations does not automatically bring with it other obligations, too. Lest I be misunderstood, I should perhaps stress that would favour the achievement of the protective goals for the sake of which the paternalism was advocated, if they could be achieved by other, less morally problematic, means.

39 As I have suggested in J. Shearmur and D. Klein, 'A Character to Lose: Good Conduct in the Great Society' in D. Klein (ed.) *Reputation*, Ann Arbor: University of Michigan Press, forthcoming, this might be seen as an informal extension of Coase's ideas about the rationale for the firm.

40 For discussion, compare J. Shearmur, 'Consumer Sovereignty'.

41 My colleague David Adams has suggested in discussion that there is a parallel here with Charles Lindblom's ideas in his 'Still Muddling, Not Yet Through', *Public Administration Review*, 39, 1979, pp. 517–26.

42 Compare Raymond Plant's suggestion of a similar idea, albeit in a rather different context, in his 'Hirsch, Hayek and Habermas: Dilemmas of Distribution' in A. Ellis and K. Kumar (eds) *Dilemmas of Liberal Democracies*, London: Tavistock, 1983, pp. 44–64.

43 *Law, Legislation and Liberty*, volume two, p. 78.

44 *Ibid.*, p. 96.

45 *Ibid.*, p. 86.

46 Raymond Plant, *Equality, Markets and the State*, Fabian Tract 494, January 1984, p. 4. Essentially the same point has also been made by Partha Dasgupta: see 'Decentralization and Rights', *Economica*, 47, 1980, pp. 107–24 and *Utilitarianism and Beyond*, Cambridge: Cambridge University Press, 1982, pp. 199–218.

47 I. Hont and M. Ignatieff, 'Needs and Justice', p. 44.

48 *Law, Legislation and Liberty*, volume two, p. 87.

49 *The Constitution of Liberty*, pp. 257–8.

50 Cf. *ibid.*, p. 258. The problem is, essentially, that Hayek discusses the issue in terms of its effects upon coercion, where we have already had reason to mention that his formal account of coercion is inadequate, and that coercion, as he describes it, anyway seems too narrow a basis upon which to argue for the importance of liberty.

51 See Ted Honderich, *Conservatism*, London: Hamish Hamilton, 1990.

52 For some useful – but I think in the end unconvincing – attempts to address this issue, compare Robert Goodin, 'What is So Special about our Fellow Countrymen?' *Ethics*, 98, July 1988, pp. 663–86, and Henry Shue, 'Mediating Duties', *Ethics*, 98, July 1988, pp. 687–704.

53 For some discussion of this issue, see J. Shearmur, 'Consumer Sovereignty'.

54 Only, of course, in the sense that they might be expected to have a coherence of moral vision not possessed by what is 'willed' by our actual sovereign bodies. However, this lack of coherence – and perhaps of moral merit – is itself an inevitable product of the complexity of what is involved in our current social arrangements, and the need for agreement on the part of many people upon whom the issues impinge. Any advantages that the Enlightened Despot might have, on the score referred to in the text, are surely more than compensated for by problems of information and motivation.

55 Compare M. Lipsky, *Street-Level Bureaucracy*, New York: Russell Sage, 1980, p. xii, and Christopher Ham and Michael Hill, *The Policy Process in the Modern Capitalist State*, Brighton: Wheatsheaf, 1984, pp. 136ff.

56 Compare, say, the discussion by Betty Friedan and Randy Shiltz, referred to in notes 10 and 19 above.

57 See note 10, above

58 Robert Goodin and Julian Le Grand, *Not Only the Poor: The Middle Classes and the Welfare State*, London: Allen & Unwin, 1987.

59 *Ibid.*, p. 225.

60 On which I hope to undertake empirical research at a later date.

61 The broad approach that I would take to their analysis is perhaps closer to David McNaughton's *Moral Vision*, Oxford: Blackwell, 1988, than to anything else known to me; but I do not wish to embark here on a more extensive excursion into meta-ethics than I can help.

62 With regard to what is covered in such cases, I am not all that far from Robert Goodin, *Protecting the Vulnerable*, Chicago: University of Chicago Press, 1985.

5 POST-HAYEKIAN POLITICAL ECONOMY

1 Compare the discussion earlier in this volume.

2 Compare Gray's discussion in *Hayek on Liberty*, p. 59, of what he there refers to as the 'indirect or system utilitarian aspect' of Hayek's moral theory.

3 See Hayek, *The Constitution of Liberty*, p. 309 and notes 8 and 10 on p. 517.

4 Hayek, *The Counter-Revolution of Science*, Indianapolis: Liberty Press, 1979, p. 52.

5 Murray Rothbard, *Toward a Reconstruction of Utility and Welfare Economics*, New York: Center for Libertarian Studies, 1977.

6 *Ibid.*, pp. 26–7.

7 Compare also, on this, Robert Nozick, 'On Austrian Methodology', *Synthese*, 36, 1977, pp. 353–92.

8 I would like to thank Mark Blaug for correcting an incautious statement in my verbal presentation at a conference which suggested otherwise, and also for some other important criticisms of ideas on welfare economics in an earlier version of this paper. He is, of course, in no way to blame for errors which may still remain. For a most interesting treatment of these issues from a rather different, but critical, perspective see Charles Rowley and Alan Peacock, *Welfare Economics: A Liberal Restatement*, New York: John Wiley, 1975.

9 Cf. Lionel Robbins, *An Essay on the Nature and Significance of Economic Science*, 3rd edn, New York: New York University Press, 1984, p. 141. The passage is quoted against me by Lawrence White in his 'Afterword: Appraising Austrian Economics: Contentions and Misdirections' in B. Caldwell and S. Boehm (eds) *Austrian Economics: Tensions and New Directions*, Boston: Kluwer, 1992, pp. 257–68; see p. 262. I would like to thank Lawrence White for discussion which has helped me to clarify my argument here.

10 Compare, for a sympathetic exposition, M. Lessnoff, *The Structure of Social Science*, London: Allen & Unwin, 1974, chapter six.

11 Compare Hayek, *Law, Legislation and Liberty*, volume two, chapter ten.

12 See I. Kirzner, *Competition and Entrepreneurship*, Chicago: University of Chicago Press, 1973.

13 Cf. Hayek, *Studies in Philosophy, Politics and Economics*, p. 173.

14 Hayek, 'The Non Sequitur of the Dependence Effect' in *Studies in Philosophy, Politics and Economics*, London: Routledge & Kegan Paul, 1967, pp. 313–17.

15 *Ibid.*, p. 314.

16 Compare, on this theme, J. Shearmur, 'Hayek and the Spirit of the Age' in N. Barry *et al.*, *Hayek's 'Serfdom' Revisited*, London: Institute of Economic Affairs, 1984, pp. 66–85.

17 Hayek, *The Constitution of Liberty*, p. 41.

18 Of course, someone's being in a condition in which they should feel miserable but do not, in fact, do so may be an indication that they require the assistance of others that much more urgently; but this opens up issues that I cannot pursue here.

19 Lionel Robbins, *The Nature and Significance of Economic Science*, 2nd edn, London: Macmillan, 1935, p. 140. See also the first part of Ilmar Waldner, 'Bare Preference

and Interpersonal Utility Comparisons', *Theory and Decision*, 5, 1974, pp. 313–28, and Amartya Sen, *On Ethics and Economics*, Oxford: Blackwell, 1987, especially chapter two. Other interesting discussions include the papers in J. Elster and A. Hylland, *Foundations of Social Choice Theory*, Cambridge: Cambridge University Press, 1986. The reader will appreciate, however, that the literature on this subject is large, and that this is not the place for me to try to do justice to it in a systematic manner.

20 Robbins, *Nature and Significance*, p. 141.
21 *Constitution of Liberty*, p. 517.
22 Compare Robert Cooter and Peter Rappoport, 'Were the Ordinalists Wrong About Welfare Economics?' *Journal of Economic Literature*, June 1984, pp. 507–30, and the ensuing discussion.
23 Robbins, *Nature and Significance*, p. 140.
24 Compare K. R. Popper and J. C. Eccles, *The Self and Its Brain*, Berlin: Springer International, 1978. See also Popper's discussion of the difference between scientific and philosophical reductions in his 'A Realist View of Logic, Physics and History', in his *Objective Knowledge*, Oxford: Clarendon Press, 1972.
25 Robbins, *Nature and Significance*, pp. 139–40.
26 Hard as it may seem, if people are to be free, some of them will make bad choices. While we might think that a desirable aim for social policy should be such that everyone is both free and makes good choices, this seems to me mistaken. A secular reading of C. S. Lewis's argument in *The Great Divorce* (London: Fontana, 1972, p. 111) against universalism is here to the point – that it amounts to 'The demand of the loveless and the self-imprisoned that they should be allowed to blackmail the universe: that till they consent to be happy (on their terms) no one else shall taste joy; that theirs should be the final power; that Hell should be able to veto Heaven'.
27 Compare, on this, Hicks' discussion of Hayek in his *Critical Essays in Monetary Theory*, Oxford: Clarendon Press, 1967, and *Money, Interest and Wages*, Cambridge, MA: Harvard University Press, 1982.
28 The reference is to 'Intertemporal Price Equilibrium and Movements in the Value of Money', now in Hayek, *Money, Capital and Fluctuations*.
29 See his unpublished George Mason University Ph.D. dissertation.
30 See Don Lavoie, *Rivalry and Central Planning*.
31 As we have argued earlier in this volume.
32 Compare, on this, H. D. Dickinson's contributions to the socialist calculation debate.
33 Compare, on this, J. Shearmur, 'Consumer Sovereignty'.
34 *Law, Legislation and Liberty*, volume three, p. 74.
35 See, notably, *The Fatal Conceit*. Hayek's discussion there and elsewhere seems to me also to systematically conflate the idea that certain of our moral ideas may have survived because they led us to conditions that would support a large population, and that there is something good about such ideas or about large populations *per se*.
36 John Stuart Mill, *Principles of Political Economy*, Book IV, Chapter VI, para. 2, *The Collected Works of John Stuart Mill*, Volume III, Toronto: University of Toronto Press and London: Routledge, 1965, p. 756.
37 As Jack Birner and Axel Leijonhufvud remarked at a conference in which these issues were discussed.
38 Any reader who might believe that it is only possible to treat of ethical judgements as undiscussible expressions of preferences should consult D. McNaughton, *Moral Vision*, Oxford: Blackwell, 1987.

39 This is a reference to some suggestions made by Peter Winch, following T. S. Eliot, about some fundamental reference-points for understanding human culture. See, for fuller discussion of this point, J. Shearmur, 'From Hayek to Menger' in B. Caldwell (ed.) *Carl Menger and his Legacy in Economics,* Durham, NC and London: Duke University Press, 1990, pp. 189–212.

6 WHY OUR FREEDOM MATTERS TO OTHERS

1 John Gray, *Hayek on Liberty*, Oxford: Blackwell, 1986, pp. 59–60.

2 *Ibid.*, p. 60.

3 See Hayek's *New Studies*, p. 77.

4 Earlier forms of the argument of the present chapter were presented at the Morell Conference on Toleration in York UK in 1985, in my 1987 Ph.D. dissertation; and in a paper delivered at the American Political Science Association in 1987 which was published in *Critical Review*, with a response by Frank Michelman, in 1990.

5 Chandran Kukathas, *Hayek and Modern Liberalism*, Oxford: Oxford University Press, 1989. I would like to thank Leif Wenar for the suggestion that I should clarify what I was saying about Hayek, Hume and Kant.

6 Hayek's *Sensory Order* and related work does not seem to me Kantian in any serious sense; not least because the basis from which Hayek starts is *realist*, and he seems to have started his work from problems raised by Ernst Mach. It is, I understand, the case that 'Kantian' thought on psychological issues, by the time at which Hayek wrote, had itself become so naturalistic in its approach that there was not as big a gulf as one might have expected between it and various forms of empiricism. However, to the extent to which this was the case, it would seem to me that 'Kantianism' had itself departed from Kant's *systematic* philosophy, and by that very fact from the principled reconciliation of Hume and Kant for which Kukathas was seeking.

7 In so far as anything of that kind can be done, it would seem to me to be via a 'moral realist' interpretation of Adam Smith's *Theory of Moral Sentiments*. But that is a task that the reader will doubtless be grateful that I do not intend to burden the present volume.

8 I would like to thank an anonymous referee for leading me to clarify this point.

9 See my 'From Divine Corporation to a System of Justice' in P. Groenewegen (ed.) *Economics and Ethics*, London and New York: Routledge, 1996.

10 For fuller discussion, see J. Shearmur, *The Political Philosophy of Karl Popper.*

11 See, for discussion, *ibid.*, chapter four.

12 See Hayek, *The Constitution of Liberty*, p. 6.

13 *Ibid.*

14 *Law, Legislation and Liberty*, volume two, p. 27.

15 See, notably, John Gray, *Mill on Liberty*, London: Routledge & Kegan Paul, 1983.

16 Cf. J. Shearmur, 'Scope and Status of Prudential Liberalism', *Review of Politics*, 54(2), 1992.

17 Compare the arguments discussed earlier in this volume.

18 At least, most of those likely to bother themselves with this volume!

19 As Peter Danielsen, who in discussion brought up this example, pointed out, in some parts of the United States everyone supposedly has the right to obtain a credit card. What they do not have the right to is a non-negligible credit rating.

20 The view that free labour must be more productive than that of slaves would seem a matter for argument, and might well lead to different consequences in different circumstances (cf. Robert William Fogel and Stanley L. Engerman, *Time on the*

Cross, Boston: Little, Brown, 1974). While, say, slaves could be driven, one would have to weigh against this what might be the heavier costs involved in the monitoring of their conduct.

21 David Gauthier, *Morals by Agreement*, Oxford: Oxford University Press, 1986, chapter nine, section 4.3.

22 For further discussion, see J. Shearmur, 'Scope and Status of Prudential Liberalism'.

23 See *The Constitution of Liberty*, p. 6.

24 In the sense of having been subject to interference that has this consequence, whether intentionally, or as 'a product of human action but not of human design'.

25 'The Non-Sequitur of the Dependence Effect'.

26 See Linda Lovelace, *Ordeal*, London: Star Books, 1982, and also Gloria Steinem's discussion in her *Outrageous Acts and Everyday Rebellions*, London: Cape, 1984.

27 I have discussed these issues in two unpublished papers delivered to the Alexander Society at the University of Manchester: 'The Sociological *a priori*' and 'Hayek, Linda Lovelace and the Moonies'. See also J. Shearmur, 'The Religious Sect as a Cognitive System' and my 'Epistemology Socialized'. For a good argument to the effect that recruitment into the Unification Church should not be seen in such terms, see Eileen Barker, *The Making of a Moonie*, Oxford: Blackwell, 1984.

28 For the rationale for my emphasis here on maintenance as opposed to origin, see J. Shearmur, 'Epistemology Socialized'.

29 Martin Hollis, 'J. S. Mill's Political Philosophy of Mind', *Philosophy*, October 1972, pp. 334–47. Karl Popper drew my attention to the significance of this article. See also John Gray, 'Freedom, Slavery and Contentment' in his *Liberalisms*, London: Routledge, 1989.

30 See Gray, *Mill on Liberty*.

31 It might be questioned whether a strictly Kantian perspective would help. For if we are going to act morally, we need to be able to identify those who should be the objects of moral consideration. This identification, for the Kantian, presumably has to take place within the phenomenal world. But there would seem to be no way in which we could identify there what is and what is not deserving of treatment as an end in itself. For everything that occurs is perceived by us as occurring as the result of causal processes. So how can we identify who are moral patients who deserve moral consideration, as distinct from non-moral objects that do not? (It is not clear that Kant's teleology, of the third critique, would help us much either, as it is not clear that he gives us any indication on the basis of which we can judge when such ideas should and should not apply.) The problem is, at one level, solved by the ideas developed in the text (as Bruce Ackerman suggested, when discussing a similar move in his *Social Justice in the Liberal State*, New Haven: Yale University Press, 1986). We can see if any candidate engages us in dialogue. But have we been listening in the right way for its reply, or what if it is severely handicapped? The Kantian problem recurs as the problem of how to identify potential partners in a dialogue. But this problem is easier to solve than is Kant's, as it is posed – and can be answered – in respect to a world that is open to our investigation. We may, for example, develop plausible theories about the degree of internal organization or structural complexity that is required for even potential participation within a dialogue; and this may make the issue of who, in principle, is a candidate for dialogue rights open to rational assessment.

32 See K. R. Popper, *The Open Society and Its Enemies*, London: Routledge & Kegan Paul, 1945, and, for discussion, J. Shearmur, 'Epistemological Limits of the State'

and 'The *Positivismusstreit* Revisited', delivered at the Australasian Political Studies Association, Monash, September 1993; and J. Shearmur, *The Political Thought of Karl Popper*.

33 As Larry Briskman has suggested to me in discussion of this material, the failure of others to find the effects in question can be interpreted as the attempt by others to test the original claim that was being made. But this is to recognize, implicitly, that such a claim has been made, and thus to recognize the person who made it. To say that a particular claim can be overruled or outweighed is not to say that its status as a claim, as opposed to its validity, is thus eliminated. However, if someone's judgement is particularly bad or becomes badly disturbed, they may come to lose their dialogue rights.

34 'In my course I have known and, according to my measure, have co-operated with great men; I have never yet seen any plan which has not been mended by the observations of those who were much inferior in understanding to the person who took the lead in the business.' Quoted from Burke (without an indication of the source) in Popper, *Open Society*, 5th edn, 1966, p. vi.

35 It will be an empirical matter who is to count as a 'person' – for personhood is simply a consequence of the empirical fact of having the capacity to contribute to such a dialogue (see note 31, above). Thus, if the claims that have been made for them should prove correct (cf. Eugene Linden, *Apes, Men and Language*, New York: Dutton, 1975), Washoe and other chimpanzees might be entitled to such rights, as a consequence of their linguistic capacities. (One might indeed consider that there could be different kinds of rights, corresponding, say, to Popper's development of Buehler's theory of the hierarchy of functions of language, from expression, communication and description, through to argument; cf. Popper's *Conjectures and Refutations*, London: Routledge & Kegan Paul, 1963.) The senile and the foetus might not fully possess such rights, as they would not possess such capacities. However, this does not necessarily mean that they would have no moral status; for as we shall see – when our argument is extended from factual to ethical subject-matter, below – those who do not have moral consideration as participants in ethical dialogue may none the less have them as the objects of such dialogue.

36 See, for a first stab at such an argument, J. Shearmur, 'Abstract Institutions in an Open Society' in *Wittgenstein, The Vienna Circle and Critical Rationalism*, Vienna: HPT, 1979, which is now included in J. Shearmur, *The Political Philosophy of Karl Popper*, chapter five. This may be seen as a development of Hayek's idea that property rights should be reshaped with an eye to the contribution that they can make to utility.

37 Cf. Thomas McCarthy's introduction to Habermas's *Legitimation Crisis*, London: Heinemann Educational, 1976; McCarthy's own *The Critical Theory of Juergen Habermas*, Cambridge, MA: MIT Press, 1978; and J. Shearmur, 'Habermas: A Critical Approach', *Critical Review* 2, winter 1988, pp. 39–50.

38 I would like to thank Larry Briskman for urging that this point should be made explicit.

39 That is, they would not have the right to form social institutions which, in their intended or unintended consequences, acted so as to insulate them from criticism. These would be the social equivalents of Popper's 'conventionalist stratagems' (cf. his *Logic of Scientific Discovery*, section 20, and J. Shearmur, 'Epistemology Socialized?' There is a parallel here with the misgivings that Hayek expresses about the consequences to people's attitudes from their participation in large-scale social formations which insulate them from contacts with markets; cf. *The Constitution of Liberty*, chapter eight.

40 I should perhaps stress that the value placed on these things *qua* experiments in living is the value placed on them by *other* people. They are, presumably, valued by most of those who undertake them because this represents what seems to them an attractive way of living. But that it is attractive to *them* does not, in itself, offer a reason why it should be thought valuable by others.

41 I believe that the kind of intersubjective appraisal suggested by Adam Smith's *Theory of Moral Sentiments* may be of relevance in this situation.

42 There is possibly some room for doubt about this, in view of Hayek's suggestion (*Law, Legislation and Liberty*, volume two, pp. 144–5) that 'It [became] part of the ethos of the Open Society that it was better to invest one's fortune in instruments making it possible to produce more at smaller costs than to distribute it among the poor'. As I have suggested in chapter four, this may mean that Hayek's admitting of a safety net is a concession to our inability to bite the bullet, concerning what a systematic application of his ideas would involve.

43 I have explored this further in a paper, 'Popper and Liberalism', given at the First Annual Conference on the Philosophy of Karl Popper, in Manchester in 1984; an article based on one section of that talk was subsequently published as 'Epistemological Limits of the State', *Political Studies*, 38, 1990, pp. 116–25.

44 See K. R. Popper, 'Facts, Standards, and Truth: A Further Criticism of Relativism (1961)' in *Open Society*, 4th and subsequent edns; especially section 13.

45 See H. B. Acton and J. W. N. Watkins, 'Negative Utilitarianism', *Aristotelian Society Supplementary Volume*, 1963, pp. 83–114, and W. W. Bartley III, *Unfathomed Knowledge, Unmeasured Wealth*, La Salle, Ill.: Open Court, 1990, chapter two, section 8.

46 I have explored these ideas tentatively in my 'Epistemological Limits of the State' and in a paper, 'From Brother Sense to Brother Man', on Adam Smith's *Theory of Moral Sentiments*, delivered at the Eastern APA in 1987. Compare also David McNaughton, *Moral Vision*.

47 Compare, say, the way in which emotivists such as Ayer and Stevenson strive to show that their theories allow for ethics to have many of the features that one might, *prima facie*, have associated with a more cognitivist approach.

48 See Robert Nozick, *Philosophical Explanations*, Cambridge, MA: Harvard University Press, 1981, p. 434: 'When in the Republic Thrasymachus says that justice is in the interests of the stronger, and Socrates starts to question him about this, Thrasymachus should hit Socrates over the head. He concedes too much when he enters an activity, discussion, that assumes that there is some mark of correctness and rightness other than (and superior to) strength.'

49 For some problems concerning which, and some possible responses, see the end of J. Shearmur, 'From Dialogue Rights to Property Rights' and J. Shearmur, 'Natural Law Without Metaphysics?: The Case of John Finnis', *Cleveland University Law Review*, 38(1 and 2), 1990.

50 This point I owe to Frank Michelman. See our exchange on these ideas in *Critical Review*, 4(1–2). I should perhaps mention that I do not think that my response there to Michelman was fully adequate as a defence of the ideas that I was there exploring, and would hope that the comments that follow in the text do a little better.

51 See, in this connection, Karl Popper, 'Toleration and Intellectual Responsibility' in S. Mendus (ed.) *On Toleration*, Oxford: Clarendon Press, 1987. In this, when discussing the exchanges between Bohr and Einstein, Popper stresses that while they both learned much from each other, they did not end up in agreement. In

this paper, Popper is critical of the idea that fruitful discussion must be expected to lead to agreement.

52 Indeed, my own suggestions depend on the idea that, whether directly or through representatives, dialogue can take place, to consensus, concerning our minimal ideas in epistemology and the allocation of rights on that basis; such a consensus might also include, within specific communities, the establishment of a 'bottom line', in respect of which a welfare safety net might operate. All this may not, however, be as daunting a task as it might seem, given that the epistemological argument amounts largely to showing that no one can demonstrate the correctness of their substantive ideas, and on the basis of some fairly trite ideas about the possibility of learning.

53 On which, see Nozick, *Anarchy, State, and Utopia*, New York: Basic Books, 1974, chapter one.

54 Cf. James Buchanan, 'From Private Preferences to Public Philosophy: The Development of Public Choice' in J. Buchanan *et al.*, *The Economics of Politics*, London: Institute of Economic Affairs, 1978, pp. 1–20.

55 See *Anarchy, State, and Utopia*, note 7 to chapter ten.

7 KNOWLEDGE AND IMPERFECTION IN A MINIMAL STATE

1 Compare J. Shearmur, 'Abstract Institutions in an Open Society'.

2 I have done this, to a fuller extent, in an unpublished paper, 'The Rise and Fall of a Semi-Nozickian Utopia'.

3 Compare Hayek's 'The Legal and Political Philosophy of David Hume' in *Studies*, pp. 106–21 and 'Dr. Bernard Mandeville' in *New Studies*, pp. 249–66.

4 See David Hume, *Treatise of Human Nature*, Book III, Part II, Section 1; cf. also Hayek's article on Hume, referred to in note 3, above, and also my 'Abstract Institutions in an Open Society'.

5 See 'Of the rise and progress of the arts and sciences' in David Hume, *Essays, Moral, Political and Literary*, ed. E. Miller, Indianapolis: Liberty Press, 1985, p. 116.

6 *Ibid.*, p. 476.

7 'Our Moral Heritage' in *Knowledge, Evolution and Society*, p. 53.

8 *Individualism and Economic Order*, p. 22.

9 *Ibid.*, p. 26.

10 *Essays*, p. 476.

11 Compare his 'Spirit of the Age' and his *Representative Government*.

12 Compare, in 'civic humanist' writings, from Polybius onwards, the role played by the 'statesman' and Mandeville's emphasis on the role of the 'dextrous politician'. Rousseau in fact provides an interesting parallel with Hayek, in that, in his problems of the legislator, he is clearly grappling with much the same problems about the social recognition and maintenance of an ideal political constitution as we are considering, here, in Hayek's work.

13 See Bernard de Mandeville, *A Letter to Dion*. As Hayek has commented, citing Rosenberg's 'Mandeville and *laissez-faire*', Mandeville's view is that 'the proper function of government is "to establish the rules of the game by the creation of a framework of wise laws" '. See Hayek, 'Dr. Bernard Mandeville' in *New Studies*, p. 259.

14 Lionel Robbins, *The Theory of Economic Policy in English Classical Political Economy*, London: Macmillan, 1952, p. 56.

15 Nathan Rosenberg, 'Some Institutional Aspects of the *Wealth of Nations*', *Journal of Political Economy*, December 1960, p. 560.

16 R. H. Campbell and A. S. Skinner (eds) Adam Smith, *The Wealth of Nations*, Oxford: Clarendon Press, 1976, volume two, part five, p. 781.

17 See D. Winch, *Adam Smith's Politics*, Cambridge: Cambridge University Press, 1978, and K. Haakonssen, *The Science of a Legislator*, Cambridge: Cambridge University Press, 1981. See also Winch's contribution to Haakonssen (ed.) *Traditions of Liberalism*, St Leonards, NSW: Centre for Independent Studies, 1988.

18 For example, that the character of the organization would not be changed in a manner that conflicts with its constitution when he joined it.

19 Cf. A. O. Hirschman, *Exit, Voice and Loyalty*, Cambridge, MA: Harvard University Press, 1970.

20 An idea explored, especially, in the writings of some early nineteenth century French liberals.

21 Compare, however, J. Shearmur and D. Klein's 'A Character to Lose: Good Conduct in the Great Society', in D. Klein (ed.) *Reputation*, Ann Arbor: University of Michigan Press, forthcoming.

22 See, for a brief overview, Richard Vernier's discussion of the controversy about liberal and communitarian interpretations of the American Founding, 'Interpreting the American Republic: Civic Humanism vs. Liberalism', *Humane Studies Review*, 4(3), summer 1987.

23 See, on Smith, J. Shearmur, *Adam Smith's Second Thoughts* (pamphlet), London: Adam Smith Club, 1985; and J. Shearmur, 'Adam Smith and the Contradictions of Capitalism' in N. Elliott (ed.) *Adam Smith's Legacy*, London: Adam Smith Institute, 1990, pp. 135–50.

24 See, for a brief but useful overview, Raymond Plant, *Hegel*, 2nd edn, Oxford: Blackwell, 1983.

25 See Alan Macfarlane, *The Origins of English Individualism*, Oxford: Blackwell, 1978.

26 See, for example, J. Habermas, *Legitimation Crisis*, London: Heinemann Educational, 1970; D. Bell, *The Cultural Contradictions of Capitalism*, New York: Basic Books, 1976, and F. Hirsch, *Social Limits to Growth*, London: Routledge & Kegan Paul, 1977.

27 For interesting arguments to the effect that this is not as cold-hearted as it might seem, compare J. Waldron, 'When Justice Replaces Affection', *Harvard Journal of Law & Public Policy*, 11(3), summer 1988, pp. 625–48, and John Tomasi, 'Individual Rights and Community Virtues', *Ethics*, 101, 1991, pp. 521–36.

28 Compare David G. Green's *Reinventing Civil Society*, London: IEA Health and Welfare Unit, 1992. I would, however, wish to distinguish between Green's arguments about mutual aid and the more general conservatism of the political argument to which he is led, from which I would strongly dissent.

29 Compare Raymond Plant, 'Hirsch, Hayek and Habermas: Dilemmas of Distribution' in A. Ellis and K. Kumar (eds) *Dilemmas of Liberal Democracies*, London: Tavistock, 1983, pp. 44–64.

30 *Law, Legislation and Liberty*, volume two, p. 42.

31 I have in mind here the phenomenon that many exponents of postmodernist deconstructions of liberalism are, in fact, liberals under the skin, such that their work is in fact best understood as a critical corrective to liberalism, rather than as the illiberal relativism that it often seems to be. Their explicit approach, however, seems to me hopeless in the face of the fact that there are genuine and powerful

challenges to liberal values, in that it is incapable of repudiating them other than as an act of will; an act just as open to their critics.

32 I must stress the half-playful character of this exercise; I have explored the pros and cons of such arrangements more seriously in an unpublished manuscript on the theme of the pros and cons of a 'Nozickian' utopia, versions of which I have presented at a variety of seminars from 1982 onwards. See also, for in some ways a complementary discussion, chapter five of J. Shearmur, *The Political Thought of Karl Popper*.

33 Jane Jacobs, *Death and Life of Great American Cities*, New York: Vintage, 1961.

NAME INDEX

SUBJECT INDEX

142, 158, 167, 175–6, 179, 180–1,
183, 190, 196, 213–15, 219; modern
9, 11, 65, 69, 71, 73, 119, 179, 214
liberty *see* freedom

markets 1–3, 10, 23, 26, 28, 30, 33–5,
47, 50–1, 67, 72–80, 82, 85, 87, 91,
98, 103–4, 108, 113–19, 128, 130,
133–5, 140–7, 151–2, 169, 172–5,
181, 193, 198, 211–15
merit 139, 141, 205, 213
methodology 3, 7, 14, 25, 29–30, 36,
143, 153, 166, 171, 198, 200, 222
minority, exploitation of 182, 190, 219
migration 120, 130, 206, 209, 212,
217–18
misery 26–8, 40, 45, 58, 64–5, 69, 85,
127, 149, 153–4, 156–7, 160, 164–8,
176, 179–80, 135, 186, 198, 240
mobility *see* migration
money 5, 29, 33, 79, 84, 108, 115–16,
170, 207
monopoly 27, 50, 68, 74–5, 78, 172,
219, 233
moral economy 8, 119, 128–33, 141
morality 8–9, 12, 22, 62, 80, 83, 86, 90,
96, 118–22, 127, 129–30, 133, 144,
145–8, 154, 158, 167, 176, 178–9,
186, 190–3, 211–13, 237, 239,
241–4

nation, nationalism 10, 36, 147–8
need 20, 47, 63, 71, 118, 164, 169, 184

organic, organism 37, 38, 42, 43, 44, 45,
57, 106, 109

paternalism 183–5, 238
personality *see* identity
persons, respect for 9, 176, 180, 186,
190, 193, 244
planning, central 1, 4, 34, 37–8, 40, 46–
7, 50–4, 56, 61–2, 64, 72, 79–81,
100, 115, 123, 152, 154, 161, 171–2,
189, 198, 239; individual 56, 67–8,
153–5, 159, 162, 170

pluralism 195, 201–2, 213, 215, 219;
political 11, 21, 46, 53–4, 73, 79–81,
101–6, 124, 153, 209
policy 36, 63, 79, 84, 124, 125, 144,
145, 200; *see also* intervention
political theory or philosophy, normative
2, 5, 6, 15–25, 100, 125, 135, 137,
159, 177, 198
politics *see* democracy
population 83, 118, 120, 140, 173–4,
205, 241
postmodernism 10, 247
power 4, 47, 61, 65, 68, 74–8, 80, 98–9,
101, 125, 169, 173, 198, 207, 209,
222, 229
preferences 8, 9, 21, 41, 54, 58, 61, 62,
126, 128, 136, 138, 154, 158–60,
163, 170, 172–3, 183–7, 189, 237,
241; *see also* choice
prices 3, 33–4, 46, 47, 51, 52, 79, 130,
135, 155–6, 172
property 11, 31, 33, 50, 52, 55, 57, 62,
83–4, 98, 120–1, 129–32, 142–3,
151, 157, 159, 175, 179, 193–7, 202–
3, 209, 213, 215, 219, 238, 244–5
propinquity 129–31, 133, 149
public interest 5, 79, 80, 114, 148, 207

rationality, rationalism 6, 12, 21, 42, 44–
5, 52–4, 56, 61–2, 66, 84, 85, 100,
107, 109–15, 126, 159, 172, 204–5,
214; critical 66, 100–1, 106–15, 179,
186–97, 215
reason *see* rationality
Rechtsstaat 60, 63, 65, 87–92, 99, 162,
177, 229
reform 3, 5, 26, 35, 38, 42, 43, 53, 55,
56, 84, 98, 99, 207
relativism 13, 112, 247
religion 9, 62, 83, 84, 118, 138, 178,
180, 232, 238
research programme 6–8, 13–5, 20, 74–
5, 152, 155, 173, 194
rights 6, 9, 11, 17, 20, 23, 57, 68, 70–1,
75–6, 121, 128–9, 131–3, 143, 151,
155, 157–8, 160, 168, 175–8, 180–1,
186–97, 202, 206, 212, 214–15,
244–6; dialogue 187–97, 243–5